Imagining the Audience in Early Modern Drama, 1558–1642

Imagining the Audience in Early Modern Drama, 1558–1642

Edited by Jennifer A. Low and Nova Myhill

IMAGINING THE AUDIENCE IN EARLY MODERN DRAMA, 1558-1642
Copyright © Jennifer A. Low and Nova Myhill, 2011.
Softcover reprint of the hardcover 1st edition 2011 978-0-230-11064-9
All rights reserved.

First published in 2011 by PALGRAVE MACMILLAN® in the United States—a division of St. Martin's Press LLC, 175 Fifth Avenue, New York, NY 10010.

Where this book is distributed in the UK, Europe, and the rest of the world, this is by Palgrave Macmillan, a division of Macmillan Publishers Limited, registered in England, company number 785998, of Houndmills, Basingstoke, Hampshire RG21 6XS.

Palgrave Macmillan is the global academic imprint of the above companies and has companies and representatives throughout the world.

Palgrave® and Macmillan® are registered trademarks in the United States, the United Kingdom, Europe and other countries.

ISBN 978-1-349-29310-0   ISBN 978-0-230-11839-3 (eBook)
DOI 10.1057/9780230118393

Library of Congress Cataloging-in-Publication Data
  Imagining the audience in early modern drama, 1558–1642 / edited by Jennifer A. Low, Nova Myhill.
      p. cm.

  1. English drama—Early modern and Elizabethan, 1500–1600—History and criticism. 2. Theater audiences—England—History—16th century. 3. English drama—17th century—History and criticism. 4. Theater audiences—England—History—17th century. 5. Theater—England—History. I. Low, Jennifer A., 1962– II. Myhill, Nova, 1970–

PR658.A88I43 2011
822'.045'09031—dc22   2010039889

A catalogue record of the book is available from the British Library.

Design by Scribe Inc.

First edition: March 2011

10 9 8 7 6 5 4 3 2 1

Transferred to Digital Printing in 2012

For Philippa and Daphne,

Ursula and Helena

Contents

Acknowledgments		ix
Introduction: Audience and Audiences *Nova Myhill and Jennifer A. Low*		1
1	Crowd Control *Paul Menzer*	19
2	Taking the Stage: Spectators as Spectacle in the Caroline Private Theaters *Nova Myhill*	37
3	The Curious Case of the Two Audiences: Thomas Dekker's *Match Me in London* *Mark Bayer*	55
4	Door Number Three: Time, Space, and Audience Experience in *The Menaechmi* and *The Comedy of Errors* *Jennifer A. Low*	71
5	Audience as Witness in *Edward II* *Meg F. Pearson*	93
6	"Lord of thy presence": Bodies, Performance, and Audience Interpretation in Shakespeare's *King John* *Erika T. Lin*	113
7	Charismatic Audience: A 1559 Pageant *David M. Bergeron*	135
8	Audience, Actors, and "Taking Part" in the Revels *Emma K. Rhatigan*	151
9	Bleared Vision in *The Taming of the Shrew* *James Wells*	171

10 Fitzgrave's Jewel: Audience and Anticlimax in
   Middleton and Shakespeare   189
   Jeremy Lopez

List of Contributors   205

Index   209

Acknowledgments

First we wish to acknowledge the support and collegiality of the members of the 2009 Shakespeare Association seminar "Audience and Audiences." The fine work presented there inspired us to develop this collection; those members whose essays are not included here offered papers that we expect to see in print elsewhere. Warm thanks are due to Diana Henderson and Lena Cowen Orlin, who permitted the late submission of the seminar topic. Without their flexibility, this project might not have been engendered. More generally, we'd like to thank the Shakespeare Association of America, whose annual conference is such a wonderful forum for the free exchange of ideas.

Katharine Eisaman Maus and Gail Kern Paster recommended scholars working on the topic who had not joined the seminar; their thoughtfulness resulted in the recruitment of several splendid contributors. Paul Yachnin and Steven Mullaney provided support and encouragement through crucial conversations and the example of their own fine work on the subject of audiences. Thanks to Carrie Beneš for her timely help with image permissions.

We would like to thank our editors, Brigitte Shull and Samantha Hasey, and the anonymous reader of our manuscript. More generally, we would like to thank Palgrave Macmillan, whose support of scholarship, particularly of early modern literature, has been a boon to the academic community for some time. Perhaps most importantly, we would like to thank our contributors, whose alacrity and professionalism have made this project a pleasure.

Both our husbands deserve credit for their support, particularly in the time they took when our planning sessions by telephone coincided with the "witching hour." Finally, this project would not have come to birth without two editors. We would like to acknowledge one another's style, savvy, intellectual liveliness, and humor, which made this project both a success and a pleasure to assemble.

INTRODUCTION

Audience and Audiences

Nova Myhill and Jennifer A. Low

Throughout the many studies of early modern drama, one interaction has gone relatively unexamined: that of performance and audience. While the early modern audience has long been recognized as central to the early modern stage, it has also, for reasons of evidence and scholarly focus, been curiously set apart from the experience of the drama of the period. There is no shortage of fascinating work on the early modern audience as a demographic entity, and there is a positive superabundance of analysis of individual plays in terms of the society in which they participate—which necessarily includes their audiences. But neither of these views exactly speaks to the other, largely because they tend to view either the audience (in the case of theater history) or the play (in the case of cultural criticism) as a relatively stable entity—one that emerges from its encounter with the other largely the same as it went in. The idea of what can be gained from studying theatrical audiences expands considerably when we recognize performance as a dialectical activity, acknowledging the role of the audience in all stages of the life of the drama as well as the certainty in the early modern period that plays had some effect on their audiences beyond passing their time for two hours.[1] Imagined audiences shape dramas at the inception of the composition process as surely as plays ask their audiences to modify their behavior and interpretive practices. Expected audiences at different venues caused early modern players to alter the dramas in their repertoire even as the plays attempted to make their audiences conform to certain behaviors at certain venues, and in performance, audiences responded to plays in ways that the playwright and the actor ultimately had little control over despite the "arts of orchestration" that aimed to produce certain types of audience response.[2]

Crucial to the project of this collection is recognizing how literally we take the concept of the audience itself. Playwrights imagine their audiences, giving us their own perceptions of the spectators' taste; actors address the audience in a complex exchange that recent performance theories, often inflected by phenomenology, have attempted to define. But the original audiences of early modern dramas are another entity—one that has proved remarkably resistant to examination. Most recent critical discussion of the early modern theater audience considers this audience as either a demographic entity or an object implied in the dramatic texts; the former, generally the province of theater historians, tends to focus on segmentation of the audience,[3] while the latter tends to present a more collective entity—largely because play texts tend to be read as communicating with, and shaping, an audience. There is an assumption in play-centered criticism that playwrights know what they want from an audience and, as competent professionals, are generally successful in getting it, while theater historians emphasize that "Shakespearean receivers were far from passive objects."[4] The title of this introductory essay is intended to distinguish between "an audience" to whom players might direct their performance and "audiences," a heterogeneous population whose constitution varied under changing circumstances. The first term implies a collective entity—one that the dramatists might know and appeal to (and even create) as a group; the second emphasizes the variety of experiences and viewing practices that individuals brought to the early modern theater.

Implicit in the distinction we draw is the notion of "the audience" as a collective entity that is brought into existence by the theatrical venue itself and "audiences" as individuals who never cease to function distinctly and who never leave behind the particularities that will shape their responses as much as anything they see on the stage. These terms, then, represent fundamentally different understandings of what happens in the theater, with the former privileging the performative authority of the play and the latter the interpretive authority of the playgoer. It is our hope that this collection will be part of a developing dialogue between scholars of "audience" and scholars of "audiences."

The audience conceived by the literary and cultural critic can be derived through the plays themselves as an aspect of the culture in which the drama participates; the audience of the theater historian is a collection of individuals who paid admission and attended plays (but seldom any particular play), whose existence can be determined from external evidence. Andrew Gurr, buttressed by a magisterial mountain of external evidence, laments the fate of this first audience, "likely nowadays to be invoked all too often in a vicious circle of internal evidence, as arbiters of this or that otherwise inexplicable or undesired feature of the plays."[5] If the imagined early modern audience is now more likely to be used to explain culturally, rather than aesthetically, inexplicable features of the plays than when Gurr wrote *Playgoing in Shakespeare's London* over twenty years ago, the basic point still holds. The two predominant modes of considering the early modern audience do not speak clearly to one another because one constructs the audience on the basis of evidence largely located outside the "subjective" internal evidence of the plays,[6] while the other finds the audience in "textual traces" provided by the plays—traces that ultimately refer to "contingent social practices" in which the audience participates to the same extent as any other group of people in London, but no more.[7] These two entities exist on almost parallel tracks, and the enormous amount of work done on both seldom spills over into something that we might truly call "interaction."

The study of early modern drama for the last two decades of the twentieth century was utterly dominated by new historicism, with its emphasis on the interrelation between literature and culture. One might wonder in retrospect why this development did not create more prominent, more sophisticated study of the role of the early modern audience in the cultural life of the drama. New historicists sought to introduce to the study of literature the "kinds of history that threatened the ideality of what Eliot called the 'ideal order' of canonical texts: kinds of history that made these texts seem too topical, too politically polemical, too imbued with prejudice, too much the consequence of a writer's particular professional or economic situation."[8] This historical specificity positions the drama as an active participant in its culture, one that shaped the public sphere rather than merely reflecting it. The critical and cultural fantasy here—that play might somehow be important—followed from a central premise of early modern political and, in a very different way, religious culture: that spectacle might have the power to shape its viewer for good or ill. In *Shakespearean Negotiations*, one of the first and most influential attempts to define a "poetics of culture,"[9] Stephen Greenblatt argues that despite our understanding "at some level . . . that the power of a prince is largely a collective invention . . . we can scarcely write of prince or poet without accepting the fiction that power emanates directly from him and that society draws upon this power."[10]

The focus in new historicism on the power of spectacles, theatrical and political, has inadvertently continued to marginalize study of the theater audience, while offering a one-sided vision of the transactions between literature and culture, one in which authorship and performance are always imagined as shaping interpretation rather than being shaped by it. In its initial focus on the court and Foucauldian "spectacles of power," the criticism of the 1980s and 1990s imagined a world strikingly similar to that of antitheatrical writers of the 1580s and 1590s, who envisioned the power of spectacles as shaping not merely the audience's interpretation but the audience itself. There are significant reasons, both historical and evidentiary, why one might find the fantasy of the overwhelmingly powerful spectacle both appealing and convincing. The contemporary texts that most explicitly consider what it meant to see a play in early modern England are, after all, the antitheatrical tracts, from John

Northbrooke's treatise in 1573 to William Prynne's screed in 1633. The tracts, particularly those of the late sixteenth century, characterize the typical theater audience as enormously vulnerable. Stephen Gosson, in *Playes Confuted in Five Actions* (1582), argues that in "the delight which springeth of Comedies . . . superiority is given to affections and so rebellion raised against reason."[11] Pleasure and reason are opposed, and viewing a play and delighting in the action puts the reason to sleep. Thus, any expectation of intellectual discrimination at a playhouse, even on the level of deciding whether a character presents an example to follow or one to shun (or indeed if he or she is an example at all), is doomed. Gosson emphasizes the fundamental passivity of the audience in his final "action" of *Playes Confuted*: a discussion of "ye Effects yt this poyson works amõg us" (sig G4r). He continues: "These outward spectacles effeminate and soften ye hearte of men, vice is learned in beholding, sense is tickled, desire pricked, & those impressions of mind are secretly conveyed over to ye gazers, which ye players do counterfeit on ye stage" (G4r). The play is consistently the active agent; the mind of the audience is consistently the passive recipient. The word "impressions" suggests a sympathetic relationship between player and playgoer greater than the mere experience of seeing or hearing, in which the minds of the spectators actually receive the "impressions of mind" imprinted by the counterfeit emotions of the actors.

The language of printing that appears with some frequency in antitheatrical tracts, as well as the concurrent suggestion that the audience will imitate what they see on stage in a startlingly literal way,[12] implies that the process that Gosson envisions in *Plays Confuted in Five Actions* is a literal reforming of the spectators' minds into the mental shape "counterfeited" by the actors.[13] Gosson certainly seems to make the argument that the audience reproduces what they see in his example of Bacchus's seduction of Ariadne: "[W]hen Bacchus rose up . . . the beholders rose up . . . when they sware, the company sware . . . when they departed to bedde; the company presently was set on fire, they that were married posted home to their wiues; they that were single vowed very solemly to be wedded" (G5r). While the first set of imitations, rising up and swearing, are physically identical—imitation in the simplest and most literal sense—the second set involve a replication of the mental state, not the physical. "Vowing very solemly to be wedded" is not precisely the same thing as going off to bed with a woman, but in this context it suggests that the effect of seeing Bacchus and Ariadne was to compel the audience to replicate not the physical action of seduction but the mental state that enabled this action. The Greek word *xaraxein* (χαράζειν), as Sir Thomas Overbury points out, means not only literally to engrave but also to make a deep impression.[14] In being metaphorized, the image represents a much more complex transaction.

The assumption that power resides in the spectacle is shared by antitheatrical writers, writers of early modern pedagogical tracts, and most of the first generation of new historicist critics. And this assumption is partially true; royal progresses and public punishments are, in significantly different ways, displays of the power of the group presenting them. But, as the noted theater semiotics scholar Keir Elam argues, that passivity of the spectator is illusory: "the audience's relative passivity as 'receiver' is in fact an active choice which imposes certain obligations on the elected 'senders.'"[15] While many discussions of the early modern audience, from the 1980s as well as the 1580s, privilege the spectacle, many accounts of various sorts of spectatorship demonstrate that what a spectacle was intended to show and what its spectators ultimately made of it do not coincide with any great regularity.

To examine the sorts of communication available between performance and audience in the theater, and in order to negotiate between the fantasy of the all-powerful spectacle and the all-powerful spectator, it will be helpful to see how both semiotic and phenomenological models of interpretation may be positioned in relation to more historically specific criticism.[16] As Keir Elam points out, the most basic requirement for meaningful communication between spectators and performers is an agreement that the audience will "recognize the performance as such"; this agreement constitutes a "theatrical frame [that] is in effect the product of a set of theatrical conventions governing the participants' expectations and their understanding of the kinds of reality involved in the performance."[17] These theatrical conventions are, of course, enormously historically specific and may well vary between venues, but recognizing them as a set of competencies shared between the playwrights, actors, and audiences gives us a way to consider the audience's role as active rather than passive—a position scarcely imaginable to Gosson and his fellow antitheatrical writers, who represent spectatorship as possession, no more volitional than contagious disease. The shared nature of these interpretive practices encourages us to think of how the audience might be imagined as a collective both like and unlike the mob Gosson envisions, but it should not obscure the divergence of audience members in terms of class, gender, or individual experience that assures that no two members of the audience bring identical horizons of expectation to the theater; "every spectator's interpretation of the text is in effect a new construction of it according to the cultural and ideological disposition of the subject."[18]

Theater professionals active between the early 1580s and 1642 knew the extent to which their audiences controlled them economically and, as a result, aesthetically. The epilogues at the ends of plays (particularly in the seventeenth century) tend to stress the power of the audience and the actors' vulnerability to their judgment; at the end of Richard Brome's *The Antipodes*, Doctor

Hughball, who has cured one character's madness by placing him in a play, tells the audience,

> Whether my cure be perfect yet or no,
> It lies not in my doctorship to know.
> Your approbation may more raise the man,
> Than all the College of Physicians can;
> And more health from your fair hands may be won,
> Than by the strokings of the seventh son.[19]

While Hughball's comment is a blatant request for applause—the approval that translates into the economic approval of repeat business—it also insists on the theater audience's involvement in the action of the play. The audience's applause, not Hughball's art, determines the success of his "cure."

Prospero's more famous epilogue at the end of Shakespeare's *Tempest* also insists that the audience's response will determine his success or failure. In his proclaimed lack of "spirits to enforce, art to enchant,"[20] Prospero insists that, unlike the actors envisioned in Gosson's 1579 *School of Abuse*, who "set . . . abroche straunge confortes of melody to tickle the ear; costly apparel to flatter the sight; effeminate gesture to ravish the sense; and wanton speache to whet desire too inordinate lust,"[21] he has no power over the audience, while they have the power to force him to "dwell / On this bare island by [their] spell" (7–8) unless they show mercy and "release me from my bands / With the help of [their] good hands" (9–10). Both epilogues ask that the audience recognize both its freedom of choice and its ability to determine the success or failure of the internal action of the play.

While playwrights attempted to encourage theatrical competence—the understanding shared between actors and audience members that allows the audience to "apprehend [the play] in its own terms and not as, say, a spontaneous and accidental event"[22]—in their spectators, the theater audience is ultimately free to focus on and ignore whatever aspects of the play or the playhouse it chooses and to bring whatever expectations and spectatorial practices it pleases to bear. "It is the spectator," Elam argues, "who must make sense of the performance for himself . . . However judicious or aberrant the spectator's decodification, the final responsibility for the meaning and coherence of what he constructs is his."[23] Ben Jonson, whose perennial dissatisfaction with his audiences appears in the prologues and epilogues of his plays, was more explicit than most in his consideration of the judicious spectator, whom he seems to have sought in vain throughout his theatrical career, and the aberrant spectator, whom he found with an increasingly resigned frequency.

Jonson makes both his hopes for and low expectations of the response of the theater audience very apparent. The mock contract between "the spectators or hearers, at the Hope on the Bankside . . . and the author of *Bartholomew Fair*,"[24] Jonson's most explicit attempt to "reveal the roles he expects [his audience] to play in his theatrical community,"[25] promises with resignation that "[h]e that will swear *Jeronimo* or *Andronicus* are the best plays yet, shall pass unexcepted at, here, as a man whose judgment shows it is constant, and hath stood still, these five and twenty, or thirty years. Though it be an ignorance, it is a virtuous and staid ignorance; and next to truth, confirm'd error does well" (107–12). In the face of the threat of complete unpredictability, Jonson professes to be satisfied with consistent misinterpretation.

Jonson's mock contract consists of five "articles," which may usefully encompass a variety of relations between playgoer and playwright (and significantly exclude the actors) in terms of Elam's description of theatrical competence. The first article asserts that all audience members, regardless of their competencies or interpretive practices, "as well the curious and envious as the favouring and judicious" (75–76), are physically bound to "remain in the seats their money or friends have put them in" (78–79) for the duration of the play.[26] While the members of the audience may judge as they please, as the next two articles stress, the purchase of the ticket is what buys audience members this right to "like and dislike at their own charge" (87–88). The overwhelmingly financial language used to describe the place of the audience insists that the limit of the audience member's authority is "the value of his place" (91). Jonson presents interpretation as entirely personal and idiosyncratic, forbidding only application; the audience he envisions may well be incompetent, but they have bought the privilege of judgment. Unlike the audience invoked in either Brome or Shakespeare's epilogue, however, Jonson's "spectators or hearers" have no power over the outcome or meaning of the play itself; their judgments are limited to themselves, and there is no suggestion of a collective audience response that might determine what *Bartholomew Fair* accomplishes. The contract ultimately does less to bind the audience to the play than to allow audience and play to operate independently from one another.

In practice, neither the antitheatrical terror of the absolute power of the spectacle over the powerless collective audience nor the epilogues' assertion of the absolute power of the idiosyncratic individuals in the audience to determine meaning is tenable; as Elam argues, "It is with the spectator . . . that theatrical communication begins and ends,"[27] but it is the theatrical spectacle that both constitutes the audience and provides the object of interpretation. In this context, it is significant that of the three monographs published on the early modern audience in the last decade, one focuses primarily on the uses individual audience members made of their experience of plays, drawing primarily from allusions to drama rather than play texts; another argues that the early modern audience is most usefully understood as a collective and grounds its argument almost exclusively in play texts; and the third actively stages the debate over whether the audience is to be understood as either a collective entity or a group of individuals.

The earliest of these monographs, Paul Yachnin and Anthony Dawson's *The Culture of Playgoing in Shakespeare's England: A Collaborative Debate* (2001)[28] is particularly explicit in its authors' divergent readings of the experience of playgoing in early modern London. Whereas Dawson argues for theatergoing as a communal experience, Yachnin argues that "the pleasures of playgoing . . . had more to do with the volatile possibilities of radical individuation than with the experience of sacramentalized collectivity"[29] and that the plays of the period in fact contribute to audience members experiencing them individually by "focus[ing] spectator attention on what cannot be seen rather than on what can."[30] Dawson argues that rather than fragmenting the audience, the plays practice "scopic control"[31] in directing the attention of the audience to moments on the stage: "such engagement is not individualizing . . . but collective."[32] While understanding audience experience in radically different terms, Yachnin and Dawson share the assumption that the play exerts significantly more control over the playgoer than the converse. This assumption is typical of most twentieth-century discussions of audience, and it is further developed in the next monograph.

In *Theatrical Convention and Audience Response in Early Modern England* (2003), Jeremy Lopez notes that "if both the Puritans and their adversaries were willing to argue publicly that a play could affect reality and the lives of its audience, it seems more than safe to assume that this is the kind of assumption playgoers would have brought with them to the playhouse"[33]—an assumption that he argues is part of the shared "perception of plays having an importantly collective effect."[34] While certainly not implying that the playwrights had full control over their audiences, Lopez argues that "plays rely on and manipulate audiences' awareness of themselves and of dramatic artifice" and that early modern theatergoers "enjoyed thinking of themselves and being thought of as a collective entity."[35] Lopez focuses on the evidence of playwrights rather than of audience members, arguing that "one can better understand the audiences of the English Renaissance if one better understands the plays they watched. That is, the plays contain within themselves most of the evidence needed to understand what audiences expected and enjoyed and experienced."[36] While allowing for the spectacular failure of dramatic control—including, presumably, Dawson's "scopic control"—Lopez finds that the playwrights still create the audience; the only audience available is the one implied in theatrical texts.

Charles Whitney's *Early Responses to Renaissance Drama* (2006) argues that the fundamental mode of theatrical reception in early modern England is focused "as much on consumption as production, on appropriation as on contemplation, and on creative re-performance as on creative performance."[37] His work emphasizes "the diversity and creativity of early reception itself."[38] In his understanding of the early modern audience as a diverse group of individuals, each actively making personal use of the narratives and characters that unfold before them, Whitney privileges reception over production, and in his use of allusions to the drama rather than the drama itself, he gives voice to audience members instead of playwrights.

The divergent methods used by Lopez and Whitney highlight the most fundamental problem of working with the early modern audience: evidence. The overwhelming majority of playgoers left no record of their attendance, let alone their reactions; Whitney's evidence, while fascinating, is a series of highly idiosyncratic records and survivals that may or may not be broadly applicable. While the best evidence about certain aspects of audience behavior must be the plays themselves, Alfred Harbage's blanket assertion in 1941 that "it is not from prologues, dedications, and epistles that we must look for a fair evaluation of Shakespeare's audience"[39] is equally impossible to refute. Harbage is largely responsible for initiating the serious study of the early modern audience, and if the claims he presented in *Shakespeare's Audience* for a "literally popular" audience "ascending by degree from potboy to prince" but dominated by the "working class" have been demonstrated to be considerably overstated, his work is still the foundation of the demographic approach to the early modern audience taken by theater historians.[40] The debate over the social and mental composition of early modern London theater audiences—carried on most notably by Gurr's *Playgoing in Shakespeare's London* (1987), Ann Jennalie Cook's *The Privileged Playgoers of Shakespeare's London, 1576–1642* (1981), and Martin Butler's *Theater and Crisis: 1632–42* (1984)—is impossible to resolve definitively with the existing evidence.[41] As Cook ruefully observes, "[T]he evidence presently gives no definitive answers to many pressing questions, especially those related to the frequency of attendance, the sizes of audiences, the economics of playgoing, or the social composition of spectators at the large open-air houses."[42] Due to the fragmentary nature of external evidence and the impossibility of determining exactly how to use internal evidence reliably, any reconstruction of the demographics of pre-Restoration London playhouses necessarily owes as much or more to the biases of the critic as it does to actual evidence.[43]

The evidence that would enable us to reconstruct the early modern audience does not exist, and it is perhaps as well to recall Harbage's suggestion that even if it did, this would not ultimately solve our problem: "[E]ven if the miracle occurred, if we could mingle with Shakespeare's audience reincarnate, its secret would prove no more penetrable than the secret of audiences now."[44] If the audiences with which both cultural critics and theater historians work are imaginary creations, assemblages of ambiguous fragments of textual and external evidence, there is a great deal to be said for allowing these pieces of evidence to speak to each other, not in search of an answer, but to develop hypotheses that let us conceive of the early modern audience as a vital partner in the production of meaning in early modern England.

The essays of this collection hew closely to the methodologies of the new historicism, but in its attempt to instantiate a marriage between historicist scholarship and theater history, our project offers an intervention in early modern literary studies. Examining the idea of audiences (rather than a single, hegemonic "audience") affords a rich opportunity to observe the interaction of culture and theater; though gaps in our knowledge render some of our work speculative, our research builds on a solid body of knowledge drawn from recent archeology and cultural anthropology as well as from historical documents. Combining cultural poetics and theater history enables us to approach the goals of the new historicism more knowledgeably, if more cautiously.

This collection presents essays dealing with performances that range in chronology from the accession of Queen Elizabeth in 1558 to the closing of the theaters in 1642. The collection also considers the audiences, real and imagined, for a wide variety of venues, including the streets of London, the Inns of Court, private indoor playhouses, and public amphitheaters. This range is part of our effort to contribute to a more complex understanding of the audience as a partner in the production of meaning on the early modern stage and of the relation between performance and reception more generally. The essays that follow are paired, with each group of two considering similar issues, though frequently in significantly different ways.

* * *

The collection begins with a pair of essays that considers the ways that the theater both creates and seeks to control its audiences, and the limits of this control. Beginning with the observation that theaters in early modern London did on occasion fail in the most basic way, simply by failing to attract enough people to view the play, Paul Menzer's "Crowd Control" explores the way that the theater, as an institution, worked to avoid these failures by "domesticating the crowd" through practices including the repertory system and the physical structure of the theaters, transforming the potentially uncontrolled, unruly, and threatening mass of people into a biddable and receptive audience by giving it "a domesticated experience of itself through the spectacularization of space and the habituation of playgoing." This transformation of the occasional crowd into "the everyday audience" might be considered in terms of Elam's "theatrical competence": the creation of spectators who bring a certain set of expectations for both their own behavior and that of the performers and performance to the theater that enables the success of the performance. Nova Myhill's essay "Taking the Stage: Spectators as Spectacle in the Caroline Private Theaters" takes a later and more restricted focus than Menzer's, examining the function of Jonson and Brome's inductions in creating multiple audience competencies. Working against the demographic readings that imply that members of a given social class can be understood as bringing identical interests and viewing practices to the theater, Myhill argues that the Caroline private theater, despite its relative demographic homogeneity, actively proposed a range of alternative methods of viewing to its audience, with the single unifying feature that all were concentrated on the performers rather than their fellow audience members, who constantly threatened to displace the players and playwrights as the center of attention.

The creation of theatrical competencies discussed in the first pair of essays relies heavily on plays being performed in particular venues; our third and fourth essays examine how plays are changed by the venues in which they are enacted—how they are interpreted and how their themes are altered by changes in staging required by moving plays from one theater to another. The essays in this section explore the techniques used by playwrights to shape the viewing methods of their audiences. In "The Curious Case of the Two Audiences: Thomas Dekker's *Match Me in London*," Mark Bayer situates his analysis in the theatrical conditions of late Jacobean drama. By the end of James's reign, theater audiences had become quite stratified, based both on company repertories and on the venues where plays were staged, with private theaters becoming the domain of the elite and the outdoor amphitheaters, especially the Red Bull and the Fortune, becoming the home of lowbrow citizens. Sometimes, however, companies were forced to cater to both audiences at once, a difficult task since plays that pleased one audience were often satirical and exclusionary of the other. This is precisely the situation that confronted the Queen Anne's Men when they moved to the Cockpit in Drury Lane in 1616 while still occupying the Red Bull: they were forced to transfer plays and players between the two radically different venues over the course of several years. Bayer examines one such play, Dekker's *Match Me in London*, performed at both venues during these turbulent years for the company. He argues that this play achieved a protean appeal, allowing it to resonate both for an audience of tradesmen and apprentices and for the more wealthy and educated playgoers at the Cockpit. While the latter group could revel in the play's subtle political commentary, the audience at the Red Bull saw instead a coherent and persuasive expression of the grievances of tradesmen and apprentices against their exploitation by those of higher social station.

In "Door Number Three: Time, Space, and Audience Experience in *The Menaechmi* and *The Comedy of Errors*," Jennifer A. Low examines how Shakespeare's adaptation of Plautus's *The Menaechmi* alters the original play's themes, its comedic genre, and the role of the audience in relation to the mimetic world. Though *The Comedy of Errors* closely follows Plautus's *The Menaechmi* in almost every plot twist, the thematic emphases of *The Menaechmi* and *The Comedy of Errors* are shaped by the parameters of Roman and Renaissance stage design. On Plautus's narrow stage, gesture and blocking reach outward toward the audience, defining spectatorial space as a specific location within the play's mimetic world. The stage and the actors' use of it allied the original audience with the Syracusan Menaechmus. In early productions of *The Comedy of Errors* on the other hand, the three doors located at the back of a much deeper stage emphasized the receding perspective, and at the play's conclusion, when Aemilia promises to recount the past in the priory, all the characters exit from the stage to the priory, excluding the audience from the play's resolution. This emphasis on the scene glimpsed all too briefly through one narrow doorway evokes Dutch painters' use of space to represent time in visual terms. This representation of time cued the audience to recognize the play's allegorical elements and respond with the detached judgment of the morality play audience rather than with the engagement of Plautus's Roman audience.

Following these essays, which examine how audience perceptions were shaped by the location or the physical parameters of the theater, we turn to the relation between audience and performer. Erika T. Lin and Meg Pearson's essays emphasize the significance of the physical presence of the actor in producing the contradictory demands placed on the audience by a range of staging practices. Pearson's essay, "Audience as Witness in *Edward II*," illustrates how pathetic spectacles may be mapped by focusing on one genre of spectacle: onstage killings. Pearson argues that certain onstage deaths, such as that of Marlowe's Edward II, require the presence of the audience as witnesses, in both the legal and theological sense, to physical acts, while others create emotional distance between audience and spectacle by focusing the audience's awareness on the theatricality of the event. Lin's "'Lord of thy presence': Bodies, Performance, and Audience Interpretation in Shakespeare's *King John*" focuses on the actor's signifying body, using the site of Shakespeare's *King John* to examine the impact of changing conceptions of identity on playgoers' interpretive practices in the early modern public theaters. Lin suggests that early modern tensions between traditional notions of identity as bound up in land and title on the one hand and emergent conceptions of identity as rooted in embodied presence on the other were not merely thematized in the play but were woven into the medium of performance itself. Even as the play repeatedly foregrounds physical appearance as an identity marker, it simultaneously undermines this notion by drawing attention to the process of semiotic decoding through which playgoers transformed actors into characters.

The fourth pair of essays in the collection explores the complex relations among the producers, performers, and audiences who combined to produce drama outside the boundaries of the purpose-built theaters. Focusing on the highly occasional performances of Elizabeth's entry pageant of 1559 and the Gray's Inn revels of 1594, David M. Bergeron and Emma K. Rhatigan's essays explore how the interactions between performers and audiences in these venues emphasize the fluidity of the positions of actor and spectator, as well as the shifting power dynamics between these positions. Settings outside the professional theaters often provide particularly striking instances of the evolving relationship between the audience and the spectacle, in part because records of such events frequently include much more detailed discussions of their occasional audiences than theatrical records do and in part because their position outside the institutional structures of the professional theaters renders the relation between spectator and spectacle less bound by convention and more subject to improvisation.

Thinking about an audience's expected or desired response, David Bergeron turns away from the public theater to the public streets, where a covenant emerges that engages the audience in charismatic response. His essay "Charismatic Audience: A 1559 Pageant" focuses on Queen Elizabeth's royal entry pageant on January 14, 1559, the day before her coronation. Elizabeth served variously as spectator, actor, and recipient of the audience's adulation, and sometimes as all simultaneously. By their reaction, the audience confirmed and sanctioned Elizabeth's position as their sovereign, thereby assisting *charisma*, that is, the interdependence of sovereign and subject so necessary to successful rule. In "Audience, Actors, and 'Taking Part' in the Revels," Emma K. Rhatigan examines the 1594 performance of *The Comedy of Errors* at Gray's Inn, arguing that the *Gesta Grayorum* revels complicate our understanding of the terms "audience" and "actors," creating performances in which both the revellers and their guests were able to explore new identities and "take part." She suggests that the performance of *The Comedy of Errors* in this particular physical and social context would have foregrounded the types of identity creation that were taking place among the audience of revellers. Both Bergeron and Rhatigan's essays suggest the extent to which these performances depend on audience response for their meaning.

This collection concludes with two essays that consider how playwrights shape a text to achieve mimetic effects onstage and examine the playwright's intentions as these become evident through the course of the play. Both James Wells and Jeremy Lopez question what the audience believes they are seeing onstage when they watch a play's dramatic resolution. In "Bleared Vision in *The Taming of the Shrew*," Wells examines how *The Taming of the Shrew* stages the conditions of the audience in the fictional world of the theater. The humor of the play's Induction rests on a character whose absurd mistakes about the world around him recreate, and therefore parody, the assumptions audiences must make to participate in any play, and particularly in the *Shrew* proper. Likewise, Kate's "taming" is complete only after she (reluctantly?) accedes to beliefs that echo those same assumptions. By staging the assumptions of the audience in a way that holds them up to ridicule, the play intensifies the divided nature of the audience's experience with theater. The play further intensifies these experiences by producing a series of scenes that, like those to which Sly and Kate are subjected, test the limits of what the audience can believe.

Lopez focuses on developing a coherent theory about the problem of "too-tidy" endings—endings in which bland figures of authority reassert themselves and stamp out the last embers of theatrical energy by expelling compelling but anti-social characters. In "Fitzgrave's Jewel: Audience and Anticlimax in Middleton and Shakespeare," Lopez traces the career of a crucial object throughout the play in order to examine a series of textual problems according to the measure of performability, reflecting on both the implications of different scene sequences and what they might imply about Middleton's process of composition. After considering whether it is fair to identify the play's protagonist, Fitzgrave, as an author surrogate, Lopez frames the methodological problems he treats with a comparison between Shakespeare and Middleton that reexamines our emotional relation to theatrical conclusions.

The power of the performance to move others has long been emphasized by commentators on early modern English drama, from the writers of antitheatrical tracts to the late twentieth-century scholars whose historicist work was heavily influenced by them. One of the most striking features of the introduction to Greenblatt's *Shakespearean Negotiations* is how agency is consistently placed with texts and performances rather than their readers and audiences. The potential for historicist criticism to inform the study of the early modern audience and vice versa has always been clear, even as it has also been subsumed by the fantasy of "how cultural objects, expressions, and practices—here, principally plays by Shakespeare and the stage on which they first appeared—acquired compelling force."[45] This model of compulsion, like much of the semimetaphorical language of new historicist criticism, suggests the power of objects and spectacles over people. If one is being compelled, after all, one can scarcely be expected to perform active interpretation. In his discussion of "the circulation of social energy," Greenblatt focuses on the "textual traces . . . made by moving certain things from one socially demarcated zone to another."[46] These things are moved by the author, in the case of words, or the company, in the case of props or costumes. But other "things" could move themselves—across the Thames, to the Blackfriars; the "social energies" that Greenblatt sees circulating in early modern London were, after all, physically embodied in the people of London in their capacity as spectators and interpreters, moving from theater to sermon to anatomy to execution to court, and these spectators were fully capable of "moving certain things from one socially demarcated zone to another." This power to move, then, was not restricted to the makers of spectacles. The essays in this collection resituate the audience as a central feature of the early modern stage—one that exerts its own moving and compelling force.

Notes

1. Jeremy Lopez, *Theatrical Convention and Audience Response in Early Modern England* (Cambridge: Cambridge University Press, 2003), 31–32.
2. Jean Howard, *Shakespeare's Art of Orchestration* (Urbana: University of Illinois Press, 1984).
3. See in particular Andrew Gurr, *Playgoing in Shakespeare's London* (Cambridge: Cambridge University Press, 1987), 59–79 and 115–90. Charles Whitney's fascinating new book, *Early Responses to Renaissance Drama* (Cambridge: Cambridge University Press, 2006), takes this practice to, and arguably beyond, its logical conclusion in its focus on "the experience of many individuals" who left behind traces of highly individual responses to early modern plays (5). Lopez disputes the utility of what he characterizes as "dividing audiences into ever smaller and more specific groups." Lopez, *Theatrical Convention*, 8. See also Lopez, *Theatrical Convention*, 16–19.
4. Gurr, *Playgoing*, 3. See also Alfred Harbage's claim that the absence of a twentieth-century Shakespeare is a result of the absence of an audience of sufficient quality. *Shakespeare's Audience* (New York: Columbia University Press, 1941), 166.
5. Gurr, *Playgoing*, 3.
6. Harbage, *Shakespeare's Audience*, 137.
7. Stephen Greenblatt, *Shakespearean Negotiations* (Berkeley: University of California Press, 1988), 5.
8. Katharine Eisaman Maus and Elizabeth Harvey, eds., introduction to *Soliciting Interpretation: Literary Theory and Seventeenth-Century English Poetry* (Chicago: Chicago University Press, 1990), x.
9. Greenblatt, *Shakespearean Negotiations*, 5.
10. Ibid., 4. While Greenblatt here is characterizing the aestheticizing model he hopes to distance himself from, in practice the centrality of the "textual trace" creates an identical effect under a different name.
11. Stephen Gosson, *Playes Confuted in Five Actions* (London, 1582), F7. Further citations in this chapter will appear parenthetically and refer to this edition.
12. Richard Halpern, *The Poetics of Primitive Accumulation* (Ithaca, NY: Cornell University Press, 1991), 38. It is also clearly visible in Greenblatt's insistence that we consider the "pressure" of images as not merely metaphorical in early modern England. *Shakespearean Negotiations*, 8.
13. Laura Levine, *Men in Women's Clothing: Anti-theatricality and Effeminization from 1579 to 1642* (Cambridge: Cambridge University Press, 1994), 13.

14. Thomas Overbury, *The Overburian Characters*, ed. W. J. Paylor (1614; repr., Oxford: Blackwell, 1936), 92.
15. Keir Elam, *The Semiotics of Theatre and Drama* (London: Methuen, 1980), 96.
16. Most of the following discussion draws heavily on Elam's *The Semiotics of Theatre and Drama*; while there is no shortage of work on theater semiotics, and significant differences exist in this field, Elam's work is particularly useful both because he works a great deal with early modern drama and because he emphasizes the importance of the audience in theatrical communication even though he is ultimately able to say much less about it than playtext or performance.
17. Elam, *Semiotics of Theatre*, 87, 88.
18. Ibid., 94, 95.
19. Richard Brome, *The Antipodes*, ed. Ann Haaker (Lincoln: University of Nebraska Press, 1966) 5.12.34–39. Parenthetical citations indicate act, scene, and lines.
20. William Shakespeare, *The Tempest*. *The Riverside Shakespeare*, ed. G. Blakemore Evans et al. (Boston: Houghton Mifflin Company, 1974), Epilogue 14. Further citations will appear parenthetically.
21. Stephen Gosson, *The Schoole of Abuse*, ed. Edward Arber (London: Alex Murray and Son, 1869), 32. Subsequent page citations appear parenthetically.
22. Elam, *Semiotics of Theatre*, 52.
23. Ibid., 95.
24. Ben Jonson, Induction to *Bartholomew Fair*, ed. E. A. Horsman (Manchester, UK: Manchester University Press, 1960), 64–67.
25. John Gordon Sweeney III, *Jonson and the Psychology of Public Theater* (Princeton, NJ: Princeton University Press, 1985), 9. Sweeney considers Jonson's attempts to manipulate his audiences through inductions, epilogues, epistles, and the plays themselves. See especially Sweeney, *Psychology*, 5–15.
26. This closely resembles Lopez's contention that "above all, playwrights seem to have wanted audiences that would pay attention to their plays." Lopez, *Theatrical Convention*, 19.
27. Elam, *Semiotics of Theatre*, 97.
28. Paul Yachnin and Anthony Dawson, *The Culture of Playgoing in Shakespeare's England: A Collaborative Debate* (Cambridge: Cambridge University Press, 2001).
29. Ibid., 80.
30. Ibid., 86.
31. Ibid., 96.
32. Ibid., 97.
33. Lopez, *Theatrical Convention*, 31–32.
34. Ibid., 21
35. Ibid., 34.
36. Ibid., 7.
37. Whitney, *Early Responses*, 1.
38. Ibid., 2.
39. Harbage, *Shakespeare's Audience*, 134.
40. Ibid., 158 and 90.

41. Ann Jennalie Cook, *The Privileged Playgoers of Shakespeare's London, 1576–1642* (Princeton, NJ: Princeton University Press, 1981); Martin Butler, *Theatre and Crisis 1632–1642* (Cambridge: Cambridge University Press, 1984).
42. Ann Jennalie Cook, "Audiences: Investigation, Interpretation, and Invention," in *A New History of Early English Drama*, ed. John D. Cox and David Scott Kastan (New York: Columbia University Press, 1997), 306. Cook's article usefully summarizes the major areas of consensus and dispute in the demographic study of the audiences of early modern England.
43. For a discussion of critical bias in deciding which demographic account to accept, see Thomas Cartelli, *Marlowe, Shakespeare, and the Economy of Theatrical Experience* (Philadelphia: University of Pennsylvania Press, 1991), 44–47.
44. Harbage, *Shakespeare's Audience*, 3.
45. Greenblatt, *Shakespearean Negotiations*, 5.
46. Ibid., 7.

CHAPTER 1

Crowd Control

Paul Menzer

Theater Fail

What would you give to see the Lord Admiral's Servants perform *The Jew of Malta*? At the Rose. In 1594. With Edward Alleyn as Barabas. More than three shillings? That was Philip Henslowe's share for *The Jew of Malta* on December 9, 1594. How about the *Blind Beggar of Alexandria* two years later, which also netted Henslowe three shillings? Or *Faustus*, with Alleyn in the lead once more, for which Henslowe collected five shillings in January 1597? Given the vagaries of Henslowe's accounting (and the debate over how to reckon his sums), the arithmetic is uncertain, but these performances are among the three or four poorest paydays that Henslowe recorded in the years he managed the Rose. (Henslowe, we are told, got half the get, but three shillings is half of six shillings; as the mathematicians teach us, half of nothing is still nothing.) There must be a simple explanation for these meager receipts: weather. The sums appear in the middle of the London winter, when it's dark by noon and the damp cold can make your fingers strangers to your palms. Marlowe, schmarlowe—have you *been* to London in January?

For all the period's references to "the multitude" or "ten thousand spectators" or "Throng'd heapes," early modern actors, far more often than not, surveyed half-empty houses from the lip of the stage or gazed across the empty pit to a sodden crowd who, in Stephen Gosson's words, "sit out of the raine to viewe the [play], when many other pastimes are hindred by weather."[1] The image sustains Leeds Barroll's dry objection to those critics who imagine a London in which plays were available for viewing "every afternoon for year after sunny year."[2] Scholars have attempted to discern the capacity of the playhouses in the period—with Andrew Gurr noting that early accounts all suspiciously specify "exactly the same round figure of three thousand"—but Ann Jennalie Cook concludes from Henslowe's receipts that "on an ordinary day . . . the big theaters could expect to pull in about half their house capacity."[3] By "ordinary" Cook means every day except holidays and term times, in other words, what Prince Hal calls "all the year."

What did the Rose or Curtain or Swan look like on these days, when the actors may even have outnumbered the auditors? As luck would have it, we do not have to imagine, since the only graphic image of the interior of a London playhouse from the period depicts just such an occasion. By my count, there are eight spectators above the stage and no one in the pit or stalls. Of course, one objects, Johannes de Witt left the audience undrawn out of mere illustrative convention, but drawing an audience is the primary point of theater, and it is striking that our lone image of an early modern London playhouse in use inscribes the absence of this collection's primary concern.

There should be a special word, a German word, for the peculiar gloom of an empty playhouse, a structure built to inhabit thousands but that echoes instead with their absence. John Webster employed a fitting oxymoron to express this contradiction as he shivered in recollection at the poorly attended premiere of *The White Devil* at the Red Bull, presented in "so dull a time a winter." It was the weather and the theater—"so open and black"—that doomed his *Devil*, since "it wanted a full . . . auditory."[4] In Webster's formulation, "open" and "black" conveys the peculiar way in which, even in a "universally lit" amphitheater, it is lights out without an audience. (It is worth comment that the success of *The White Devil*, for Webster, is defined purely by its reception.) With Henslowe and Webster in mind, we might read Jonson's belligerent vow to be satisfied with one approving spectator—"So he judicious be; He shall b' alone / A Theatre unto me"—as a documentary account of a bad day at the playhouse rather than, as some critics do, an incipient program for the antitheatricality of *Sejanus*.[5] For once, Jonson might not be exaggerating just to make a point.

Early English theater failed. Good plays, anthologized plays like *Faustus* and *The White Devil* failed—failed occasionally—in the primary sense that they, like de Witt, did not draw an audience. They failed due not to dramaturgical flaws, thematic imprecision, or narrative superfluity but because of occasional problems: weather; traffic; boredom; sickness; or, just possibly, there was something better to do, like eat, drink, or flog a servant. There are always good reasons not to see *Doctor Faustus*. Then, as now, plays in performance are hostage to a thousand daily accidents. Theater is, ultimately, an art of radical contingency.

While *Doctor Faustus* the eternized literary phenomenon succeeded (and succeeded wildly beyond, we might suppose, even the outsized dreams of its ambitious maker), on January 5, 1597, *Doctor Faustus* the mortal theatrical event failed—and failed utterly. It will be the argument of this essay that, on such occasions, contingency trumped habituation. And it was the work of early modern playwrights, players, and playhouses—in other words, *the industry*—to make certain it never, ever happened again (until it did). After all, the industry did not want the occasional crowd; they wanted an everyday audience. They generated this audience, I will argue, principally by converting the occasional into the everyday by, in effect, domesticating the crowd. An audience is, ultimately, a cultivated crowd; and players, playwrights, and playhouses colluded to give the crowd a domesticated experience of itself through the spectacularization of space and the habituation of playgoing.

Crowd Control

The control of crowds is the necessary work of civic officials. J. S. McClelland writes, in *The Crowd and the Mob: From Plato to Canetti*, that "[c]rowds . . . cause more trouble in sites dominated by great cities, simply because there a marginalized population existed which could become a crowd much more easily than . . . in the countryside. . . . There [in cities] a way had to be found of coping with the crowds which were always more or less a permanent feature of their existence."[6]

Crowds may not have been a "permanent feature" of London life but, by metastasizing over the last quarter century of the 1600s, London had, by Shakespeare's age, become a city of crowds—crowded outside St. Paul's to hear a sermon, gathered on corners to listen to chapmen, packed in yards to wager on cockfights, lining the Fleet for coronation processions, jammed in an amphitheater for *Lear* or blood sports. With a population cresting two hundred thousand by 1580, London had evolved with astounding speed from the large market town that Chaucer knew to an international center of commerce and nascent colonial power.

The experience of being in a crowd may have been a novelty to many Londoners, for it was immigration that fueled London's growth. London's crowds may have shocked even those immigrants from smaller cities, however. Only three other cities in England had populations over ten thousand, their total population a mere third of London's. London was growing far faster than any other urban center and much faster than the country at large.[7] Alfred Harbage speculated that the novelty of London's sprawl promoted a peculiarly Elizabethan wariness for mass sociability: "Elizabethans had a very real fear of the potentialities of a crowd—any crowd," he concludes. "They were less used to crowds than we are."[8] That fear may have been justified. Early modern Londoners were, apparently, somewhat renowned for bad behavior. In 1525, Jean Froissart spoke to their notorious reputation: "The Englishmen are the perilousest people of the world and most outrageousest if they be up, and specially the Londoners."[9] Closer to home, city fathers, preachers, poets, and players complained of "tumults" and "outrages" at public gatherings, particularly the theaters. London's late sixteenth-century population boom produced and sustained the city's emergent commercial leisure industry, but it presented novel challenges to those charged with maintaining urban order.

McClelland has also suggested that "there has been a particular way of looking at crowds in every period of history,"[10] and the early moderns who cared to address the topic in print did, indeed, have an orthodox view of collective behavior. They did not like it. Describing the place of the crowd in Renaissance politics, Christopher Hill summarizes the period's dubiety: "Most writers about politics during the century before 1640 agreed that democracy was a bad thing."[11] This is a mild assessment, since the contempt, derision, and bile that writers categorically heaped upon crowds in the drama, sermons, verse, and prose of this period approach pathology or, what is more likely, tropic conventionality. There is no need here to compile a list of quotations to prove the prevalence of the "many-headed multitude" in Renaissance literature. Hill, among others, has done just that.[12] The Horatian tag *bellua multorum capitum* (Epistles 1.1.76) was a Renaissance commonplace, and the many reiterations include those of Sidney in his *Arcadia*, Thomas Browne in *Religio Medici*, Spenser in Book V of the *Faerie Queene*, and Milton in *Paradise Regained*. Heterodox in genre, politics, poetics, and theology, these touchstones of English Renaissance literary achievement share a decidedly dim view of the common crowd. The metaphor, points out a modern critic, is "common to the point of vulgarity."[13] When Shakespeare's Coriolanus reproves the crowd as "many-headed," a citizen notes wearily that "[w]e have been called so of many" (2.3.16–17).

For the early moderns, as in so many respects, the phenomenon emerged before a theory to understand it. The English crowd was a literary topos for early writers, not a sociological topic. Serious study of the crowd would wait until the eighteenth century, proximate with the French Revolution. In the hands of Gustave Le Bon, a leading exponent of crowd psychology at the turn of the eighteenth century, "crowd" signified not purely as a sociological description of collective behavior but rather as a "hostile symbol for what he saw as the irrationality of mass politics."[14] George Lefebvre was the first modern historian to take up the crowd as a subject worth serious scrutiny in his 1924 book *Les Paysans du Nord pendant la Révolution française*. Tracing social and historical patterns of crowd phenomena, he drew a sharp line between "crowds" as spontaneous social gatherings and "assemblies" as "more voluntary association[s],"[15] the transition from the former to the latter being the operative concern of the early English theater industry.

Such precision of definition did not seem of any particular interest to the early moderns, for whom "crowd" seemed simply to mean a gathering of folk below their breeding. Defining the "crowd" is, however, of central concern to Le Bon, Lefebvre, and perhaps the most renowned student of "collective behavior" (the preferred nomenclature of contemporary social scientists) George Rudé (for whom any large gathering in one place constituted a "crowd"). Robert Holton, reviewing the history and contemporary thrust of collective behavior studies, offers this cogent summary of evolving terminology and the ends of such studies:

> If "crowd" is defined as collective assembly in the streets or some other public place, such behavior may be clearly distinguished from other forms of social action, namely the privatized activities of individuals and small groups within households, and the formal processes of bureaucratic institutions. Crowd study may then be seen as an investigation of why it is that particular social movements, communities, and societies become involved in collective behaviour . . . and what function and meaning such behaviour in its different forms has for the movement, community, or society involved. This enterprise is likely to shed further light on the origins, meanings, and function of territorial and community identity from the level of street and neighborhood to that of nation, thereby contributing to an understanding of social order.[16]

Definition work is also central, I suggest, to an understanding of the work of the early theater industry, which actively solicited a "crowd" but just as actively wanted to cultivate an audience.

Is it "audience" or "audiences," as this collection's subtitle tacitly asks? One thing or many things? In his *Origins of Contemporary France* in 1876, Hippolyte Taine had introduced the now familiar notion that crowds think in *idées fixe*, that the crowd has a "group mind" whose working does not echo that of the individual.[17] Taine gets credit for the term, though Francis Bacon observed in 1603 that "the minds of men in company are more open to affection and impression than when alone," though Bacon does not imply that "minds of men" would all be working in conjunction.[18] Taine's focus on the "group mind" has a relevant application to the theatrical crowds of early modern London, for, as Bacon implies, it was the melting into collective consciousness of individual subjectivity that impressed and concerned early modern commentators.

The tension between the concept of "audience" and that of "audiences" was of primary concern to the theater industry, which worked hard to turn a collective into a collective noun. Taine's notion of groupthink, for instance, jars with dramatic characterizations of the crowd, which stress multifariousness. In *Coriolanus*, the third citizen unpacks the image of the "many-headed multitude," noting the variety—not conformity—of the varied minds: "[T]ruly I think if all our wits were to issue out of one skull, they would fly east, west, north, south, and their consent of one direct way should be at once to all the points o'th' compass" (2.3.17–21). Against later notions of the collective mind, we have to hold up early modern figural locutions that posit quite a different dynamic. Scholars of early modern audiences who are concerned less with actual and more with perceptual demographics frequently split over this very concern: whether to treat the audience as one thing or a group of many things, whether the audience communed in "sacramentalized collectivity" or enjoyed the pleasures of "radical individuation," in Paul Yachnin's terms.[19] It is the argument in what follows that the internal tension between collectivity and individuation formed the gyre around which the audience experience rotated. This internal, central dynamic of the crowd, toggling between individual thinking and groupthink, fueled particular industry-wide dramaturgical, histrionic, and programmatic strategies that proceeded along two fronts: the "public transportation," or mass conversion of a collection of individuals into a complacent audience, and the programmatic habituation of playgoing into the lives of early modern Londoners.

Public Transportation

If the control of crowds is the necessary work of civic officials, then it is also the necessary work of the dramatist. The public theaters arguably hosted the most commercialized and habitual opportunities for mass sociability in Elizabethan London. Among other things, playgoing provided an opportunity for Londoners to confront the dilemma that makes urban life simultaneously exciting and intolerable: other people, and lots of them, in extremely tight quarters.

Guy Debord has argued that communities that eliminate geographical space reproduce it in the form of spectacular separation. Such communities therefore develop "technologies of separation," or what, in the context of the present argument, we might call "theater."[20] Applied to the world of early modern London, these technologies included the particular time and space of the playhouses themselves (considered later) and the significant and signifying action of the player, which in collusion with the playhouse architecture worked simultaneously to gather bodies and create space among them, sanitizing the crowd of its violent potentialities and rendering them habitually complacent (or complacently habituated, in the inevitable postmodern chiasmic inversion).

After all, however real the Renaissance fears of crowds may have been, the records in fact reveal few violent disturbances at the playhouses. The playhouse riots of 1584, 1592, and 1597 and the occasional attacks against the playhouses on apprentice holidays like Shrove Tuesday and Mayday seem the product of traditional apprentice grievances. Moreover, such affrays took place at, not in, the playhouses. Given the frequency of playing indicated, for instance, by Henslowe's records, and given the fact that by 1595 the theaters were drawing upward of fifteen thousand spectators a week—ratings that would make Neilsen blush—few serious "outrages" are recorded relative to the many opportunities for audiences to erupt.[21] As Andrew Gurr notes, "[C]onsidering the alarm so regularly voiced by the civil authorities, particularly in the 1580s and 1590s, the number of affrays that actually engaged audiences inside the playhouse was almost nil."[22] Considered from history's safe remove, theatrical strategies of crowd control seem wildly successful.

In fact, direct references to the audiences who attended the public playhouses more often point out the fearful press of the bodies that loomed over and around the players and the potential violence directed not at one another but at the actor's rather vulnerable body, which may seem to refract audience hostility or energy from one another to the representative onstage figure(s). Northrop Frye has characterized the Elizabethan age as one whose attentions were focused by a "centripetal gaze," an optical metaphor for the increasingly central power of London and the spectacular presentations of the dramaturgically conscious Tudor court with the queen as cynosure of all eyes.[23] But Frye's "centripetal gaze" describes well the physics beneath the slightly alarmed current that runs through descriptions of actors before crowds. John Earle affirms a material source for Frye's "centripetal gaze." "The eyes," writes Earle, "of all men are upon him [the actor]."[24] In *Kind-Hartes Dream*, Henry Chettle goes a step further and diagnoses a phobic condition inherent to acting, that of being "publike in everie ones eye, and talkt of in every vulgar mans mouth."[25] Chettle's focus on the eyes and ears of the public introduces a queasy digestive metaphor implying that acting involves not only indecent exposure but also a reciprocal supply and demand between artistic production and the audience's appetite. With a worrying look at the audience above and around him, a Clown in *The Three Ladies of London* fulfills the digestive figure introduced by Chettle. The actor worries aloud, "But yonder is a fellow that gapes to bite me, or else to eat that which I sing."[26] The player feels his body to be at risk—fodder for a demanding audience member. Representation—"that which I sing"—is the defensive proxy for the actor's exposed body, singing for supper instead of becoming the entree. Consumer culture indeed. Competing with the audience for space (onstage in the private playhouses, at his feet in the public), the player spectacularizes the proximity through display, providing a defense against the crowd's press.[27] Representation deflects the centripetal gaze.

Like their numbers, the conduct of the Elizabethan audience has been subject to colorful and perhaps overly fanciful review. Popular characterizations portray the audiences that populated the suburban theaters as nut-cracking hooligans, favoring a romantic notion of a rough-and-tumble Elizabethan stage. History's bias can favor the piquant at the expense of the plain, selecting anomaly over habit. Certainly, contemporary accounts capture for us something of the occasionally unruly and always pungent crowds, who "choked" the players "with the stench of garlic" and were given to bombarding the players with missiles to demonstrate critical disapproval.[28] Just as often, however, accounts retrieve for us an audience more rapt than rapping, transported by the centripetal attention. For Thomas Dekker, it is the audience's mute wonder, not their boisterous interference, that disturbs him; he imagines a playwright soliciting an audience "on tiptoe, to Reach-up, / And (from *Rare silence*) clap their Brawny hands, / T'Applaud, what their charmd soule scarce understands."[29] Gosson similarly records the responses of an enthusiastically attentive audience in the "publike Theaters" who "[s]tand upright with delight and eagernesse to view . . . a noble shew."[30] Or George Puttenham, who grumps of an audience, "[T]heir eares so attentive to the matter, and their eyes upon the shewes of the stage, that they take little heede to the cunning of the rime."[31] The same John Webster who urged his readers to "sit in a full theater, and . . . thinke you see so many lines drawne from the circumference of so many eares, whiles the actor is the center" wrote of the actor that "by a full and significant action of body . . . [he] charmes our attention."[32] Acting here is imagined to possess a quasi-Orphic capacity to "charm" a restive crowd into complacency.

Webster's emphasis on the signifying mimicry of the representing player (with a detectable trace of the Orphic notion of the orator) brings us back to the mollifying purpose of playing. Muriel Bradbrook points out that "bewitching" and "entrancing" are adjectives that both Gosson and Thomas Nashe use to condemn and to praise the stage respectively.[33] In *Plays Confuted in Five Actions*, Stephen Gosson captures the baiting relationship between audience and the player as well as the entrancing effect of fictional representation. Deploying the feeding metaphor discussed above, Gosson describes an audience watching Bacchus woo Ariadne: "the beholders rose up, every man on tiptoe and seemed to hover over the prey."[34] Gosson's description invokes what one critic calls "the dark origins" of theater as blood sport.[35] The purpose of playing—or the purpose of playing well—was in part to ensure that the audience continued merely to hover, never to descend.

While Gosson describes an audience collectively transported by mimesis, Nathan Field's slippery grammar brings us back to the curious ontological status of collective gatherings engaged in a singular activity. Describing an entertainment in 1608, he recalls the threatening "monster" who "clapped his thousand hands / And drowned the scene with / His confused cry."[36] The singular possession of plural attributes—"his thousand hands"—characterizes the unifying effect of publicly exercised critical judgment. In fact, while accounts of playgoing and playgoers stress the diversity of the audience, accounts of audience behavior at plays stress the singularity of audiences unified by pleasure or contempt. Thus, even as Gosson emphasizes that the crowd "take[s] up a wonderful laughter and shout[s] all together with one voice," John Davies in 1595 can epigrammatize the crowd's diversity:[37]

> For as we see at all playhouse doors,
> When ended is the play, the dance, and song,
> A Thousand townsmen, gentlemen, and whores,
> Porters and servingmen together throng.[38]

In the *Gull's Hornbook*, Dekker also attests to audience diversity, the theater "allowing a stoole as well to the Farmers sonne as to your Templer."[39] An anonymous observer notes that "Gentiles mix'd with Groomes" at the playhouse, while Gosson himself anatomizes the "monster of many heads" as comprising "Tailors, Tinkers, Cordwayners, Saylers, Olde Men, yong Men, Women, Boyes, Girles and such like."[40] Contemporary observations have it both ways, uneasily noting the "mixing" of diverse persons while attesting to the singularity of an audience at play.

John Davies's diagnosis of playhouse diversity focuses on the end of the play. At some point between the play's end and the audience's exit, collectivity reverts to diversity, as the singular audience disintegrates into Davies's varied collection of class and vocational representatives. Here we can cite Elias Canetti's important point that it is the "expectation of reassembly" that eases the transition from audience to throng.[41] In a passage of indecipherable oddness, Thomas Dekker in 1613 described the breakup of the audience upon completion of a play, when—still under the spell of the playhouse fiction—the departing audience metamorphizes back into throng, offering the form of a tumult but none of its violent actuality:

> I have often seen after the finishing of some worthy tragedy or catastrophe in the open theatres that the scene after the epilogue hath been more black . . . than the most horrid scene in the play was; the stinkards speaking all things, yet no man understanding anything; a mutiny being among them, yet none in danger; no tumult, yet no quietness; no mischief begotten and yet mischief born; the swiftness of such a torrent, the more it overwhelms, breeding the more pleasure.[42]

For Dekker (who like Webster juxtaposes "open" and "black"), the "scene after the epilogue" blurs the threshold between performance and postperformance, an ambivalent dilation of the play. Hovering somewhere between "tumult" and "quietness"—between rapping and rapture—the departing audience feel their unity collapsing into diversity, their status as audience giving way to a status as throng. Yet as an extension of the playhouse "scene," the experience offers the wild excitement of the torrent without the grave and bloody consequence, sparagmos deflected from the single body of the actor and dispersed and diffused among the spectators. The experience of playgoing—of attending to the actor's "significant action" of the body—has emptied the event of violent potential, substituting a habit of pleasurable participation for the violent potential of impromptu gatherings.

The peculiar architecture of London's playhouses colludes in this habituation of the crowd. From the few contemporary illustrations, we know that the suburban theaters of London looked like no other urban structures. Their profile, purpose, and the space they occupied were well known. Outside, facing the city, the arenas displayed an impassive wall. Inside, as Canetti observes, "the spectators turn their backs to the city. . . . They have left behind all their associations, rules, and habits. Their remaining together in large numbers for a stated period of time is secure and their excitement has been promised them. But only under one definite condition: the discharge must take place inside the arena. . . . The crowd is seated opposite itself. Every spectator has a thousand in front of him. . . . There is no break in the crowd that sits like this, exhibiting itself to itself."[43] Canetti is not expressly describing the theaters of Elizabethan London, but his speculations accord with the physical disposition of Southwark's and Shoreditch's theaters. The crowd "exhibits itself to itself," a mimetic reproduction of an impromptu throng. The closed crowd may freely digest the performance onstage, participating in the heady charge of the baiting crowd with none of the dire consequence.

Canetti also suggests a helpful typology of the successfully habituated playgoing crowd. The "closed crowd," as he terms it, renounces growth for habit:

> It has a boundary. It establishes itself by accepting its limitations. . . . The entrances to this space are limited in number, and only these entrances can be used; the boundary is respected whether it consists of stone, of solid wall, or of some special act of acceptance, or entrance fee. Once the space is completely filled, no one else is allowed in. . . . The important thing is always the dense crowd in the closed room. . . . The crowd sacrifices its chance of growth, but gains in staying power. . . . It is the expectation of reassembly which enables its members to accept each dispersal. The building is waiting for them; it exists for their sake and so long as it is there, they will be able to meet in the same manner.[44]

Through repetition and commodification, the crowd is institutionalized, given its own form. The habitual repetition of the act gives the crowd what Canetti calls a "domesticated experience of itself."[45] The crowd becomes an audience playing a crowd. Habituation, routine, and domestication enervate the crowd's potential for violence, for collective mischief. Theater crowds, in Canetti's terms, forego the improvisatory wildness of unruly throngs for the promise of repetition. The closed crowd polices itself through an unspoken decorum of behavior; repetition calcifies into habit.

The interaction of the architectural and human fabrics—playhouse and player—collaborate in what Debord calls the "technology of separation." The playhouse's circumambient structure focuses the audience's attention on a single or small group of representative figures, which collude to pacify through the creating of spectacular distance. Intriguingly, Londoners had, technically, to leave the city proper to enjoy a spectacular representation of urban proximities, for while they largely failed to bring playhouses into the city, players and playwrights brought the city into the playhouse. The epilogue to *Eastward Ho* directly analogizes the view from the stage with a glimpse of a city crowd gathered on balconies for a festive occasion. In this rare, eyewitness view of the surrounding galleries, the actor imagines the interior face of the theater as a streetscape of house fronts curved into a ring: "I perceive the multitude are gatherd together to view our coming out at the counter. See if the streets and the fronts of houses, be not stacked with people, and the windowes fild with Ladies, as on the solemne day of the pageant!"[46] The city is here reproduced in the playhouse, what Michael Drayton called the "proud round" encircling the stage transformed into a festive urban scene.[47] James Shirley goes one step further when he proposes that playgoing may substitute for a young man's continental tour, since "the three howers spectacle . . . were usually more advantage to the hopefull young heire, then a costly, dangerous, forraigne Travell, with the assistance of a governing Mounsieur, or Signior to boot."[48] Shirley opens up the meanings of "vicarious" here, articulating the ways in which theatrical experience can substitute for the heavy investments of foreign travel. With his emphasis on instruction, vicarious experience, and representative space, Shirley gives full expression to the ways in which playgoing gives to the audience a domesticated experience of itself while simultaneously creating distance, an idea more familiarly bruited by the prologue to *Henry V*.

Enclosed, ultimately, within the etymology of the "playhouse" is the domestication of festivity—a "house" for holidays, for leisure, for the crowd to experience itself in its metropolitan plenitude. But while Hal's sententious "[i]f all the year were playing holidays, / To sport would be as tedious as to work" serves the strategies of an aspirant monarch, it was, perversely, the theater industry's operative strategy to convert sport into work, to rebrand theatrical attendance from "playing holidays" into the tediousness, or at least regularity, of a workaday enterprise.[49]

The Everyday Audience

While I suggest that the actor inserts and creates spectacular separation between his body and the audience—creating representative distance where none actually exists—the theater industry also carefully cultivated a space and time to habituate its audience to the routines of regular attendance. Cook has estimated that over the years of London's population growth from one hundred fifty thousand to three hundred fifty thousand no more than between 1 and 2 percent of London's total population regularly attended the theater. Early modern theatrical success required repeat business, which prologues explicitly urge upon the auditory ("And when sixe times you ha' seen't / If this *Play* doe not like, the Divell is in't").[50] Surely one of the reasons the industry developed repertorial programming was to urge and reward daily attendance. Just as greater London's growth relied on immigration, London's theatrical industry relied on repeat business and therefore needed through its practices to encourage and routinize playgoing.

Routines require a conceptualization of daily experience that works along a grid where the twin axes of space and time discipline the daily activities of the subject, governing when and where the subject engages in a particular behavior. The emergent theatrical/leisure industry inscribed itself on this spatiotemporal grid by providing particular buildings that could be relied on to provide a particular experience at a particular time every day (even if, as outlined later, the "particular time" for performances in the period was no more precisely defined than "the afternoon"). Theatrical success depended on the theater industry's ability to incise itself on the "leisure grid" of London's elite and others, inculcating playgoing as reflex, or that which does not require decision.

Through its repertorial practices and spatiotemporal location on London's leisure grid, then, the theater industry converted the occasional into the everyday. For a register of theater's successful inscription on the conceptual map of London life, we may observe the period's satiric quasi-Theophrastian verses, which often sketch the rigorously organized sloth of the privileged Londoner:

> My Lord most court-like lyes in bed 'till noone,
> Then, all high-stomacht riseth to his dinner,
> Falls straight to Dice, before his meate be downe,
> Or to digest, walks to some femall sinner.
> Perhaps fore-tyred he gets him to a play,
> Comes home to supper, and then falls to dice,
> There his devotion wakes 'til it be day,
> And so to bed, where until noone he lies.[51]

The poem generates its comic torque from the idea of programmatic lassitude, but the verse articulates the theater industry's absorption into the circadian routine of the indolent gentleman. As in this example by Edward Guilpin, these comic "to do lists" routinely include playgoing as the afternoon's employment (just squeezed in here between fornication and dice), but the playhouses occupy a spatial coordinate on the grid as well. John Earle notes that a gallant's "business is the street: the Stage, the Court and those places where a proper man is best shown," fully articulating the spatiotemporal logic of the man at leisure's diurnal schedule for whom playgoing occupies both a time and place: his afternoons are spent at the playhouse, and so are his shillings.[52]

Such poems borrow from—and mock—the numbing regularity of the period's sacred and pedagogical schedules, such as that of Edward Waterhouse while at the Inns of Court, which serve to discipline the subject within a paratactic but rational order of events:

> From 5 in the morning to 6. Ad Sacra. Begin with God by reading and prayer.
> From 6. To 9. Ad Jura. Read the law carefully and understandingly.
> From 9. To 11. Ad Arma. Carry on harmless acts of Manhood, Fencing, Dancing &.c.
> From 11. To 12. Ad Artes, Forget not Academique learning, Logick, Rhetorick.[53]

Hour by hour, the schedule ambitiously grows, minutely regulating the day's activities, which end with a stress upon repetition: "Ad Repetitionem & Sacras, Repeat your Parts and say your Prayers . . . To Bed betimes, and rise betimes again."[54] From such forms, verse parodies borrow their emphasis on repetition and regularity of both time and space: "Your Theaters hee daily doth frequent"; "The places thou dost usually frequent / Is to some playhouse in an afternoon"; "You are our daily and most constant Guests." "Daily," "usually," and "constant" register the metronomic regularity of playgoing on which the industry relied.[55] Indeed, the dreary regularity of this routinization enervates the courtier of Sir John Davies's similar epigram "In Fuscum," for whom, like Ben Jonson, plays have become work:

> [H]e's like a horse, which turning round a mill,
> Doth always in the self-same circle tread. . . .
> Thus round he runs without variety.
> Save that sometimes he comes not to the Play,
> But falls into a whore-house by the way."[56]

Vive la différence. The emphasis is on the way that diversion has become routine, that regular playgoing makes a business out of pleasure, which is, after all, the theater industry's business model. For this playgoer, to sport has become "as tedious as to work." Certainly, the poems cited here all sound of satire, but for the period's playmakers, these words sound like money. They sound like success.

The theater industry's place, space, time, and programming all colluded to inculcate playgoing with an almost pedagogic rigor. Its success in doing so is reflected by both advocates for and critics of the stage, who frequently observe the pedagogical parallels in ritualized playgoing, in Gosson's tendentious "school of abuse" metaphor. William Prynne complains of Inns of Court men—like Waterhouse—for whom playgoing is "one of the first things they learne as soone as they are admitted, to see Stage-playes, & take smoke at a Play-house, which they commonly make their Studie."[57] Less severe critics nevertheless censure not playgoing but *repeated* playgoing: "I wholly condemn the daily frequenting of them [plays]: as some there be (especially in this Citie) who, for want of better imployment, make it their Vocation."[58] Richard Brathwaite has no objection to "occasional" playgoing, which in itself is no vice, but to turn "occasional" into "vocational" is, again, to mistake a holiday for workaday. Quoted earlier, James Shirley, naturally enough an advocate of playgoing, wanders perilously close to undercutting his own argument when he refers to the plays of Beaumont and Fletcher, who "made Blackfriers an Academy,"[59] reminding us, once again, that protheatrical and antitheatrical tracts are frequently indistinguishable. These prose and poem portraits all reflect the astonishing degree to which the playgoing culture had, in just a decade of commercial operation, successfully incised itself upon the everyday life of early modern London, coming to occupy a fixed coordinate on the experiential leisure grid.

Finally, we might understand the domestication of the crowd's festive energy within the paradigm of popular culture powerfully articulated by Michael Bristol and others. Bristol traces the manner in which the commercial theaters commodified traditional ludic elements that resided in nearly all social groups and communities in early modern London. As an example, Bristol traces the building of the Chester pageant giant in 1602 as an instance of popular festive expression, and he summarizes the technical achievements and civic cooperation required to build and maintain such artifacts as marvels of technical proficiency and sophisticated civic cooperation. Such expressions were important registers of collective civic identity but also, as Bristol makes plain, required a complex outsourcing of specialized labor. One of the functions of the professional theaters in London, then, was to offer "the commodities of spectacle, narrative, and conviviality without the time-consuming burdens of skilled engagement or social commitment that would be required to obtain these same goods in a social world organized by the ethos of gift exchange."[60] In other words, with the rise of a commercialized leisure industry, you no longer had to build your own giant.

In Bristol's terms, the rise of a centralized, commercial theater industry in London—with a coterminous trade in and with the provinces—converted bespoke festivity into an off-the-rack experience. While the wholesale conversion of early English drama into a real estate–dominated endeavor with the advent of permanent playhouses in the 1570s has been overstated, it is true that the building of architecturally distinct, purpose-built playhouses in London in the last 25 years of the sixteenth century wrought a powerful change upon the habit of playgoing in England—by making it a habit (among other things). Whether playing in great halls, innyards, or marketplaces, traveling companies had temporarily to convert mixed-use spaces into theatrical venues, taking on the additional challenges of controlling access and collecting monies, temporarily cordoning a quotidian place as a theatrical space. Drawing an audience requires a temporary intrusion on or within the daily grid of experience. Defined as a single-use playing space, the Rose or Swan or Theatre or Curtain promised and delimited access, release, and replication and, in the process, codified, reified, and appropriated the prerogative of the crowd to make its own space in its own time and at its own choosing.

The Imaginary Audience

Describing the effect of Elizabethan London's magnificently messy sprawl on newly arrived immigrants, Ann Jennalie Cook suggests that "[f]irst-time visitors from the country must have felt like travelers to some fabled land."[61] But the land is no less fabulous to the modern scholar who seeks the bodies of those who first attended the plays around which our professional lives circle. In some respects, as the editors note in the introduction, this puts us in the company of the writers who first wrote these plays, since "imagined audiences" shaped the origins of those plays every bit as thoroughly as they do our reconstructions of those same plays' original receptions. As noted in this chapter's opening paragraphs, the "ten thousand spectators" who imagined brave Talbot bleeding afresh is roughly an order of magnitude larger than the size of the audience likely in attendance (one suspects that the early modern "ten thousand" was, like the modern "gazillion," a largely imaginary figure). Between the literal and the actual resides the academic imaginary—the cinematic projection that comprises the theatrical culture of the past. In one version of the academic imaginary, packed houses with broken teeth but whole hearts eagerly attend Joseph Fiennes's *Romeo and Juliet* or Olivier's *Henry V* (fingerless gloves de rigueur for the pit-dwellers). In yet another, a sparse and soggy crowd sit on their numb hands through yet another *Faustus*—tourists, surely, who, like Johannes de Witt, came on a bad day. Whether de Witt drew from life or not, he realistically portrayed the position of the scholar who contemplates the early modern audience. Ultimately, he did us a favor. He saved some space for us.

Notes

1. Henry Peacham, "Epigram 94," in *Thalia's Banquet* (London, 1620); Thomas Nashe, *Pierce Penilese*, in *The Works of Thomas Nashe*, ed. R. B. McKerrow (Oxford: Basil Blackwell, 1904–1905), 1:212; Thomas Dekker, *Roaring Girl*, in *The Dramatic*

Works of Thomas Dekker, ed. Fredson Bowers (Cambridge: Cambridge University Press, 1953), 3:17; Stephen Gosson, *Plays Confuted in Five Actions*, in *The English Drama and Stage under the Tudor and Stuart Princes, 1543–1664*, ed. William C. Hazlitt (London: Whittingham and Wilkins, 1869), 202.
2. Leeds Barroll, *Politics, Plague, and Shakespeare's Theatre: The Stuart Years* (Ithaca, NY: Cornell University Press, 1991), 172.
3. Andrew Gurr, *Playgoing in Shakespeare's London*, 3rd ed. (Cambridge: Cambridge University Press, 2004), 25; Ann Jennalie Cook, *The Privileged Playgoers of Shakespeare's London, 1576–1642* (Princeton, NJ: Princeton University Press, 1981), 190–91.
4. John Webster, "To the Reader" in *The White Devil, English Renaissance Drama: A Norton Anthology*, ed. David Bevington et al. (New York: Norton, 2002), 1664.
5. Ben Jonson, "Apologetical Dialogue," in *Poetaster*, vol. 9, *Ben Jonson: Works*, ed. C. H. Herford, Evelyn Simpson, and Percy Simpson (Oxford: Oxford University Press, 1950), 533.
6. J. S. McClelland, *The Crowd and the Mob: From Plato to Canetti* (London: Unwin Hyman, 1989), 73–74.
7. Roger Finlay, *Population and Metropolis: The Demography of London, 1580–1650* (Cambridge: Cambridge University Press, 1981), 7.
8. Alfred Harbage, *Shakespeare's Audience* (New York: Columbia University Press, 1941), 14.
9. Jean Froissart, *The Chronicles of Froissart*, trans. John Bourchier (London, 1524): chap. 242, 312 verso.
10. McClelland, *Plato to Canetti*, 1
11. Christopher Hill, "The Many-Headed Monster," in *Change and Continuity in Seventeenth Century England* (Cambridge, MA: Harvard University Press, 1975), 181–204, esp. 181.
12. See also C. A. Patrides, "'The beast with many heads': Views on the Multitude," in *Premises and Motifs in Renaissance Thought and Literature* (Princeton, NJ: Princeton University Press, 1982), 124–36; and Brent Stirlin, *The Populace in Shakespeare* (New York: Columbia University Press, 1949). Frederick Tupper Jr. long ago compiled an impressive series of references to the crowd in "The Shakespearean Mob," *Publications of the Modern Language Association of America* 27 (1912): 486–523. See also Kenneth Muir, "The Background of *Coriolanus*," *Shakespeare Quarterly* 10, no. 2 (1959): 144–45.
13. Patrides, "Beast," 132.
14. Robert J. Holton, "The Crowd in History: Some Problems of Theory and Method," *Social History* 3, no. 2 (1978): 219–34, esp. 220.
15. Quoted in Holton, "Crowd in History," 220.
16. Ibid., 221.
17. Quoted in McClelland, *Plato to Canetti*, 47.
18. Francis Bacon, *The Advancement of Learning* (Oxford: Clarendon Press, 1926), 116.
19. Paul Yachnin and Anthony Dawson, *The Culture of Playgoing in Shakespeare's England: A Collaborative Debate* (Cambridge: Cambridge University Press, 2001), 80.

20. Guy Debord, *The Society of the Spectacle*, trans. Ken Knabb (Paris: Black and Red, 1967), 167.
21. Muriel Bradbook writes that the "record of grave disturbances in the later sixteenth century is negligible in relation to the number of performances given." *The Rise of the Common Player: A Study of Actor and Society in Shakespeare's England* (London: Chatto and Windus, 1962), 51.
22. Gurr, *Playgoing in Shakespeare's London*, 56.
23. Northrop Frye, *The Anatomy of Criticism* (Princeton, NJ: Princeton University Press, 1957), 58.
24. John Earle, *Micro-cosmography* (London, 1628), 39.
25. Henry Chettle, *Kinde Hartes Dream* (1604; repr., London: Scolar Press, 1979).
26. Robert Wilson, *Three Ladies of London*, vol. 6, *A Select Collection of Old English Plays*, ed. Robert Dodsley, 14 vols. (London: Robert Dodsley, 1744), 206.
27. See Jonathan Haynes, "The Elizabethan Audience On Stage" in *The Theatrical Space: Themes in Drama*, ed. James Redmond (Cambridge: Cambridge University Press, 1987), 59–67, esp. 59.
28. John Marston, *Jack Drum's Entertainment* (London, 1616), H3v.
29. Thomas Dekker, *If This Be Not a Good Play the Devil Is in It*, in *The Dramatic Works of Thomas Dekker*, ed. Alfred Harbage (Baltimore, MD: Penguin Books, 1969), 952.
30. Gosson, *The Trumpet of War*, quoted in Gurr, *Playgoing in Shakespeare's London*, 45.
31. George Puttenham, *The Arte of English Poesie* (London, 1589), 82.
32. E. K. Chambers, *The Elizabethan Stage* (Oxford: Clarendon Press, 1923), 4:257–58.
33. M. C. Bradbrook, *Rise of the Common Player*, 110.
34. Gosson, *Plays Confuted*, 214.
35. Ralph Berry, "Twelfth Night: The Experience of the Audience," *Shakespeare Survey*, 34 (1981): 111–20.
36. Nathan Field, dedicatory verses to *The Faithful Shepherdess*, in *The Works of Beaumont and Fletcher* (London: George Routledge and Sons, 1880), 2:519, lines 33–34.
37. Gosson, *Plays Confuted*, 184.
38. *Epigrammes* 17, "In Cosmum," in *The Poems of Sir John Davies* (Oxford: Clarendon Press, 1975).
39. *Proemium* and chapter 6, in *The Gull's Horn Book*, in *The Non-Dramatic Works of Thomas Dekker*, ed. A. B. Grossart (London: 1884–86), 2:247.
40. *Pimlico, or Runne, Red-cap. Tis a Mad World at Hogsdon*, in *Ancient Drolleries*, ed. A. H. Bullen (Oxford: Oxford University Press, 1891), sig. C.; Gosson, *Plays Confuted*, 184.
41. Elias Canetti, *Crowds and Power*, trans. Carol Stewart (New York: Farrar, Straus, and Giroux, 1984), 17.
42. Thomas Dekker, *Strange Horse Race*, in *The Non-Dramatic Works of Thomas Dekker*, ed. A. B. Grossart (London: 1885), 3:340.
43. Canetti, *Crowds and Power*, 28.
44. Ibid., 17.
45. Ibid., 21.

46. H. Harvey Wood, ed., *The Plays of John Marston* (Edinburgh, UK: Oliver and Boyd, 1934), 3:171.
47. J. William Hebel, ed., *Works of Michael Drayton* (1961; repr., Oxford: Clarendon Press, 1931–1941), 2:123.
48. James Shirley, "To the Reader," in Beaumont and Fletcher's *Comedies and Tragedies Written by Francis Beaumont and John Fletcher Gentlemen*, by Francis Beaumont and John Fletcher (London, 1647), A3.
49. William Shakespeare, *Henry IV, Part One*, in *The Norton Shakespeare*, ed. Stephen Greenblatt, Walter Cohen, Jean E. Howard, and Katharine Eisaman Maus (New York: W. W. Norton, 2008): 1.2.182–83.
50. Ben Jonson, prologue to *The Devil Is an Ass*, in *Ben Jonson: Works*, ed. C. H. Herford, Evelyn Simpson, and Percy Simpson (Oxford: Oxford University Press, 1950), 6:459.
51. Edward Guilpin, "Of Gnatho," in *Skialetheia, or, a Shadowe of Truth in certain Satires and Epigrames* (London, 1598), A8.
52. Earle, *Micro-cosmography*, 54.
53. Edward Waterhouse, *Fortescus Illustratus* (London, 1663), 151–52.
54. Ibid.
55. Francis Lenton, *The Young Gallant's Whirligig* (London, 1629), 7; Thomas Cranley, "Amanda," in *The History of English Dramatic Poetry to the Time of Shakespeare*, by John P. Collier (London: G. Bell and Sons, 1879), 3:217–18; Henry Glapthorne, "To a Reviv'd Vacation Play," in *Plays and Poems* (London: John Pearson, 1874), 2:194.
56. Sir John Davies, *Epigrams*, in *The Complete Poems*, ed. Alexander B. Grosart (London: Chatto and Windus, 1876), 2:37–38.
57. William Prynne, "Epistle Dedicatory," in *Histrio-Mastix* (London, 1632), 3v.
58. Richard Brathwaite, *The English Gentleman and The English Gentlewoman* (London, 1641), 103.
59. Shirley, "To the Reader," A3.
60. Michael Bristol, "Theatre and Popular Culture," in *A New History of Early English Drama*, ed. John D. Cox and David Scott Kastan (New York: Columbia University Press, 1997), 231–51, esp. 239, 247.
61. Cook, *Privileged Playgoers*, 53.

CHAPTER 2

Taking the Stage

Spectators as Spectacle in the Caroline Private Theaters

Nova Myhill

Ben Jonson's *The Magnetic Lady* (1633) begins with two gentleman playgoers, Probee and Damplay, entering the Blackfriars stage in search of "the poet o' the day" (Induction 13) to "entreat an excellent play from you" (49).[1] The two gentlemen are seated on the stage throughout the play, presumably among the playgoers who have paid for stools on the stage. At first glance, the Induction and between-act sections of *The Magnetic Lady* would seem to function as a simple didactic model, an explicit attempt, like Jonson's other prologues and inductions, to encourage certain behaviors in his audience and discourage others: the two gentlemen comment, and the playhouse boy who serves as Jonson's mouthpiece approves the sentiments of Probee and discredits those of Damplay. In what follows, however, I wish to suggest that inductions such as Jonson's are ultimately less concerned with either enforcing or catering to a particular mode of spectatorship within the private theater audiences than with acknowledging the variety of available methods of watching, "provid[ing] the spectator with a sharpened perception of his [or her] own processes as a spectator,"[2] and ultimately refocusing the attention of the members of the audience onto the play rather than onto each other.

In "'Wits Most Accomplish'd Senate': The Audience of the Caroline Private Theaters," which remains the most useful study of the Caroline audience, Michael Neill argues that the Caroline private theater is frequented by and caters to a "highly sophisticated audience" that conceives of itself as "a court of taste . . . a closed group of *cognoscenti* who came to the playhouse not merely to be entertained but to appreciate and judge the offerings of the poet's fancy."[3]

The essay suggests a single, idealized model of spectatorship, which all members of the audience, regardless of their education and social status, wish to present themselves as embodying, thus becoming corporate members of the "court of taste" ultimately defined by "the aristocrats who . . . exercised an influence out of all proportion to their actual numbers."[4] This model is reinforced by "the dedications, prefaces, prologues, and epilogues . . . [that] are the record of the [playwrights'] relationship with this audience of discerning patrons and intimates";[5] Neill presents this relationship, in practice, as one of appeasement on the part of the playwrights in the face of "a hypercritical audience—[an attempt] to woo them into acquiescence."[6] The audience attends the theater for the purpose of judging plays, and authority in the playhouse lies exclusively with the audience.

But the inductions I discuss here, Jonson's Inductions to *The Magnetic Lady* and *The Staple of News* (1626) and Richard Brome's Praeludium written for the 1638 revival of Thomas Goffe's *The Careless Shepherdess*,[7] suggest two important corollaries to this model: this self-conscious audience functioned as spectacle as well as spectators and, as a result, the plays make judgments about their spectators as thoroughly and visibly as the audience judges the plays. The theater offered not only the chance to develop the "essential accomplishment" of "the appreciation and judgment of works of dramatic art"[8] but also, as importantly, the chance to publicly display one's possession of this accomplishment. As Neill observes, "[T]he profession of critical connoisseurship was open to any gentleman who could buy admission to the private playhouses"[9]: Brome's Induction to *The Careless Shepherdess* suggests that the stage offers not only a place for gentlemen to show their membership in this "profession" but also a chance to display their clothes and for their social inferiors to "occupy a place near you: there are / None that be worthy of my company / In any room beneath the twelve penny."[10] In dramatizing members of the audience sharing the physical space of the stage with the actors—the gallants on stools who make up a prominent part of the stage spectacle, at times actively competing with the players for both space and attention—Jonson and Brome's staging of spectatorship reclaims the stage for the players and suggests that the experience of playgoing is as subject to judgment as the plays themselves. Like the actual audience of the private theater, the audience members represented in these inductions come to the theater for a variety of reasons, including interest in costumes, topical application, stylistic judgment, and self-display. Jonson and Brome's interest in the variety of methods of spectatorship opens all of them to criticism, or at least self-consciousness.

While evidence certainly suggests that the Caroline private theaters served a much more socially homogenous clientele than their Elizabethan predecessors, the representations of this audience emphasize, to a much greater extent than representations of Elizabethan audiences, the diversity of tastes and viewing practices both between members of different social groups and within members of the same group. Probee and Damplay, for instance, are socially and economically united, speaking on behalf of "the better and braver sort of your people! Plush and velvet outsides!" (31–32), who are willing to pay eighteen pence or two shillings for seats in Blackfriars, not "your sinful sixpenny mechanics" (30). Probee and Damplay are represented as typical members of that segment of the Blackfriars audience. In most important ways, they are identical to one another—the significant difference is only how they watch a play. This divergence in their viewing practices might be important in how we imagine the relation between the Caroline audience and the actors and playwrights, particularly since Probee and Damplay's social uniformity presents a challenge to Neill's claim that "such distinctions [in viewing practices] tended to be largely fictitious and designed to flatter the aristocrats."[11]

Neill's analysis does not distinguish between literary and theatrical prefatory materials; a crucial feature of his argument indeed depends on understanding the literary qualities of Caroline drama as the central feature admired by the audience of connoisseurs whose tastes shaped the drama. The most interesting aspects of the inductions, and to a lesser extent the prologues and epilogues, however, are precisely their theatrical features, through which the audience and the play explicitly occupy the same space and are visible in the same ways. In their recent work on Elizabethan prologues, Douglas Bruster and Robert Weimann emphasize the liminal qualities of the prologue—both as a piece of writing and as a figure on the stage—"alternately deferential and commanding," recognizing both the audience's power over the play (including the power to simply silence it by refusing to stop talking) and the play's power over the audience, to take it to another world.[12] This sense of liminality is even more pronounced in inductions than in prologues and epilogues; if the prologue and epilogue function as a "threshold, a liminal space between the actual and the potential that characterized the 'playing holidays' of dramatic fiction in the early modern playhouse," they do so for the space of about thirty lines, with the body of a single actor.[13] The induction extends over much more time and, importantly, space.

In her discussion of "critical inductions," those with a specific focus on theatrical production and reception, Thelma Greenfield notes that by 1604 such inductions are considerably more common in plays performed at private theaters than in plays performed at public theaters. She attributes this to Harbage's suggestion that "the Globe theater audience was less in need of a lesson in good manners than the more elegant patrons of the private theaters."[14] It seems to me that the greater frequency of inductions that include representations of the audience in private theaters than public is more significantly a product of the physical than the social configuration of the audience. Only in the private theaters do members of the theater audience physically share the space of the stage with the performers, competing for space and the attention of the rest of the audience. While the presence of spectators on the stages of the private theaters, particularly the Blackfriars, was a well-established theatrical convention, it was also the subject of regular satire and other forms of complaint from some of the playwrights, particularly Jonson, who seems never to have accepted the situation and whose anxieties about reception are amply visible in his inductions, prologues, and printed prefatory matter.[15] I would like to view these anxieties as reasonable rather than hyperbolic here and consider the stage sitters as a potentially serious alternative focus for the theater audience.

Theater historians have in general been at pains to minimize the potential disruption from these spectators, consistently making the smallest possible estimate of their numbers that the evidence will allow. This reading of the evidence seems to stem from a visceral distaste for an audience that might authentically compete with the play for the rest of the audience's attention: "[W]hether or not the space available for acting is sufficient, one winces at the thought of drama huddled in such an extensive frame of spectators in all postures."[16] Precisely because of this uneasy sense that any large number of stage sitters might fatally compromise the production, it seems worth taking Jonson's complaints, which routinely mention physical contact between actors and stage sitters, seriously for a moment.[17] The prologue to *The Devil is an Ass* (1616) is almost entirely concerned with the physical constraints the stage sitters—the "grandees"—impose on the actors. Jonson asks the audience not to force them to "act / In compass of a cheese-trencher"[18] and specifically complains about the physical contact "when you will thrust and spurn, And knock us on the elbows" (11–12) and the assumption that the audience controls the stage space "and bid [the actors], turn; / As if, when we had spoke, we must be gone, / Or till we speak, must all run in, to one, / Like the young adders to the old one's mouth!" (12–15). The prologue complains that the audience wants not live actors but "Muscovy glass," translucent images, "that you might look our scenes through as they pass" (17–18). The substance of the audience threatens that the play "through want of room . . . must miscarry" (23), as the stage affords room for only one set of bodily presences. In the *Gull's Horn Book* (1609), Dekker similarly observes that should the gallant seated on the stage "rise with a skreud and discontented face . . . and draw what troop you can from the stage after you: the *Mimicks* are beholden to you, for allowing them elbow room."[19]

Recently, Tiffany Stern has imagined the spectacle of the stage sitters in considerable detail, considering how this "living decoration" of "colored silks, satins, and feathers" provided both a backdrop for the plays and serious competition for the attention of the playgoers.[20] In this context, inductions that represent stage sitters, as in *The Staple of News*, *The Magnetic Lady*, and *The Careless Shepherdess*, represent not the audience's intrusion into the stage space but the actors' intrusion into the space of the audience, if the stage itself can be said to be demarcated into actor space and audience space. The inductions themselves suggest that this division is physically impossible; if the liminal stage space is to be divided, then this must happen based on newly drawn boundaries not in space but in behavior.

At this point, I would like to return to Probee and Damplay in their position as precise representations of the gentleman playgoers who command the stage of the Blackfriars. The fundamental difference between these gentleman playgoers is their sense of what their payment buys; Damplay sees himself as having bought the right to do whatever he wishes in the theater, certain that the play is there for him, not he for the play, while Probee defines his experience in the terms the playwright provides for judging the play: "[O]ur parts that are the spectators, or should hear a comedy, are to await the process and events of things, as the poet presents them, not as we would corruptly fashion them" (4 Chor. 10–13). Probee thus claims that the search for personal satire is "an unjust way of hearing and beholding plays," while Damplay is certain that nothing can be "out of purpose at a play[.] I see no reason if I come here and give my eighteen pence or two shillings for my seat but I should take it out in censure on the stage" (2 Chor. 59–62). Probee and Damplay may have paid the same amount of money, but they have not paid for the same experience.

When Probee urges him to "mark the play" (3 Chor. 18), Damplay makes explicit his sense of his relation to the play: "I care not for marking the play: I'll damn it, talk, and do that I come for. I will not have gentlemen lose their privilege, not I myself my prerogative, for ne'er an overgrown or superannuated poet of 'em all. He shall not give me law; I will censure, and be witty, and take my tobacco, and enjoy my Magna Carta of reprehension, as my predecessors have done before me" (3 Chor 19–25).

Damplay's legalistic language of privilege, prerogative, and precedent emphasizes the power dynamic between the play and its audience, which depends on both parties allowing the other certain rights. When the Boy objects to his determination to read the play as personal satire in the second-act chorus, Damplay protests that "this were a strange empire, or rather a tyranny, you would entitle your poet to over gentlemen, that they should come to hear and see plays and say nothing for their money" (2 Chor. 53–56). The "tyranny" that Damplay objects to is the silencing of the audience; his understanding of his "rights" as a playgoer includes the right to be heard as well as seen, and to offer an interpretation that differs from that of "your poet." The fear of tyranny and insistence on the gentlemen's "Magna Carta of reprehension" emphasizes the audience's rights as subjects to the play. The play is imagined as the sovereign, but Damplay's status as a gentleman and his payment for his place in the theater protects him from the arbitrary and absolute power he sees the Boy demanding for the playwright.

While Probee is certainly presented in a more favorable light than Damplay, they are both equally exaggerated figures; Probee's willingness to subordinate his judgment to the play is no more or less plausible than Damplay's refusal to do so, and Probee's utter rejection of "the solemn vice of interpretation" or application (2 Chor. 34) is clearly inconsistent with both the mode of spectatorship practiced by many of the private theater audience and the interests of Jonson's satire, however it may accord with the rhetoric of Jonson's other prologues and epilogues. The central difference between Probee and Damplay is that Damplay is focused on his rights (what the Boy cannot prevent him from doing), while Probee is focused on his responsibilities (what he should be doing himself): "We come here to behold the plays and censure them, as they are made, and fitted for us" (4 Chor. 14–15). Probee, like the Boy, sees the play as a whole, and his main objection to looking for personal satire is that doing so "deforms the figure of many a fair scene by drawing it awry" (2 Chor. 34–35). Damplay's experience of the play is visceral and immediate: a series of moments that he cannot connect, a hunger for activity and conclusion. But despite this fundamental difference in their habits of viewing and interpretation, the gentlemen share the assumption that the play cannot change them; both Damplay's insistence that he need not "mark the play" and Probee's definition of their "parts as spectators" imply that the play, not they, is subject to judgment, and if the Boy proposes Damplay as a negative model, he is able to do so because he shares the space of the actors and speaks; Probee is in some important sense invisible by contrast.

Damplay, while not an entirely desirable spectator, is not an impossible, naïve, or inexperienced one. He still remembers Jonson's complaint that "you make a libel of a comedy" from "a prologue long since" (2 Chor. 28–30), although remembering the words is apparently an entirely different thing than applying them to himself, and he never interrupts the play or fails to understand exactly what his situation is. If he presses his rights as a gentleman "even to license and absurdity," he is free to do so. The Boy gives up Damplay as a hopeless case but hopes that he will serve as a negative example that will reform other playgoers: "[B]e yourself still, without a second. Few here are of your opinion today, I hope; tomorrow I am sure there will be none when they have ruminated this" (2 Chor. 79–82). Damplay's ways of watching are made ridiculous, both by presenting them on stage at all and by Probee consistently siding with the Boy when the latter puts Damplay down, but they are significantly contractual in nature, as is the Boy's formulation of the theater as a shop where, like the playgoers envisioned in the prologue to *Bartholomew Fair*, every person may censure in proportion to, but not beyond, his or her payment (2 Chor. 63–65).[21]

It seems worth noting that in almost all early modern plays in which characters watch a theatrical performance, "the audience plays its part badly and misinterprets the play."[22] Despite the flattering gesture of the prologue's address to "gentles," the early modern stage presents an audience that accords with the antitheatrical image of the playhouse as a gathering place of the foolish or wicked, in pursuit of mindless pleasure, anxious to corrupt or be corrupted, and impervious to the beneficial effects of the stage that its defenders insisted were available to those who would only watch the play in the correct frame of mind. Compared to the represented audiences of Elizabethan plays, who routinely lack "the most basic form of theatrical competence—the ability to recognize the play as such,"[23] Damplay has considerably more potential. The audiences represented in Caroline drama present a much more varied and sophisticated set of problems—"competence" has come to be defined in increasingly specialized and complex ways. This is particularly noticeable in the way that audiences are represented as having significantly different experiences of the play because of the ways in which they watch.

As Neill suggests, these representations are frequently satirical, and it is certainly possible that "such distinctions tended to be largely fictitious,"[24] but if we divorce the variety of interpretive practices from the vexed question of satire and social class, several things are apparent that suggest some limitations of Neill's reading of the "taste" of the Caroline playgoer as uniform. First, many behaviors represented on the stage or attested to in prologues were certainly not confined to these types of dubious evidence. The claim that there existed an audience who preferred the drama of twenty or thirty years past is amply verified by the records of repertories of the 1630s, and the King's Men's seasonal move from the Blackfriars to the Globe shifted not only repertory but also audience members between public and private playhouses. The frequent, if less systematic, transfer of plays and companies between the Cockpit and the Red Bull under Christopher Beeston's management suggests that the King's Men were not entirely anomalous in their use of multiple playhouses.[25]

Similarly, an interpretive practice consistently inveighed against was that of "application," or "interpretation"—that is, matching the characters on stage to public persons in Caroline London as Damplay does in the second interval. This in no way suggests that such a practice did not exist, and the mention of it, particularly in the self-protective gesture of satirical playwrights such as Jonson, encouraged rather than diminished its practice. The conventions for attending the private theaters (rather than the public amphitheaters) are far more likely to be brought on the Caroline stage than the old joke of audience members who have never seen a play and cannot recognize the distinction between fact and fiction.

Theatrum Redivium, Richard Baker's response to William Prynne's massive antitheatrical tract *Histriomastix* (1633), argues for the public benefit offered by the stage: "[I]t is a general delight, general to sex, to age, to quality . . . it is a sociable delight, many do at once enjoy it, and all equally."[26] But the representations of contemporary theater audiences—in prologues, epilogues, interscenes, and in the plays themselves—strongly emphasize the segmentations to be found in this "general" audience. "The ladies" are frequently differentiated as a type of audience member, as are citizens, country gentry, Inns of Court men, and courtiers, all of whom are assumed to have their own reasons for coming to the play. If Probee embodies a fantasy of the Caroline audience entertained by playwrights of the period, there is equally a recognition that any production will inevitably play to responses that vary based on the playgoer's interpretive practices.

And the audience is potentially even more segmented by viewing practices than by social class. While Brome's Induction to *The Careless Shepherdess* presents one member each of the court, the Inns of Court, the country gentry, and the London citizenry, Jonson's inductions to both *The Staple of News* and *The Magnetic Lady* present multiple members of the same playgoing class—the gossips and the court gentlemen—watching the plays in significantly different ways that reflect their individual interests and previous theatrical experience rather than their shared social class. In what follows, I am not so much interested in either the qualities of the ideal audience envisioned by Jonson in a figure like Probee or the satirical butts of jokes like Thrift, the citizen from *The Careless Shepherdess*, who certainly does function as a means of flattering the taste of the courtly playgoers as Neill suggests. Instead, I am interested in the variety of ways of watching plays available in Caroline London and what this might suggest about the flexibility of the relationship between spectators and spectacles, the possibility of judgment going both ways, and the mutual shaping power of plays and their viewers.

Courtiers, Citizens, and Ghosts: The Audiences of *The Careless Shepherdess*

Richard Brome's Praeludium to the 1638 revival of Thomas Goffe's *The Careless Shepherdess* at Salisbury Court provides a particularly interesting representation of the private theater audience in terms of both social class and viewing practices. The induction addresses the increasingly vexed question of why one would attend the private theater, or, to put it another way, what a shilling buys for each of the spectators represented in the Induction.

Set in the Salisbury Court theater itself, the scene consists of conversation among four playgoers and Bolt, the doorkeeper. The "actors" in the scene represent varied approaches to the theater: the courtier, the Inns of Court man, the country gentleman, and the citizen. Entering separately, they find seats on the stage. While Spark, the Inns of Court man, and Spruce, the courtier, are previously acquainted, the stage provides an occasion for Thrift, the citizen, and Landlord, the country gentleman, to become part of a social circle defined by money and physical space. The last to enter is Landlord, who proclaims it "my ambition / To occupy a place near you" (3); cost no longer functions to differentiate classes. Landlord can buy a "place" near the cash-strapped Spark and Spruce, and Thrift's haggling that begins the play insists that the play is itself a commodity. Ultimately, however, the commodity is not the play but rather the "company" that Landlord and Thrift can easily buy their way into. Landlord's interest in the play is utterly secondary to his interest in the "place" his shilling buys him among courtiers and Inns of Court men.

As the correlation of place with social status taken for granted by Damplay and Probee breaks down, Spruce and Spark become increasingly anxious to differentiate themselves from Thrift and Landlord. When Landlord proclaims that "I have found fault with very good Sermons / In my daies, and now I desire that we / May passe our sentences upon this Play" (3) and Thrift eagerly takes up the metaphor, wishing that he "had my Gown" (3), Spruce and Spark both vehemently deny Landlord and Thrift's competence to "censure poetry," which is "the Prerogative of the wits in Town" (3). But this censure is not what Probee envisions; Spark is pleased with his choice to "spend [his] money at the play / [rather] Then at the Ordinary" because he has found Spruce, and "if the play should prove dull / Your company will satisfy my ears" (3).

After a long discussion of poetry and dramatic construction, in which Spruce and Spark demonstrate their familiarity (and Thrift and Landlord's lack of familiarity) with a very specific set of literary standards based in text rather than performance, Spark asks Landlord, "cause you will be prodigious," to tell him "what part you think essential for a play? / And what in your opinion is styled wit[?]" (4). Landlord defines the pleasure of the play as visual rather than verbal; his desire for "a Fool in every Act" is based not on the language that such a character would produce but rather on his desire "to see what faces the Rogue will make" (4). Thrift, seconding this desire, shares Landlord's pleasure in physical activity—he "would rather see him leap, laugh, or cry / Than hear the gravest speech in all the play." But Thrift also attends to language, albeit in a very different sense than Spruce or Spark: "His part has all the wit / For none speaks carps or Quibbles besides he" (5).

Spark and Spruce's ridicule is predictable but interesting. Spark sees both Landlord and Thrift as "ghosts"—those with the same tastes as their forefathers, "whose dull intellect did nothing understand / But fools and fighting" (5). The pleasures of the contemporary theater have evolved, insists Spark, so that that audience is moved "to admire, not to laugh"; puns went out of style with trunk hose, "And since the wits grew sharp, the swords are sheathed" (5). Here, as in the Induction to *The Magnetic Lady*, the Elizabethan theater (there expressed as Damplay's appeal to precedent—his rights to do "as my predecessors have done before me") is marked as conducive to a style of interpretation ill-suited to the new drama of the Caroline private theater. But while Jonson suggests that Damplay's tastes might be reformed in the rest of the audience if not in Damplay himself, Brome's Praeludium suggests these tastes are class-based and might instead be redirected to another venue; Thrift, true to his name, determines to take back his money, "for now I have considered that it is too much," and go instead to the much cheaper Red Bull or Fortune, "and there see a play for two pence / And a jig to boot" (8).

Dismayed at the promise of a comedy with no fool, no wordplay, and no swordplay, Landlord determines to leave: "[T]he Comedy / Will be as tedious to me as a sermon, / And I do fear that I shall fall asleep / And give my twelve pence to be melancholy" (5). Spark promises him other forms of "mirth," and Landlord consents to remain, if only "that I may view the Ladies and they me" (5–6); the spectacle of the audience is ultimately more compelling than the play. Ultimately, however, none of the participants in the Praeludium remain on the stage: Spruce and Spark determine to watch the play from "some private room" (8) lest their presence should intimidate a third actor into forgetting his lines, though Landlord suspects it is less concern for the actors than fear that "some Creditor should spy them" that leads them to "take sanctuary amongst / The Ladies" in the boxes, where he will join them, concealed by "a Ladies head / Or . . . a lattice window," which interrupts both their vision and their visibility (8).

Despite the Induction's interest in the range of possible responses to the play, all of these responses are ultimately banished from the stage to either the boxes or other theaters altogether. The Induction ends with the onstage spectators leaving the "open stage" to the Prologue, but the Prologue is himself "an actor plac't in the Pit" (8) who takes over from the second actor; he is a plant who comes from the offstage audience to begin the play by speaking for the absent author. While Spark, Spruce, Landlord, and Thrift all proclaim their right to judge the play, all the varieties of this model of audience as judge are utterly rejected by the structure of the prologue itself.

The prologue, that thing that will actually allow the play to begin, is interrupted by a combination of incompetence from the actors and the onstage audience; the first actor to attempt to deliver the prologue stops after one line: "Must I always a hearer only be?" (7). When the onstage audience laughs at him and the prompter fails to rescue him with the next line, the actor playing the Prologue exits, cursing the prompter, and is succeeded by a second actor, who manages to add the second line: "Mayn't a Spectator write a Comedy?" before losing his place and being laughed off the stage by the "actor plac'd in the

Pit." He too departs, challenging "him that laughs [to] speak the Prologue for me" (8). At this point, the actor speaks his only lines from the pit, promising to "do the Author justice" (8) in the absence of a script. The opening conceit of the prologue is that of the spectator as author, the hearer gaining voice; this is emphasized by being three times repeated and by its finally being delivered by an actor playing a member of the portion of the audience ordinarily confined to the pit. The implication here is that the self-conscious wits who occupy the stage, far from serving as models of superior judgment, ultimately serve as distractions from the play, incapable of providing substantial and informed criticism. The play itself, not the self-conscious display of wit no less absurd in Spark and Spruce than in Landlord and Thrift, becomes the model of judicious criticism, and, significantly, the pit, rather than the "open stage," becomes the site from which the spectator's comedy originates.

The prologue itself is a preemptive defense of the play from the inappropriate assumptions of the audience members in the pit; the actor mocks the poor judgment of those he heard in the Pit say,

> There n'ere was poorer language in a Play;
> And told his Neighbour, he did fear the vile
> Composure would go neer to spoil his stile.
> Another damn'd the Scene with full-mouth'd oaths,
> Because it was not dress'd in better cloaths;
> And rather wish'd each Actor might be mute,
> Then he should loose the sight of a fine suit. (9)

The prologue cites this as judgment appropriate to "the Antipodes," claiming that "what they do raise / To prejudice, is here the chiefest praise" (9): the play's merits lie in its suiting its language and costume to its pastoral genre rather than its place on the stage. In the same way that the Induction offers a variety of methods of viewing, all of which are ultimately rejected for their usurpation of the place of the play and the privileging of the audience over the author, the prologue demands that the audience bring a more discriminating taste to the play, one that is shaped by the terms of the play rather than its location. In this context, the academic judgment of Spark and Spruce is more of an infringement of the prerogative of the author than are the plot- and actor-centered views of Thrift and Landlord. The fantasy here is not a fantasy of an audience drawn from the court and the Inns of Court; it is the fantasy of the stage occupied by the play alone, spectators tidily dispersed to the boxes and pit, "hearers only," while the play occupies both their attention and that of the rest of the theater audience.

"Come to See and to Be Seen": Women of Fashion at *The Staple of News*

If the Prologue of *The Careless Shepherdess* can begin the play only after multiple audiences are silenced and removed from sight, his counterpart in Jonson's *The Staple of News* has no such luck. Jonson's four Gossips, like Probee and Damplay, occupy the stage for the duration of the play and dominate the intermeans between acts as well as the Induction. If the Gossips, with their love of costume, desire for news, and interest in topical application, are marginalized as a satire of the audience Jonson dreads, they equally serve to emphasize the centrality of the audience to the playhouse experience and offer a range of more or less desirable viewing habits that are, significantly, all focused on the play and its performance. The true object of Jonson's scorn is the real audience of Blackfriars, who watch each other, not his fictional creations who watch the play.[27]

Six words into his speech, the Prologue to *The Staple of News* is interrupted by "four gentlewomen ladylike attired," the most theatrically experienced of whom, Mirth, demands that he cease his function as "gentleman usher to the play" and become their usher instead and "help us to some stools here," which they will occupy for the duration of the play.[28] Mirth insists on the propriety of the Gossips taking their place in explicitly social terms. In response to the Prologue's apparent surprise that she and her companions want to sit "O' the stage" (7), Mirth identifies herself and her companions as "persons of quality . . . and women of fashion . . . come to see and to be seen" (8–10). The stage direction "ladylike attired" supports Mirth's claim here; as satirical portraits of the Blackfriars audience emphasize, dressing for the theater was a crucial aspect of playgoing, especially for those who purchased the relatively small number of seats particularly designed to be seen as the actors were seen.

The Prologue objects to Mirth's desire for seats on stage in terms that echo Gosson's "To the Gentlewomen Citizens of London," which warns, "you can forbid no man, that vieweth you, to note you and that noteth you to judge you."[29] "What will the noblemen think, or the grave wits here, to see you seated on the bench thus?" (15–17), he asks. Mirth confidently counters this attempt to present the Gossips as mere spectacle—they have come to see, as well as to be seen, and to "arraign both them and their poets" (22). If the Gossips are to be judged, in Mirth's formulation, then so are the male audience members who share the stage, the plays, and the poet himself—a fantasy literalized in Mirth's discussion of her sight of Jonson in the tiring-house "rolling himself up and down like a tun" (63).

While Mirth, Tattle, Expectation, and Censure are allegorical rather than literal figures—Mirth identifies herself as the daughter of Christmas and Spirit of Shrovetide—Mirth insists on their likeness to the other stage sitters, both in class and motive and because "they had mothers, as we had, and those mothers had gossips (if their children were christened) as we are, and such as had a longing to see plays, and sit upon them, as we do, and arraign both them, and their poets" (18–22). The Gossips are fellow humans, and fellow Christians, and thus fellow judges. While the Prologue mocks this judgment, entreating Expectation to "expect no more than you understand" (32), he also recognizes that he is powerless to prevent its influence; Expectation "can expect enough . . . and teach others to do the like" (33–35). He also underestimates their scope of judgment; while he expects "Curiosity, my Lady Censure" (39) to care only for "whose clothes are the best penned (whatever the part may be)" (40–41), she cares too for "which amorous prince makes love in drink, or does overact prodigiously in beaten satin" (45–46). Censure, that is, judges not only the costumes (though these, of both the actors and the audience, are certainly her main concern) but also the actors' ability and technique.

Mirth, Tattle, Censure, and Expectation place themselves on the stage among the gentleman audience members, who apparently share the Gossips' desire "to see, and to be seen" (9). The Induction's explicit focus on the likeness between the Gossips and the parts of the audience the Prologue defines as normative—"the Noblemen . . . or the grave wits here"—is supported by the probable staging of their entrance. While the note in Parr's edition of *Staple* suggests that the Gossips, like Nell and her prentice Rafe in Beaumont's *The Knight of the Burning Pestle* (ca. 1607), enter from the auditorium, Jonson's stage direction, "Enter Prologue. After him Gossip Mirth, Gossip Tattle, Gossip Expectation, and Gossip Censure, four gentlewomen, ladylike attired" (1 s.d.), suggests that the Gossips follow the Prologue onto the stage from the tiring-house (where Mirth has "see[n] the actors dressed" [63]),[30] from which patrons seated on stools would also have entered. While the entrance of Beaumont's Nell from the audience immediately marks her entrance as a violation of the decorum of space, the case with the Gossips is more ambiguous. Nell is, after all, the wife of a citizen; she is emphatically not part of the audience the Blackfriars envisioned for itself in terms of both gender and, significantly, class.[31] Her entrance to the stage, like her husband's, is founded on ignorance of the theatrical and the social conventions of the Blackfriars. But Mirth, if not one of Jonson's judging spectators, is nonetheless exceptionally aware of what to expect in the theater, capable of making distinctions between "the old way" of representing vices with their wooden daggers, and the present practice: "[N]ow they are attired like men and women o' the time" (2 Int. 13–16). If Jonson hopes for a more discriminating audience, he does not expect one, and the stage itself, a male preserve, becomes open to women not as a means of staging incursion, as Nell's entrance in *The Knight of the Burning Pestle* does, but as a means of suggesting the extent to which the gallants on the stage resemble the "ridiculous gossips that tattle between the acts."[32]

In a play obsessed with true and false judgments, the purchase of status, and the right and wrong uses of wit and wealth, the Gossips literally stage the competition over the play's meaning (and the audience's attention) between Jonson and his actors on the one hand and the audience and their preconceptions on the other. At stake is the function of the theater—social or pedagogical. While Jonson deprives the Gossips of the last word in the play, the note "To the Readers," which complains that the play (particularly the Staple scenes) has been so misinterpreted "as if the souls of most of the spectators had lived in the eyes and eares of these ridiculous Gossips that tattle betweene the *Acts*" (5–6), suggests that Jonson, to no one's surprise, was finally unable to control the play's outcome on the stage. The Gossips, Jonson's representations of the theater audience, are the only part of that audience over which he can exercise complete control.

While the Prologue questions Expectation's understanding and mocks what he presumes to be Censure's fascination with the relation between costume and action, he also recognizes Expectation's power to make other audience members see as she does, and Censure seems quite as interested in the actors' readiness (or drunkenness) in their parts as in their costumes. The Gossips are abundantly qualified to make certain types of judgment, particularly Mirth, who despite her shortcomings seems far closer to the audience Jonson might envision than "most of the spectators" (To the Readers, 4–5), who apparently do watch as the Gossips do and "censure by contagion."[33]

The practice Jonson explicitly condemns in his address to the reader is that of application, an interpretive practice that Mirth at least explicitly speaks against. The most theatrically experienced (and up to date) of the spectators, Mirth exposes the variety of viewing practices in play and trains her less astute cohort how to watch as surely as Probee does; she rejects Censure's claim that Pecunia is a satire of the Spanish infanta and provides an interpretive lens that corrects Tattle's understanding of allegorical drama as it was practiced in the previous century. Jonson may disavow the "ridiculous gossips" to the reader, but Mirth actually functions as an internal gauge that raises issues of interpretation for the viewer as Jonson does for the reader. It is through Mirth that the author Jonson is constantly rendered visible as the creator of the *Staple*; and if the Gossips are always fully aware that they are watching a play, then this is not to their discredit.

When the Prologue is finally allowed to resume his speech seventy lines after Mirth interrupts it, he expresses the poet's grave doubts about whether the audience at large will pay appropriate attention to the play when there are so many other distractions—all of them to be found among the audience itself. Wishing that his audience "had come to hear, not see, a play," the poet

> prayes you'll not preiudge his Play for ill,
> Because you marke it not, and sit not still;
> But haue a longing to salute, or talke
> With such a female, and from her to walke
> With your discourse, to what is done, and where,
> How, and by whom, in all the towne; but here.
> (Prologue 7–12)

The sense of the competition between the play and the audience for the attention of the rest of the audience is acute—the anxiety that the playhouse is only a gathering place to exchange gossip about "what is done, and where, / How, and by whom, in all the towne; but here." Despite his apparent contempt for the judgment of the Gossips, the inattentive audience the Prologue here envisions is male, distracted from the play by the prospect of "talk with such a female." The fantasy of an audience that sits quietly in their seats and listens to the actors competes with the fantasy of the constantly shifting, never silent audience incapable of benefiting from the play. Even as the Gossips watch the play in the expectation of "new and fresh" news (Ind. 25), the Prologue voices the anxiety that the audience will be sharing news that falls quite outside the play:

> Alas! what is it to his Scene, to know
> How many Coaches in *Hide-parke* did show
> Last spring, what fare to day at *Medleyes* was,
> If *Dunstan*, or the *Phoenix* best wine has?
> They are things—But yet, the Stage might stand as wel,
> If it did neither heare these things, nor tell.
> (Prologue 13–18)

Although the play mocks the pretensions of Cymbal and his desire to develop a monopoly on news analogous to the monopoly the stationer's company has on printing[34]—the news to "be examined, and then registered, / And so be issued under the seal of the office, / As Staple News, no other to be current" (1.1.34–36)—it also hopes for an audience that will come to the Blackfriars to be entertained by the play rather than each other. Paradoxically, Jonson's introduction of the Gossips among the stage sitters serves to shift the focus from the audience to the play rather than the other way around.

The Gossips drive the act breaks with their constant conversation, and it seems worth considering how audible they are to the rest of the audience during the intermeans. The Blackfriars audience is, as Jonson frequently laments, extremely prone to taking advantage of the intermeans to stand, stretch, chat with their neighbors, and possibly change seats. None of this is going to change if the Gossips keep talking. But Mirth leads the discussion toward judgment, and if this is a judgment that Jonson is not anxious that the rest of his audience share, it is at least a discussion centered on the play, not "how many coaches in *Hide-parke* did show last spring."

Regardless of how the Caroline audience was composed, or how it may now be imagined, the prologues, epilogues, and representations of audiences in the 1630s consistently present not one audience but multiple ones. In some cases, one type of audience member is clearly encouraged over the others—as in the case of Probee's vastly more astute comments than Damplay's—but there is never any pretense that other types of audience do not exist or can consistently be retrained. If Probee embodies a fantasy of the Caroline audience entertained by playwrights of the period, there is equally a recognition that any production will inevitably play to varied responses and that all of these responses might be understood in terms of judgment that might or might not coincide with that of the playwright.

The presentation of versions of the onstage audience in the private theaters only incidentally stages model behaviors to imitate or avoid; more significantly, it suggests the closely intertwined relation between play and audience and the threat that this poses to the play itself. The reversibility of the positions of spectator and spectacle focuses attention on the centrality of the position of the author—one that is marginalized in the assumption that the spectators alone control the meaning of the play and that the theater serves more as a place to display one's clothing and "wit" than a showplace for the play itself. The onstage audience staged in these Inductions ultimately expands the frame of the play to include the entire theater, placing the theater audience on display in the terms of the playwright rather than the reverse.

Notes

1. Ben Jonson, *The Magnetic Lady*, in *Ben Jonson*, ed. C. H. Herford, Percy Simpson, and Evelyn Simpson, vol. 6 (Oxford: Oxford University Press, 1954). Citations refer to act, scene, and line numbers and appear parenthetically in the text.
2. Thelma N. Greenfield, *The Induction in Elizabethan Drama* (Eugene: University of Oregon Books, 1969), 67-95.
3. Michael Neill, "'Wits Most Accomplish'd Senate': The Audience of the Caroline Private Theaters," *Studies in English Literature 1500-1900* 18 (1978): 341, 344. Neill's description of this group for whom "theater-going ceased to be a mere matter of occasional entertainment" (345–46), becoming instead a daily event that allowed one to develop and demonstrate one's connoisseurship of dramatic literature contrasts interestingly with Paul Menzer's discussion of the "everyday audience" in this collection (29–33); while Neill sees this habituation as ultimately granting authority to the audience at the expense of the playwrights, Menzer sees it as demonstrating the institutional success of the playhouses.

4. Neill, "Caroline Private Theaters," 342.
5. Ibid., 344, 346.
6. Ibid., 347.
7. For the case for Brome's authorship of the Induction, see Matthew Steggle, *Richard Brome: Place and Politics on the Caroline Stage* (Manchester, UK: Manchester University Press, 2004), 121.
8. Neill, "Caroline Private Theaters," 346.
9. Ibid., 345.
10. Richard Brome, Praeludium to *The Careles Shepherdess*, by Thomas Goffe (London, 1638), 3. Subsequent page citations appear parenthetically.
11. Neill, "Caroline Private Theaters," 342.
12. Douglas Bruster and Robert Weimann, *Prologues to Shakespeare's Theatre: Performance and Liminality in Early Modern Drama* (New York: Routledge, 2004), 33.
13. Bruster and Weimann, *Shakespeare's Theatre*, 37.
14. Greenfield, *Elizabethan Drama*, 87.
15. Peter Happé usefully compiles Jonson's comments on and staging of his audience in "Jonson's On-Stage Audiences," *Ben Jonson Journal* 10 (2003): 23–41.
16. Herbert Berry, "The Stage and Boxes at Blackfriars," *Studies in Philology* 63 (1966): 174. Andrew Gurr, while interested in the remarkable obtrusiveness of the gallants seated on stage, restricts their number to "as many as ten." *Playgoing in Shakespeare's London* (Cambridge: Cambridge University Press, 2004), 157.
17. Emma Rhatigan's discussion in Chapter 8 of the inability of the performers in the Gray's Inn Revels of 1594 to complete the performance because the number of spectators on stage left no room for the actors is another forceful reminder of this potential competition.
18. Ben Jonson, *The Devil is an Ass,* in *Ben Jonson,* ed. C. H. Herford, Percy Simpson, and Evelyn Simpson, vol. 6 (Oxford: Oxford University Press, 1954), Induction, 3, 7–8. Subsequent citations appear parenthetically.
19. Reprinted in E. K. Chambers, *The Elizabethan Stage* (Oxford: Clarendon Press, 1923), 4:368–69.
20. Tiffany Stern, "Taking Part: Actors and Audience on the Stage at Blackfriars," in *Inside Shakespeare: Essays on the Blackfriars Stage*, ed. Paul Menzer (Selinsgrove, PA: Susquehanna University Press, 2006), 42.
21. Ben Jonson, *Bartholomew Fair*, ed. E. A. Horsman (Manchester, UK: Manchester University Press, 1960), Induction, 86–97.
22. Alvin Kernan, "Shakespearean Comedy and Its Courtly Audience," in *Comedy from Shakespeare to Sheridan*, ed. A. R. Braunmuller and J. C. Bulman (London: Associated University Presses, 1986), 93.
23. Keir Elam, *The Semiotics of Theatre and Drama* (London: Methuen, 1980), 87.
24. Neill, "Caroline Private Theaters," 342.
25. Gurr, *Playgoing*, 183–90. See also Mark Bayer's "The Curious Case of the Two Audiences: Thomas Dekker's *Match Me in London*," Chapter 3 in this volume, especially 57–61.
26. Richard Baker, *Theatrum Redivivum* (London, 1662), 138.
27. Jonson's blanket condemnation of the gossips in his note "To the Readers" has led most critics to adopt uniformly unfavorable interpretations of the women, and,

perhaps more significantly, to discuss them as a single unit rather than as representing diverse habits of viewing. Despite Happé's claim that Jonson "induces us to see them so adversely that we are more or less bound to disagree with everything they say" ("Jonson's On-Stage Audiences," 30). Julie Sanders "challenge[s] a purely antifeminist reading of the *Staple* gossips characterization," noting that "in terms of the knowledge of theater repertoire (and some of its political resonances and applications) these women are astute theatergoers." "'Twill Fit the Players Yet': Women and Theatre in Jonson's Late Plays," in *Ben Jonson and Theatre: Performance, Practice, and Theory*, ed. Richard Cave, Elizabeth Schafer, and Brian Woolland (London: Routledge, 1999), 186.
28. Ben Jonson, *The Staple of News*, ed. Anthony Parr (New York: St. Martin's Press, 1988), Induction 1 s.d., 5–6. Subsequent citations refer to act, scene, and line numbers and appear parenthetically.
29. Stephen Gosson, *The Schoole of Abuse*, ed. Edward Arber (London: Alex Murray and Son, 1869), F2.
30. Parr, *Staple of News*, 64n2.
31. Laurie E. Osborne, "Female Audience and Female Authority in *The Knight of the Burning Pestle*," *Exemplaria* 3 (Fall 1991): 495–98.
32. Jonson, *The Staple of News*. This comment appears in the address "To the Readers," curiously located between the end of the second intermean and the beginning of act 3 (line 6).
33. *Bartholomew Fair*, Induction, 99.
34. Anthony Parr, introduction to *The Staple of News*, by Ben Jonson (New York: St. Martin's Press, 1988), 22–31.

CHAPTER 3

The Curious Case of the Two Audiences

Thomas Dekker's *Match Me in London*

Mark Bayer

"Curious" is an unusual term to describe an early modern play, and it is perhaps an even odder way to characterize its audience. Unlike most productions, however, Thomas Dekker's *Match Me in London* (ca. 1611) was performed in two radically different performance contexts: at the Red Bull, a large public amphitheater in Clerkenwell, and at the Cockpit, a much more intimate and expensive private venue in Drury Lane.[1] Curiously, it was successful at both. Why? And why was this play's success contrary to expectations?

Many plays, of course, were performed at more than one venue as theater companies disbanded, re-formed, and merged with one another and as titles passed from company to company when their personnel changed. Significantly fewer were staged before audiences that were vastly different in their social and economic composition or playgoers from completely different walks of life with nearly incompatible tastes in plays. The citizen spectator in Beaumont's *Knight of the Burning Pestle* (ca. 1607), staged at the private theater at Blackfriars, echoes the opinion of that theater's audience in remarking that a play "[i]s stale; it has been had before at the Red Bull."[2] By deliberately casting aspersions at productions at rival venues—and by assuming that the audience at Blackfriars would share his opinion—this fictional spectator suggests just how polarized audiences had become.

As the London playgoing industry grew from humble beginnings, from a collection of innyard playhouses in the 1560s and 1570s to the first purpose-built structures in the 1570s to a variety of indoor and outdoor performance venues in many neighborhoods in and around the city in the next decades, it became increasingly specialized. By the 1620s, the myth of the heterogeneous audience comprising spectators from across the social spectrum was exactly that: a myth projected by modern scholars concerned predominantly with Shakespeare and his popularity. Audiences at London's playhouses had become increasingly stratified, with more genteel spectators attending private indoor playhouses like Blackfriars and the Cockpit while large crowds of tradesmen and apprentices continued to pay just a few pennies to attend bombastic and popular performances at amphitheaters like the Fortune and the Red Bull.[3]

This trend represented not simply preferences for different kinds of dramatic entertainment but markers of mutual exclusivity. Thomas Middleton's epistle to *The Roaring Girl* (1611) discusses the vogue for "huge bombasted plays, quilted with mighty words to lean purpose" at the large, outdoor amphitheaters. On the other end of the dramatic spectrum, a young gallant "will upon the Friars stage . . . sit" in "his silken garments, and his satin robe."[4] Thomas Tomkis's *Albumazar* (1615), a play performed before the university wits at Trinity College, Cambridge, satirizes the lowbrow fare at the public theaters when the clown, Trinculo, vows to "confound [his beloved] with compliments drawn from plays I see at the Fortune and the Red Bull where I learn all the words I speak but understand not."[5]

Due to this increasingly stratified market, playwrights were forced to take an accurate gauge of the playhouse for which they were writing and the expectations of their audience. The printer's prologue to *The Two Merry Milkmaids* (1620) advises that "every writer must govern his pen according to the capacity of the stage he writes to, both in the actor and the auditor."[6] John Webster learned this lesson the hard way when *The White Devil* flopped at the Red Bull in 1612, a play that according to the playwright "lacked a full and understanding auditory: and that since that time, I have noted, most of the people who come to that playhouse resemble ignorant asses" ("To the Reader," ll. 6–9).[7] Apparently the collection of artisans and apprentices that thronged that theater could not appreciate the court intrigue and intricate Italianate dialogue in Webster's play. The dramatist wrote for the same company again in 1617 with *The Devil's Law Case*, but only after they had migrated to the more elite Cockpit, suggesting that the failure of his previous effort had nothing to do with actors and everything to do with the venue, its audience, and their nostalgic tastes for more heroic plays boisterously acted. What's curious then about *Match Me in London* is that it was performed at both of these very different venues and was, apparently, successful at each.

In this chapter, I want to outline the particular circumstances that led to the performance of some plays at both the Red Bull and the Cockpit and then suggest how *Match Me in London* might be read in two very different ways attuned to the different audiences at the two venues—lending it a certain crossover potential that very few plays from its period enjoyed. I claim that unlike most of the drama of this period, *Match Me in London* is double-coded: intelligible in two distinct cultural idioms and therefore capable of appealing to varied audiences in different ways.

Given the growing disparity in audience composition at the public and private theaters, why would a theater company even try to please such disparate groups with the same play, knowing that what appealed to one would probably not satisfy the other? For a few years after 1617, and for reasons beyond the players' control, the Queen Anne's Men didn't have a choice. Since the conversion of the Red Bull from an inn sometime around 1605 or 1606, the troupe had built a large and loyal following there based on plays by Thomas Heywood and others and on the popularity of comedian Thomas Greene.

The Queen's Men's Fraught Move Indoors

Lured by the prospects of higher profits in playing before the gentry at a private playhouse (where the cost of admission was six times higher than at the Red Bull), Christopher Beeston, the company's manager, moved the troupe to the Cockpit in 1616. This indoor venue was considerably smaller and more intimate than the Red Bull and was located in a radically different social environment on the fashionable Drury Lane to the west of the city in Westminster. The company misjudged the reaction of their audience at the Red Bull, and on Shrove Tuesday (March 4, 1616/1617), a large group of apprentices registered their dissatisfaction with the company's move in a riot that began at the Fortune playhouse but had as its target the Red Bull and, especially, the Cockpit. In the aftermath of the event a contemporary writes, "The prentices on Shrove Tuesday last, to the number of 3 or 4,000 committed extreme insolencies . . . a justice of the peace coming to appease them, while he was reading a proclamation, had his head broken with a brick bat. The other part, making for Drury Lane, where lately a new playhouse is erected, they beset the house round, broke in, wounded diverse of the players, broke open their trunks & what apparel, books, and other things they found, they burnt and cut in pieces."[8] The sheer number of apprentices involved in this altercation proved a force too large for either the players or the municipal authorities to deter: "Though the fellows defended themselves as best they could, and slew three of them with shot, and hurt diverse, yet they entered the house and defaced it."[9] Plays were presented at neither house for several months, as the rioters caused severe damage to the new theater and forced the company to return temporarily to the Red Bull.[10]

The uncomfortable circumstances attending the Queen Anne's Men's move from the Red Bull did not deter the company from continuing their enterprise at the Cockpit. Nevertheless, through a combination of its own poor financial health and the damage to its theaters and stage property caused by the rioters, Beeston and the players were forced into the unenviable situation of using both venues at once. Beeston transferred plays and players between the Red Bull and the Cockpit, just as their rivals so successfully played at both the Globe and Blackfriars, albeit with one significant difference. Instead of the King's Men's stable and productive winter/summer arrangement, Beeston would essentially split the Red Bull group into two: one playing outdoors at the Red Bull and the other indoors at the Cockpit, swapping plays and personnel between the two venues throughout the playing season. The death of Queen Anne on March 2, 1618/19, gave Beeston, who had a financial interest in both playhouses, suitable cover to reorganize the troupe extensively and merge most of what had been Queen Anne's Men with Prince Charles's Men at the Cockpit, while Richard Perkins, Ellis Worth, John Cumber, and others stayed on at the Red Bull as part of the Revels company. A few years after that, amid ongoing litigation between Beeston and some of his disgruntled players, the troupes reorganized again with the group known as Prince Charles's Men returning to the Red Bull with Lady Elizabeth's Men, whose membership was folded in with Charles's, at the Cockpit.[11] Because Beeston's players were unable to develop a new repertory for their new venue throughout this tumultuous period, the company probably had every intention of playing Red Bull material at the new venue, and it is likely, since it was now deliberately targeting upscale clientele, that it intended to alter the productions significantly in order to appeal to this new market. It is, of course, a credit to the actors that they were able to modify their usual bombastic style to appeal to an audience that had previously reveled in productions in which these very histrionics were regularly satirized.[12]

Credit is also due to the protean characteristics of the plays themselves. The obvious differences in the composition of audiences at different theaters notwithstanding, theatrical professionals had long recognized that part of their challenge was to appeal to multiple and stratified audiences simultaneously, that the tendencies of certain playgoers to attend certain playhouses was neither absolute nor fully predictable. Audiences, despite discernable and important similarities in their composition, were, ultimately, a collection of individuals. The Prologue to Middleton's *No Wit, No Help Like a Woman's* (ca. 1612) wonders "how is't possible to suffice / So many ears, so many eyes?" He goes on to recognize not only that certain audiences prefer certain types of plays but that the motivations that bring different individuals and social groups to the playhouse differed markedly:

> Some for mirth they chiefly come,
> Some for passion, for both some;

Some for lascivious meetings, that's their arrant;
Some to detract and ignorance their warrant.

Middleton's solution to this challenge, in what could easily be understood as a precursor to reader-response approaches to literary works in general, was to turn tragedy into comedy and comedy into tragedy. Some plays, he argues, strive to satirize certain groups and their values while also endorsing and even valorizing them, depending on the perspective of the individual witnessing it: "Yet I doubt not . . . We shall both make you sad and tickle ye."[13] The Prologue-discloses the remarkable diversity of theatrical products on offer throughout the city as a whole—even within the repertory of a single company. He also notes that some plays themselves—the kinds of plays Beeston's groups at the Cockpit and the Red Bull desperately needed now—offer a kind of protean appeal operating on the basis of social comportment and pretension rather than just individual or collective standards of taste.

The Red Bull and the Cockpit could not have been more dissimilar. The Red Bull was located in Clerkenwell, a teeming suburb to the northwest of the city populated largely by tradesmen and apprentices. Since its beginnings sometime around 1605 or 1606, the Red Bull immediately became associated with the nearby Fortune as a venue specializing in the performance of plays "mostly frequented by citizens and the meaner sort of people."[14] Although an association with the Red Bull became something of a demerit in polite company, audiences composed predominantly of tradesmen and apprentices delighted in a repertory that featured a mix of heroic history plays that regularly included affirmative portraits of London's laboring classes, like Heywood's *If You Know Not Me, You Know Nobody* (1604), John Day's *Travels of Three English Brothers* (1607), and William Rowley's *A Shoemaker, a Gentleman* (ca. 1608), rounded out with farcical comedies like John Cooke's *Greene's Tu Quoque* (ca.1611) highlighting the antics of Thomas Greene, the company's beloved comedian. The Red Bull became something of an institution in Clerkenwell and the surrounding environs, and the fierce loyalty of its audiences is suggested by the violent actions of the rioters, who seemed to have no particular animus against playgoing in general but were reacting specifically to the Queen Anne's Men's move to a new playhouse and only damaged property that belonged to that troupe.[15]

The Cockpit, on the other hand, was adjacent to Lincoln's Inn (one of the Inns of Court) amid the fashionable houses of the wealthy, who would typically arrive at the theater by coach attired in finery. Beeston took out a thirty-year lease on property for his new private theater on Drury Lane in the parish of St. Giles in the Fields from John Best, a grocer, on August 9, 1616. The location was poised to draw spectators from the affluent neighborhoods of Whitehall and St. James as well as the numerous aristocrats who lived along Drury

Lane. The theater was within walking distance of all four Inns of Court and the euphuistic law students who regularly resorted to the private theaters. By the 1610s, Westminster was no longer simply the seat of law and government; it was beginning to develop a distinctive urban character of its own, one in sharp contrast to the city and its other suburbs. By the turn of the century, John Stow notes "a continual new building of divers fair houses" to complement the "hostelries and houses for gentlemen and men of honor" that were already there, suggesting that this was the neighborhood of choice for many wealthy sojourners from the provinces eager to take advantage of the bountiful amenities of the growing metropolis.[16]

The playhouse itself, as its name implies, was a former cockpit and already had a circular auditorium to which Beeston added a square stage, tiring-house, and boxes. Obviously, the venue was significantly more intimate for both the actors and the audience than were any of the outdoor theaters, and its stage was about a quarter of the area of the Red Bull's, considerably diminishing the scope of the stage action. Keith Sturgess sums up the difference between public and private houses, claiming that "at the first, however attentive they are, the spectators form a crowd; at the second, an audience."[17] By the 1630s, the Phoenix (as the Cockpit was sometimes called after it rose from the ashes of the riot) along with Blackfriars had established itself as the venue of choice for the aristocracy and featured a repertory designed with these elite playgoers in mind.[18] Later in its history, the venue became perhaps the most popular hall playhouse in Caroline England, featuring the satirical and courtly plays of James Shirley (who provided the troupe with two plays a year, in the spring and fall), masque-like productions by Thomas Heywood, and drama presented by a traveling company of French players. Beeston himself developed a close relationship with Sir Henry Herbert, the master of the revels; his troupe frequently performed plays from the Cockpit at court, and the venture made Beeston extremely wealthy.[19] In the early years of its existence, however, when the success of the theater was far from assured and before new plays could be commissioned for the new venue—all compounded by the loss of some of their playbooks in the riot—Beeston was forced to use material from the Red Bull at the Phoenix.

Although many dramatists earned reputations for certain types of plays and often tended to write for certain companies at certain venues, most were versatile enough to write for various segments of the audience and were familiar enough with the market to tailor their works accordingly. Dekker had been writing plays since the late 1590s and had experience with both private and public theaters. He began his career writing for Philip Henslowe and the Admiral's Men, providing a string of chronicle history plays culminating in *The Shoemaker's Holiday* (1600), a play that celebrates the meteoric rise of Simon Eyre and extols the values of hard work that catapulted him to the mayorship. This same kind of "citizen comedy" would become popular among the tradesmen and apprentices at the Red Bull. At the same time that Dekker proved himself adept at writing for the large outdoor amphiteatres, he wrote a very different kind of satirical comedy for the boy's company at Paul's, including *Satiromastix* (1601), *Westward Ho* (1604), and *Northward Ho* (1605)—plays designed for more sophisticated audiences of courtiers and law students.

Sometime around the end of the decade, Dekker became estranged from Henslowe and the Admiral's Men (now known as Prince Henry's Men) and began writing for Queen Anne's Men at the Red Bull. Unlike playwrights like Shakespeare or Heywood, who were also sharers in their respective companies, or Jonson and Middleton, who supplemented their incomes by writing masques and civic pageants, Dekker derived the majority of his income writing for the commercial theater. He was plagued by financial troubles throughout his career—what biographer George Price calls "the burden of an endless struggle for subsistence."[20] The necessity of making ends meet likely meant that Dekker's survival relied on a steady stream of playwrighting, which, in turn, depended on his ability to adapt plays to particular audiences.

Match Me in London: Indoors and Out

Match Me in London, assuming it was written around 1611 or 1612, before Dekker was imprisoned for debt in 1613, became part of the Red Bull repertory earlier in that decade but was one of those plays transferred to the Cockpit, most likely in an attempt to capitalize on numerous references to an impending royal marriage between Prince Charles and a Spanish infanta. This political context might have been lost on an audience of apprentices. Instead, audiences at the Red Bull could plausibly view the same play as an exoneration of their own dogged work ethic and mental dexterity.

Set in Spain, the play's main plot concentrates on the personal anxieties of Cordolente, a shoemaker who "goes upright on the soles of his conscience" (2.1.7). His marriage to Tormiella is threatened by the efforts of her father, Malevento, to block the union in favor of his choice, Luke Gazetto, a gallant clearly distinguished from the "commons." Both suitors, however, are thwarted when the king of Spain sees Tormiella and pursues her himself, summarily banishing Cordolente. But the tenacious shoemaker returns in disguise to rescue his bride, who repeatedly and adamantly rejects the king's sexual advances. Meanwhile, Don John and Valesco, the king's brother and father-in-law, plot to usurp the throne. After being implicated in their plot, the queen is banished from the court, but she too returns and is reunited with her foolish and adulterous husband when the treachery is unraveled.

Several critics assume that, to appeal to the Cockpit's elites, the play must be understood metaphorically as political commentary on James's reign and especially on the Spanish match of 1617–1624.[21] The play's subplot does deal extensively with the intramural disputes among various malcontented courtiers and members of the royal family with frequent, and often plausible, topical allusions to political figures and events throughout James's reign. Near the beginning of the play, the king recounts a fable in which political power originally dispersed to all members of a community inhabited by a "lion, fox, and silly ass" is gradually usurped by the lion (1.4.28). Drawing on Aesop, Philip Sidney's "Ister Bank" in *The Arcadia*, and the second eclogue of Edmund Spenser's *Shepheardes Calender*, the king's fable could readily be apprehended as a portrait of royal tyranny in a growing absolutist climate under the Stuarts, especially given James's tendency to fashion himself as a lion—the emblem of Scottish royal authority. For those immersed in these debates, this scene functions as an allegorical vignette expressed in familiar, albeit coded, language. For those unfamiliar with either this literary tradition or these political metaphors, the king's story—which is not essential for the development of the plot—could nevertheless foreshadow his violent pursuit of his personal whims.

Assimilating the play's main plot to a larger political subtext is more problematic and requires a more sophisticated understanding of Jacobean politics and English common law. Auditors familiar with *Basilicon Doron* (1603), *The True Law of Free Monarchies* (1598), and James's other statements concerning royal versus parliamentary prerogative (as many in attendance at the Cockpit no doubt were) might recognize verbal echoes with Dekker's foolish king. Seeking to display the vast gulf between himself, as monarch, and those of lesser rank, the king challenges, "Dost thou think / Thy poisonous rotten breath shall blast our fame, / Or those furred gums of thine gnaw a king's name?" (2.2.96–98). The king's words recall James's view that many of his subjects carried a "natural sickness . . . a feckless arrogant conceit of their greatness and power . . . [that] they will think the king far in their common."[22]

Later, Cordolente raises the legal relationship of the monarch to parliament:

> You oft call Parliaments, and there enact
> Laws good and wholesome, such as who so break
> Are hung by the purse or neck. But as the weak
> Or smaller flies i'the spider's web are taken
> When great ones tear the web, and free remain.
> (4.1.56–60)

Any audience could grasp that in any dispute with the king, commoners were akin to flies in a spider's web, and less well-to-do playgoers could certainly appreciate the financial pain to their purse associated with breaking the law and competing with royal monopolies, even while the great commit crimes with relative impunity. More educated auditors would recognize the significantly more intricate legal proceedings behind this statement that sought to delineate whether the king or the parliament was sovereign, realizing that potentially treasonous statements like this could leave them to hang by the neck.

James obviously thought power resided solely with the monarch, explaining in *The True Law of Free Monarchies* "that the king is above the law, as both the author and the giver of strength thereto," adding in a speech before parliament on March 21, 1610, "I would not have you meddle with such ancient rights of mine."[23] This kind of topical reading, especially the application of elements of the play to the debates surrounding parliament, the Spanish match, and James's granting of monopolies, relies on abstruse distinctions between private and public tyranny contained in tedious legal wrings and publicly debated for decades in Jacobean literary and legal culture.[24]

The law students who regularly attended performances at the Cockpit would appreciate the play's implicit legal contest; could easily understand, and probably welcomed, this intricate metaphorical dimension of the play; and would readily grasp the references to current events. It would not be the only time that plays at the Cockpit strayed into sensitive topics through direct topical allusion. Shirley's *The Ball* (1632) piqued the ire of Herbert because "there were diverse personated so naturally, both of lords and others in the court, that I took and would have forbidden the play, but that Beeston promised many things that I found fault withal should be left out."[25] That Herbert did not choose to censor *Match Me in London* suggests that the political allusions in that play either were not as pregnant as modern commentators have suggested or were so convoluted that only the most avid and educated political enthusiasts could decipher them. For Herbert and much of the audience at the Phoenix, as for many commentators today assessing the play retrospectively, the play must have seemed little different from the tragicomedies that they had grown so used to in the decade before, especially at the private theaters.

Intricate legal and topical allusions, however, are hardly integral to an interpretation of the play in its historical context and are easily beyond the grasp of many—probably most—of the lesser-educated artisans and apprentices who frequented the Red Bull (or any other public playhouse). Judging by the repertory at that theater, which included visually spectacular plays punctuated by fireworks and plentiful stage action, like Thomas Heywood's five-part *Ages* (1609–1613) and *Fortune by Land and Sea* (ca. 1609), it took something more than legal disputation to earn the approbation of the audience at the Red Bull. Although Kathleen McLuskie does note the "conflict between citizen and aristocratic values," little critical attention has been paid to the representations of tradesmen and apprentices, the part of the play that was probably most salient at the Red Bull. Studies that concentrate solely on the play's tragicomic aspects and geopolitical allusions—to the point of privileging the subplot over the main plot and one of the play's audiences over the other—treat the presence of the numerous "lower" characters as incidental because they seem to have no place in a critical agenda focused around the tastes and concerns of a genteel Cockpit audience. This critical practice has the drawback of dissociating the play from Dekker's ouevre, anaesthetizing the social and political importance of citizens and their values, and failing to recognize the importance of outdoor playhouses like the Red Bull in the late Jacobean dramatic marketplace.

When we try to interpret *Match Me in London* from the perspective of the audience at the Red Bull, the play instead provides a coherent and persuasive expression of the grievances of tradesmen and apprentices against their exploitation by those of higher social station.[26] Throughout the contest for Tormiella's hand in marriage, wealthier characters and assorted nobles—and not just the tyrannous king—adopt various strategies to manipulate and possess their social inferiors. Both Tormiella and tradesmen like Cordolente are commodified by their betters, who are less concerned with these characters' expressed desires than with their malleability as human property due to their relative positioning in the social hierarchy. Malevento's servant, Bilbo, explains to his master that Cordolente has "stolen her," words that suggest that Tormiella could and should be possessed and so initiates the plot to end Tormiella's unsanctioned marriage and restore her to her rightful suitor, Gazetto, even against her wishes (1.2.101). The emergence of the King of Spain as a competitor for Tormiella forces a realignment in the terms of the exploitation as Gazetto and Malevento, who had previously conspired against Cordolente, are themselves relegated to a subordinate position (although Malevento is later elevated to lord admiral when he agrees to do the King's bidding).

In words that address the marriage suits of both Cordolente and Gazetto, the King's lady believes that "tis a pity / A citizen should have so fair a tree / Grow in his garden" (2.2.9–11). The King and his entourage, along with Malevento and Gazetto, at different times imply that Tormiella's emotions ought to be dictated by the fiscal economy, believing it is the province of social superiors to adjudicate the value of these "trees" and to use this valuation to apportion them accordingly. Cordolente and his fellow tradesmen are forced to recognize that their lack of wealth determines the relative value accorded their marriage suits and other social prospects. Presumably accustomed to this kind of treatment from their betters, both Cordolente and Tormiella are able to perceive their position in this economy accurately. Tormiella recognizes that their lack of wealth effectively excludes them from the debate concerning their own marriage: "I want skill / To trade in such commodities," she admits (2.1.222–25), while Cordolente, using yet another mercantile metaphor, despairs that he is "the poor / Shopkeeper, whose ware is taken up by the king" (5.2.82).

As many commentators have noted, Dekker's king is a fairly transparent portrait of royal tyranny. For a Red Bull audience, he is hardly the play's only tyrant. The negotiations and elaborate orchestrations of the King, Malevento, and Gazetto to lay claim to Tormiella consistently and persuasively demystify the operation of justice in the interests of dominant social factions at the expense of common citizens. Without regard to the actual dynamics of the situation, those of a higher station appropriate the terminology of juridical discourse in order to advance their interests, allowing Malevento to label Cordolente "a civil thief" (2.1.55) and the King to "spoil the spoiler" and claim Tormiella as "a lawful prize / That's taken from pirates" (3.3.81–82). The audience soon realizes that justice is merely an empty signifier applied randomly to various situations by powerful characters to protect their interests. Gazetto's insistence that Tormiella is rightly his and that his suit for her and his plot against Cordolente is "justice" becomes a parody of the ethical imperatives that the law supposedly upholds when Gazetto "thanks vengeance" after persuading an officer to assist him in finding Cordolente (2.1.114, 131).

The King utilizes similar tactics when he uses his role as the state-sanctioned provider of justice to further his own interests so blatantly. Assured that he has full control of the judicial mechanisms of the state and that his "hand / . . . Can shake kingdoms down" (2.2.72–73), the King, as a matter of royal fiat, considers any affront to his authority bound to fail. In language that could easily remind elite Cockpit audiences of James I, the King's words to Tormiella display his single-mindedness and stalwart belief in royal prerogative over any other consideration:

> Thou beat'st thy self in pieces on a rock
> That shall forever ruin thee and thine,
> Thy husband and all opposites that dare
> With us to cope, it shall not serve your turn
> With your dim eyes to judge our beams (2.2.75–79).[27]

Nor does the King need to fashion his aggression as the vengeance of a selfish monarch. He assures Tormiella, "I will not force thee against thy blood," realizing that the mechanisms at his disposal allow him to achieve this prize through the legal system and through other more covert and outwardly palatable means of persuasion. Tormiella, however, is not fooled and unmasks "the court [as] an enchanted tower / Wherein I am locked by force, and bound by spells / A heaven to some, to me ten thousand hells" (3.3.25–27). Through this disparaging representation of the abuses of aristocratic and royal prerogative, a

Red Bull audience of tradesmen and apprentices could recognize their disenfranchised place in the social hierarchy and their proscribed access to a judicial system that ostensibly works in the interest of all citizens. While some courtly audiences might be inclined to parse lines like these as an implicit critique of the impostures of royal authority and a corrupt court, plebeian audiences would be more likely to see them as a condemnation of the entrenched system of rank and privilege that maintains the status of all courtiers.

What's most remarkable about *Match Me in London*, however, is that its conclusion subverts the expected tragicomic denouement in favor of the king that its own plot would appear to generate. Despite its bleak portrayal of the plight of the commons, the play's ending is potentially emancipatory for Cordolente, Tormiella, and the Red Bull audience. Cordolente disrupts the impending marriage between the King and Tormiella and is happily united with his bride. The king relents and is humiliated, even though he is ultimately reconciled with his queen, who is feared dead. Thwarting the generic expectations of tragedy, most commentators comfortably classify the play as a tragicomedy, a genre to which elite audiences familiar with the plays of Shakespeare, Beaumont, and Fletcher could readily assimilate Dekker's play. It's also possible that the gentry at the Cockpit might have understood the play's reversal in favor of Cordolente and Tormiella as a quaint but preposterous satire of the social pretensions of artisans, just as the exploits of Rafe in *Knight of the Burning Pestle* (ca. 1607) would have aroused their amusement rather than their admiration.[28]

I would argue, however, that in another social context, the play subtly redirects both these tragicomic and satiric expectations. Even though gestures are made to certain "charms of divinity" and "thunders and lightnings" punctuate a dumbshow that accompanies the play's climax, as they did so many productions at the Red Bull, the miraculous turn of events in favor of the shoemaker and his bride is not solely a product of "divine intervention," as Julia Gasper claims. The happy ending comes about through the agency of Tormiella and Cordolente, who shrewdly foil the King's shameful intentions through their very own, very human, resourcefulness (5.4.11). Unlike Bianca and Beatrice-Joanna in Middleton's *Women Beware Women* and *The Changeling*, respectively, who are complicit in the chicanery of their well-positioned suitors to possess them, Tormiella rejects her royal suitor and actively conspires with her estranged husband for her release, vowing, "I'll kill ten monarchs ere I'll be one's whore" (2.2.57).

Cordolente, for his part, does not resign himself to his fate but is willing to confront the king. In a stunning series of actions that display to the Red Bull audience the ingenuity of lowly commoners (and to the elites at the Cockpit probably a form of sentimental comedy), Cordolente puts his profession to good use, using his shoemaker's credentials to bypass the elaborate security measures the king has implemented in his palace and gain admittance to Tormiella's chamber. Recognizing that "the ant, / On his poor mole-hill [cannot] brave the elephant," the shoemaker does not actively use force to resist the king but bides his time and, in an unusual dramatic move, invests his bride with the agency to maneuver out of the predicament (4.4.48–49). Tormiella, accordingly, feigns madness and intends to kill the king if he continues to pursue her, assuring him that "by heaven, that night's [i.e., their wedding night] his last." The nuptials are interrupted during a dumb show in which "Cordolente steals in, . . . steps in rudely, breaks them off [while] Tormiella flies to his bosom" (5.3). In response, the king, realizing that his prize is unattainable, banishes the couple from the court but reserves the most severe punishment for Gazetto, who had participated in the planned regicide.

The play, therefore, does function as a tragicomedy but in a way uniquely attuned to the expectations of a diversified audience of artisans and, in a quite different way, to the social elites at the Cockpit. Plebeians are encouraged to leave the play heartened; despite the structural biases inherent in both social and economic spheres, individual initiative might overcome these impediments and the system might indeed be manipulated to serve their interests. A Red Bull audience might bond around the representation of the shoemaker, while the elaborate political and legal discourse provides at the same time a source of solidarity for a considerable segment of the Cockpit audience engaged in the legal profession. So prominent in Dekker's *Shoemaker's Holiday* (1599) and Rowley's *A Shoemaker, a Gentleman* (ca. 1608), staged at the Fortune and the Red Bull, respectively, the figure of the shoemaker is once again appropriated by *Match Me in London* to express and promote camaraderie among tradesmen and apprentices. Dekker's play offers another portrait of the honest and forthright shoemaker, able to fix "that which few men care to mend, a bad sole" (1.1.20). Such a far-fetched representation of citizens might well strike a more elite audience as overly sentimental, if not humorous, quite possibly allowing playgoers at the Cockpit to enjoy such working-class heroism as farce.

What can *Match Me in London* ultimately tell us about Jacobean audiences? Perhaps counterintuitively, the fact that a single play might succeed at two very different playhouses does not suggest that playwrights could generally anticipate a heterogeneous group of spectators who would applaud plays from across the generic and intellectual spectrum. *Match Me in London* is something of an anomaly among drama of the 1620s in being able to appeal to two audiences at once. It was not, in other words, the audience that was adapting to new trends in the dramatic literature but the plays that were forced to appeal to the growing stratification of audiences. *Match Me in London* was most likely a success at the Red Bull precisely because of its important deviations from the tragicomedy that was popular at London's private venues. The play is best seen, therefore, as a curiosity in the evolving dramatic market rather than an indicator of a relatively homogenous appetite for dramatic performance. The difficult circumstances surrounding this play's production and the company's move between the Red Bull and the Cockpit offer a unique opportunity to speculate about the response of specific audiences. Reading the double coding of the play indicates that, overall, audiences were changing as theaters and their occupants catered to specific segments of the broader dramatic market, making audiences more segregated than they had been in the sixteenth century. Playgoers were increasingly divided into distinct interpretive communities based on education, economic class, and social status. When they did applaud the same production, they were probably watching two different things.

Notes

1. The play was first printed in 1631. Its title page claims "it hath been often presented; first, at the Bull in St. John's Street; and lately, at the private house in Drury Lane called the Phoenix [as the Cockpit was sometimes known]." Determining when, exactly, the play was performed at these venues is subject to debate. No original license from the Master of the Revels survives, but when it was relicensed for performance by the Lady Elizabeth's Men on August 21, 1623 it was described by Herbert as "an old play," having "been formerly allowed by Sir George Buc," his predecessor who controlled the mastership from 1608 to 1622. Relying on internal evidence and topical allusions, many scholars date its first performance between 1619 and 1621 (since it is unlikely that the play was written between 1613 and 1619 when Dekker was interred in the King's Bench prison for debt). The play's obvious engagement with the question of a Spanish match for Charles and oblique references to the Admirality and to James's increasingly unpopular granting of monopolies are the usual reasons given for this late date. But there is no reason to assume that any of these factors preclude an earlier performance date. The Spanish match was a hotly debated topic as early as 1605 when that possibility was first tabled with reference to Henry; dramatic works make references to James's abuse of monopoly power as early as the first quarto of *King Lear* (1608) and by Dekker himself in *The Seven Deadly Sins* (1606). These commentators tend to privilege internal references over the facts stated in the quarto and provided by the Master of Revels. The fact that the play was "first" staged at the Red Bull suggests that it may have been written before 1616. There is no reason, therefore, to dismiss Harbage's case for a first performance at the Red Bull as early as 1611. Throughout this period, Dekker was a parishioner at St James's, Clerkenwell and, after a falling out with Henslowe and the Prince's Men at the Fortune, was a frequent provider of plays for the Red Bull, both for Anne's Men and the transplanted Red Bull company after the queen consort's death. The play also has certain affinities with *If This Be Not a Good Play, The Devil Is in It* (ca. 1610), another of Dekker's early attempts at tragicomedy. On the date of the play, see Julia Gasper, *The Dragon and the Dove* (Oxford: Oxford University Press, 1991), 166–67; Fredson Bowers, *Introductions, Notes, and Commentaries to Texts in the Dramatic Works of Thomas Dekker*, 4. Vols. (Cambridge: Cambridge University Press, 1980), 3:143–44; Alfred

Harbage, *Annals of English Drama, 975–1700* (Philadelphia: University of Pennsylvania Press, 1940), 82–83; George R. Price, *Thomas Dekker* (New York: Twayne, 1969), 30–32; Larry S. Champion, *Thomas Dekker and the Traditions of English Drama* (New York: Peter Lang, 1985), 105. All quotations from the play are taken from Fredson Bowers, ed., *The Dramatic Works of Thomas Dekker*, 4 vols. (Cambridge: Cambridge University Press, 1955).
2. Francis Beaumont, *The Knight of the Burning Pestle*, ed. Michael Hattaway (New York: Norton, 1969), 4.4.31–32. References are to act, scene and lines.
3. Andrew Gurr, *Playgoing in Shakespeare's London* (Cambridge: Cambridge University Press, 1987), 175–81.
4. Thomas Middleton and Thomas Dekker, *The Roaring Girl* (London: Thomas Archer), A1v; Francis Lenton, "The Young Gallant's Whirligig," qtd. in Gurr, *Playgoing*, 247.
5. Thomas Tomkis, *Albumazar* (London: Nicholas Oakes, 1615), C1r.
6. John Cooke, *The Two Merry Milkmaids* (London: Lawrence Chapman, 1620), A2r. This play, performed by the Revel's Company at the Red Bull, was most likely written by John Cook, an actor with the Queen Anne's Men and its successor companies, who was familiar with both these venues and their audiences.
7. John Webster, "To the Reader," in *The White Devil*, ed. C. Luckyj (New York: Norton, 1996), lines 6–9. Of course we might believe Webster's other reason for the play's failure, that "it was acted in so dull a time of winter, presented in so open and black a theatre" (ll. 4–5). As Paul Menzer reminds us in this volume, productions failed for any number of reasons, not least the dreadful London weather.
8. Qtd. in Gerald Eades Bentley, *The Jacobean and Caroline Stage* (Oxford: Clarendon Press, 1968), 6:54.
9. Bentley, *Jacobean and Caroline*, 1:161–62.
10. For more on the causes and effects of this riot, see Mark Bayer, "Moving UpMarket: The Queen Anne's Men at the Cockpit in Drury Lane, 1617," *Early Theatre* 4 (2001): 138–48.
11. See Bentley, *Jacobean and Caroline*, 1:167–69; Gurr, *Shakespearean Playing Companies* (Oxford: Oxford University Press, 1996), 324–27, 402–3. For details on Beeston's legal troubles, see C. W. Wallace, "Three London Theatres of Shakespeare's Time," *University of Nebraska Studies* 9 (1909): 287–342.
12. This ability to greatly modify their presentation style is something that was clearly within the capacity of actors of the era as evidence of so many players moving from amphitheater to hall playhouses attests. See John Astington, "Playing the Man: Acting at the Red Bull and the Fortune," *Early Theatre* 9 (2006): 130–43, esp. 138.
13. Thomas Middleton, *No Wit, No Help Like a Woman's* (London: Humphrey Moseley, 1657), A2r.
14. James Wright, *Historia Histrionica* (London, 1699), B3r.
15. For more on the history of this theater, see Bentley, *Jacobean and Caroline*, 6:214–47; Mark Bayer, "The Red Bull Playhouse," in *The Oxford Handbook of Early Modern Theatre*, ed. Richard Dutton (Oxford: Oxford University Press, 2009), 225–39.
16. John Stow, *Survey of London* (London: John Wolfe, 1598), 404.
17. Keith Sturgess, *Jacobean Private Theatre* (London: Routledge, 1987), 31–49.
18. Bentley, *Jacobean and Caroline*, 6:61.

19. Ibid., 6:64; Gurr, *Shakespearean Playing Companies*, 421.
20. Price, *Thomas Dekker*, 33.
21. Cyrus Hoy, *Introductions, Notes, and Commentaries* (Cambridge: Cambridge University Press, 1980), 3:144; Gasper, *Dragon and the Dove*, 166–89; Kathleen McKluskie, *Dekker and Heywood: Professional Dramatists* (London: Macmillan, 1994), 175.
22. King James VI and I, *Political Writings*, ed. Johann P. Sommerville (Cambridge: Cambridge University Press, 1994), 28. Another absolutist monarch, Shakespeare's Richard II, expresses similar sentiments when he wonders, "Is not the King's name forty thousand names?" and attempts to "arm, arm [his] name" (3.2.81–82). *Richard II*, in *The Norton Shakespeare*, ed. Stephen Greenblatt et al. (New York: Norton, 1996). Parenthetical citations refer to act, scene, and line.
23. King James VI and I, *Political Writings*, 74, 191.
24. Gasper, *Dragon and the Dove*, 173–83. Dekker's own *Satiromastix*, performed in 1601 at a private theater by Paul's Boys, deals with many of these legal questions at a more intellectually elevated level.
25. Qtd. in Richard Dutton, *Mastering the Revels: the Regulation and Censorship of English Renaissance Drama* (Iowa City: University of Iowa Press, 1991), 92.
26. The play asks to be understood in the tradition of earlier citizen favorites by Dekker and performed at the Fortune. Dekker evokes *The Shoemaker's Holiday* (1600) through the occupation of the protagonist and frequent punning on "soles" as "soul." He alludes to *The Roaring Girl* (1611) at 1.2.85, suggesting, perhaps, that these two plays were written at around the same time.
27. James was fond of Caesar's similar speech to his mutinous army in book 5 of *The Pharsalia*, which he translated in his 1584 book of poetry. Caesar asks if "the loss occasioned by your desertion will hinder Caesar's career? It's as if the rivers should all threaten to hold back the waters as they merge with the sea: if they stopped flowing. Would sea-level fall? No, no more than it rises with their influx." Quoted in David Norbrook, "Lucan, Thomas May, and the Creation of a Republican Literary Culture," *Culture and Politics in Early Stuart England*, ed. Kevin Sharpe and Peter Lake (Stanford, CA: Stanford University Press, 1993), 46–47.
28. McLuskie, *Dekker and Heywood*, 173; Gasper, *Dragon and the Dove*, 181.

CHAPTER 4

Door Number Three

Time, Space, and Audience Experience in *The Menaechmi* and *The Comedy of Errors*

Jennifer A. Low

When comparing *The Comedy of Errors* to *The Menaechmi*, its Plautine source, critics generally suggest that the primary difference between the two plays is their genre.[1] I suggest that the difference between the plays is more organic. Each playwright was accustomed to composing dramas for a specific theater design; this design shaped the way that each play made use of the audience and, consequently, the way that each audience experienced the dramatic action. Like Thomas Dekker's *Match Me in London*, the play that Mark Bayer discusses in this collection, the picaresque tale of twins searching for one another after a lifetime of separation can be read in at least two decidedly different ways. In this case, however, the meaning of the plot depends on which playwright is using it to structure his play and on how that playwright was using his theater. My argument is that the audience experience—the way the playwright *positions* the audience with regard to the action—is shaped partly by the relation between the stage and the spectators' area but also by the way the playwright makes use of that relation.

In the original productions of *The Menaechmi*, the space in which the audience sat was clearly defined by characters within the drama. The spectators are implicitly the allies of the Syracusan brother; the space itself is Syracuse, the idealized heterotopia to which, at the play's end, the brothers return. In original productions of *The Comedy of Errors*, the dimension emphasized at the play's denouement was time (though it was represented largely in spatial terms); the amazing conclusion uses tricks of perspective to make the audience cognizant of time past through the drama's emphasis on what might be glimpsed, Monty Hall fashion, behind curtain number three—in this case, the doorway of the priory.

Stage Space, Audience Space

The mimetic nature of dramatic performance itself suggests that the edge of the stage is a boundary between two different kinds of places—one that should not be crossed on a whim.[2] But, as several scholars have noted, Plautus's long, shallow stage encourages acting that acknowledges the audience as a presence. In *The Menaechmi* (more so even than in most other plays of the period), gesture and blocking reach outward toward the audience, transforming spectatorial space into dramatic space. In *The Comedy of Errors*, the use of Roman stage convention, specifically the three doorways, calls attention to the door of the priory, which is never used until the final act. The presence of the door to the priory creates a sense of expectancy gratified first when Antipholus takes refuge in the abbey and, more fully, when Aemilia comes out of it. Both the design of the stage and this use of the door lend this feature extra significance, which is heightened when Aemilia promises a resolution that can be achieved only when the characters pass through the door and leave the space of the stage.

The presentation of interior space in *The Comedy of Errors* has recently become a subject of critical concern. While critics like Mary Crane and Amanda Piesse have extensively discussed the scene in which Antipholus of Ephesus is locked out of his house while his wife dines inside with his brother, few have noted how thoroughly Aemilia's speeches evoke a space and the events to come within the priory.[3] The gestures and the staging implied by her words could be said to acknowledge the advances of Serlio and Scamozzi or to prefigure the perspective sets of Inigo Jones. Aemilia's priory provides a door into the past when she, a deus ex machina, steps forward to resolve the conflicts and relocate all the characters within the family circle. The play's use of that doorway, creating almost a visual tableau of the expression "Time reveals all things," promotes a sense of perspective and focus. Rather than opening out expansively, the narrow doorway finally represents an opportunity for the characters to go back in time, an emphasis that excludes the audience from the plot's conclusion and reinforces for us the thematic importance of temporality in the play.

Plautine Stage-Space

At the end of *The Menaechmi*, the Epidamnian brother will be redeemed "through the agency of Tyche (Chance deified)."[4] But what he is going *to* is suggested by the staging, which characterizes offstage and the audience area as two opposed worlds. The detachment of the Syracusan Menaechmus and his brother's deeper engagement with his community are reinforced by the play's staging, which was structured by the design of the Roman theater. Plautine comedies were performed on a narrow wooden stage (the *scaena*), perhaps sixty yards long, with a background of painted boards that generally represented two or three houses, depending on the demands of the play. Actors entered and exited both through the wings and through actual doors into the "houses" onstage. There is evidence from Vitruvius indicating common conventions: that one wing entrance commonly led from the forum, while the other led from the harbor, where people arrived from foreign parts.[5] Certainly, playwrights like Plautus used the many entrances to localize the action, with each representing a particular place.

The doors "were probably recessed to provide small vestibules" or porches, often supported by columns.[6] George E. Duckworth comments, "the length of the stage . . . made the numerous soliloquies and asides, the instances of eavesdropping, and the failure to see other characters on the stage, far more natural than is possible on the modern stage."[7] Richard C. Beacham cites Plautus's *Amphitruo* in support of the possibility of a roof strong enough to climb onto over at least one of the stage doors.[8] As for the tableau of the whole, Beacham says that "[t]he area in front of the three doors was thought of . . . as an open street which the characters normally refer to as *platea*; less frequently as *via*."[9] The rest of the theater was notable for special seats reserved for members of the Senate.[10]

In sum, Plautus's stage was long and narrow and painted with mimetic effect to depict a street—as Plautus himself says, often in Athens but, equally often, "Greekish. Not Athensish, though."[11] The combination of these conventional elements is, as Niall W. Slater has already shown, a drama of frequent metatheater. As Slater says, "Plautus's remarkable achievement is to include self-conscious awareness of theatrical convention in a new concept of comic heroism, which I believe emerges most clearly in performance. A number of Plautus's characters . . . demonstrate a self-awareness of the play as play and through this awareness demonstrate their own ability to control other characters in the play."[12] Slater also cites several key elements that define Plautine dramas as metatheatrical: "the monologue, the aside, eavesdropping, role-playing, and the play-within-the-play."[13]

What interests me is twofold: first, how the place actually staged in *The Menaechmi* defined itself in relation to the rest of the mimetic world of the play, and second, how the mimetic world makes use of the spectators. Like so many of Plautus's plays, *The Menaechmi* is set in a section of a street—clearly a mere segment of a microcosm. Commercial and civic life take place offstage and not on the street, for that is the liminal space on which the Menaechmi's drama unfolds. Their stage is merely a part of a community. It is the use of the twins in *The Menaechmi* that extends the mimetic world of the Eastern Mediterranean into the spectator area. Plautus's alien twin, in contrast to Shakespeare's, keeps aloof from the community he is visiting, except for his presumably erotic tryst with Erotium. He almost never begins a conversation with Epidamnians, only speaking to them when he is accosted. Yet while he remains aloof from the citizens of Epidamnus, surprisingly, he solicits the views of the audience in frequent addresses. Eventually, he makes them his accomplices, amusing them with a show that is meant to confuse and confound the Epidamnians onstage. Unlike Shakespeare's Syracusan Antipholus, whose actions, body language, and dialogue demonstrate his willingness to be integrated into Ephesian society, the Syracusan Menaechmus, encouraged by Roman stage design, gradually forms a relationship with the audience instead. The partial nature of the staged community, completed for Menaechmus of Epidamnus by the world offstage, is completed for his twin by the audience members who sit watching his plight, themselves a cross-section of the Greco-Roman society on which all the characters are based. For the alien twin, the audience, by virtue of its silence, merits his confidence. It is the only group whom he freely approaches.

To picture the process at work, we must consider Roman stage design once again, reverting to Duckworth's comment: "[T]he length of the stage (believed to be as much as sixty yards) made the numerous soliloquies and asides, the instances of eavesdropping, and the failure to see other characters on the stage, far more natural than is possible on the modern stage which is usually smaller and often represents indoor scenes."[14] Like Peniculus the parasite, Menaechmus addresses the audience repeatedly, but unlike the parasite, Menaechmus voluntarily addresses the audience almost exclusively: his servant Messenio is the only character with whom he initiates any extensive exchange. He clearly feels at ease with the audience: his comments to them range from the general, musing type—"Who's this woman talking to?" (l. 369)—to more pointed addresses that summarize his strategic exploitation of the Epidamnians' apparent mistaking of his identity (ll. 479–85). Gradually, he reaches the point where he asks questions that all but invite a response: when he sees Peniculus approaching, he inquires of the audience, "Who is this who is coming up to me?" (*Quis hic est, qui adversus it mihi?*) (l. 487). In contrast, neither of Shakespeare's Antipholi soliloquize often, and they never address the audience so directly. Such questions occur more often in the works of Shakespeare's contemporaries than in those of Shakespeare himself. When questions do figure as part of a Shakespearean soliloquy, the addressee tends to be ambiguous, as in Iago's query, "And what's he then that says I play the villain, / When this advice is free I give and honest?" (2.3.336–37).[15] On the page, such a question can be taken as rhetorical, as directed toward the spectator, or both. Onstage, the actor's interpretation would determine the question.

The unique role of the audience becomes evident after the Syracusan twin encounters his brother's parasite who, confusing him with his brother, berates him for not including him at the meal he has just had with the native twin's mistress, Erotium. After an acid exchange, Peniculus exits. The Syracusan then turns to the audience and asks for an explanation of the parasite's bizarre behavior. "Everyone," he says, is making a fool of him (*satine, ut quemque conspicor, / ita me ludificant?*) (ll. 522–23). But of course the audience is excluded from this "everyone"; they are the passive, receptive, yet approving friends to whom he turns to reveal his puzzlement and the resulting vulnerability. With them, he avoids the bellicosity that he has addressed to the parasite and will soon address to the Matrona. Believing that they can be trusted not to make aggressive demands, he seems to expect empathy and, perhaps, even an answer to the mystery from them.

Menaechmus of Syracuse soon reverts to the audience again, turning to them in midsentence as he concludes a brief conversation with Erotium's maid: "Say I'll take care of these things—take care that they're sold as soon as possible for what they'll bring. Gone now, has she? Gone! She's shut the door" (ll. 548–550). The audience is played again as Menaechmus's accomplice, as if its members are telling him what is going on behind his back. He plays them off against the characters onstage, counting on them to let him know when he can no longer be observed by the other characters.

Conjuring Space

Menaechmus of Syracuse restructures both the role of the audience and the drama's use of the stage space when his angry and mystified sister-in-law calls on her father to back her up. To reinforce the old man's initial impression that he is deranged, the alien twin conjures up a complete world in order to fall in with the family's expectations; concession, he expects, may enable him to evade their wishes more effectively than flat denial: "Seeing they declare I'm insane, what's better for me than to pretend I am insane, so as to frighten them off?" (*Quid mihi meliust, quam quando illi me insanire praedicant, / ego med adsimulem insanire, ut illos a me absterream?*) (ll. 830–31).[16] What renders his performance complex is that he pretends to be possessed by Apollo. Madness—frequently invoked both by Epidamnians and by the Syracusan twin—is a powerful trope for possession, poetic inspiration, and acting ability, sometimes even representing artistic ability more generally. The madness that Menaechmus of Syracuse impersonates complicates the character's relation to the audience because it creates yet another world and resituates the audience in relation to it.

Pretending to be inspired by religious ecstasy—that is, to be visited by a god—the Syracusan twin invokes many classical myths in which such events actually occur. In Euripides's play *The Bacchae*, Dionysus, pretending to be his own celebrant, executes spells invisible to his cousin Pentheus, who responds by thinking that he, Dionysus, is insane. Roman society in Plautus's time was well aware that, historically, this kind of experience could easily be misinterpreted as madness, simply because onlookers might be skeptical of a verbal exchange with an invisible interlocutor. The result in this context is an absurd play-within-a-play, as the actor pretending to be the Menaechmus unfamiliar with Epidamnus allows the other characters to impose the identity of Menaechmus of Epidamnus upon him but plays the role of that Menaechmus as one who is insane. The absurdity of this enactment of madness depends both on the knowledge that the audience shares with the character and on Plautus's manipulation of mimetic conventions.

Menaechmus begins with gesticulations (*Ut pandiculans oscitatur* [l. 833]) that alarm "his" wife and father-in-law. His plan works: the old man immediately urges his daughter, "Come over here, my child, as far as you can from him!" (*Concede huc, mea nata, ab istoc quam potest longissime*) (l. 834). Then Menaechmus calls for Bacchus and his companions and, addressing them, mixes the two worlds as he drolly comments, "I hear, but I cannot quit these regions, with that rabid bitch on watch there at my left, aye, and there behind a bald-headed goat" (*Audio, sed non abire possum ab his regionibus, / ita illa me ab laeva rabiosa femina adservat canis, / poste autem illinc hircus calvus*) (ll. 836–38). When his insults again irritate the wife past bearing, she and her father plan to carry him off for treatment with the help of servants; he finds he must enact "some scheme, [or else] they'll be taking me off to their house" (l. 847). After dispatching the wife, he recreates a contest in an arena:

> Many are thy commands, Apollo. Now thou dost bid me take yoked steeds, unbroken, fiery, and mount a chariot that I may dash to earth this aged, stinking, toothless lion. Now am I in my car! Now do I hold the reins! Now have I goad in hand! On, steeds, on! Let the ring of your hoofbeats be heard! Let your fleetness of foot rush you rapidly on!
>
> > Multa mi imperas, Apollo; nunc equos iunctos iubes
> > capere me indomitos, ferocis, atque in currum inscendere,
> > ut ego hunc proteram leonem vetulum, olentem, edentulum.
> > iam adstiti in currum, iam lora teneo, iam stimulus in manust.
> > agite equi, facitote sonitus ungularum appareat,
> > cursu celeri facite inflexa sit pedum pernicitas. (ll. 862–67)

This vivid evocation does not merely confuse our sense of mimetic reality; it conjures up a reality in which Menaechmus is completely engaged with the beings he describes. The extensive stage directions provided by every editor indicate how remarkably this scene conjures action and props out of thin air. If Apollo is not necessarily imagined as physically present, the chariot and horses certainly are. This performance of Menaechmus would almost certainly have confused members of Plautus's audience; some of them might really have believed his pantomime, while others might have been convinced of the reality of his insanity.

To cap the scene, as soon as he has chased his father-in-law off the stage, Menaechmus abruptly returns to the world of Epidamnus:

> For Heaven's sake, are they out of my sight now, those two that absolutely compelled me, sound though I am, to go insane? I'd better hurry off to the ship while I can do so safely. I beg you, all of you, if the old man comes back, don't tell him which way I bolted.
>
> > Iamne isti abierunt, quaeso, ex conspectu meo,
> > qui me vi cogunt, ut validus insaniam?
> > quid cesso abire ad navem, dum salvo licet?
> > vosque omnis quaeso, si senex revenerit,
> > ne me indicetis qua platea hinc aufugerim. (ll. 876–880)

His words open up a chasm—an ambiguity that suggests both that the act was just a performance and also that "his" wife and father-in-law literally drove him insane. Once again, the audience members are Menaechmus's accomplices, serving to protect him from the residents of Epidamnus. With this direct address ("Don't tell him which way I bolted"), the audience members become his supporters, alien to Epidamnus and allied to him. They complete the scene, filling out the incomplete world onstage with their judgments, their initiative. They are part of his world, though not of the world of Epidamnus.

For the audience, the performance is a play-within-a-play, yet the character provides such detail in his speeches that the world of gods and men that he invokes is fully as real as that of Epidamnus itself. Whereas before they were aligned with Epidamnus of Syracuse as his allies, for a short period they become isolated from all other characters, trying to assess whether the prosaic world of Epidamnus or the alien world of the gods is the true world of the play. Moreover, the Syracusan's performance assaults the boundary between the world of reality and the world of the play because the Syracusan Menaechmus himself becomes an actor. Though he is performing for the benefit of a family whom he wants to alienate, he is also performing for the audience, whose relationship with him is temporarily suspended. Menaechmus's involvement in the world of the gods is to all appearances deeper and more fully committed than his involvement in the community of Epidamnus; watching his fiction, the audience could not tell what there would be to prevent the world of Menaechmus's fake madness from becoming as real as Epidamnus, the mimetic world of the entire play.

If the spectators had been attentive, they would have been aware that Menaechmus was choosing to play a part. At the same time, the part he played was as convincing—at least visually—as the part of Menaechmus the sane man. Spectators might have seen that the Syracusan Menaechmus was merely acting insane and sharing his pretense with them; however, he successfully convinces the Matrona and her father that he *is* insane—unable to distinguish between fantasy and reality. This scene demonstrates that, to the naked eye, staged possession and staged insanity look exactly the same. In fact, it shows that neither insanity nor possession nor mimesis can be distinguished from one another: all three evoke a mimetic reality through words and gestures.

Because of this confusion, the alien twin's actions would have radically undermined the audience's sense of how they fit into the action. Were they Menaechmus's accomplices, as they had been until this moment? Or were they part of a fantasy world in his head? And if he was self-consciously creating that fantasy world, to what degree had he created the audience themselves? For the Menaechmi, after all, what reality had the audience members? What did the audience represent to the *characters* (as distinct from the actors, whose consciousness remained outside of the play)? What was their relation to the drama enacted onstage? As Tweedledee says to Alice of the Red King's dream, "'If he left off dreaming about you, where do you suppose you'd be? . . . You'd be nowhere. Why, you're only a sort of thing in his dream.'"[17]

This metatheatrical show is matched less fantastically by the play's conclusion, when the former slave Messenio enacts the role he will play in one week as auctioneer: "Auction . . . of the effects of Menaechmus . . . one week from today" (*Auctio fiet Menaechmi mane sane septimi*) (l. 1157). Both Paul Nixon and Lionel Casson specify in their editions of the play that Messenio bawls out the news in an auctioneer's chant, as if he were opening the sale itself—which he will not do for a week. The twins agree to return to Syracuse, though they return to the Epidamnian's house "for the present," excluding both the Epidamnian community and the wider, possibly Syracusan, community of the audience. In retiring this way, they create for the first time a sense of possible intimacy, gesturing toward their ability to do without other society now that they have discovered each other. Unlike the Epidamnian Menaechmus, who was always caught up in a net of social relations, and the Syracusan Menaechmus, who preferred to be alone, the united pair enjoy each other's company and resolve their social difficulties by joining together. This conclusion leaves the audience's role open-ended: they could see themselves as the ones to welcome the twins back to Syracuse, or they might perceive their role as no longer necessary, as the twins were finally united. Plautus's text leaves this point undecided, and how the original audience felt at the end of the play must remain a matter of conjecture.

Shakespeare's Roman Stage-Space

In his adaptation of Plautus's plot, Shakespeare treats his audience differently. Changes in the plot result in a more passive role for the audience until the play's conclusion, which differs markedly from that of *The Menaechmi*. In *The Menaechmi*, the two brothers return to Syracuse, leaving behind the wife, mistress, parasite, and responsibilities of the Epidamnian Menaechmus. In *The Comedy of Errors*, the alien brother is integrated into Ephesus, the community represented onstage. Thus the audience has no explicit role in the play as it did in the Roman version, where the audience served as the community—indeed, as a group of accomplices—of the Syracusan Menaechmus. Shakespeare diverges from Plautus as well in adding new elements to the dramatic structure, specifically a framing story that begins and ends with the father of the twins; he even surprises the audience with the last-minute introduction of their mother. (Neither parent is present or much dwelt on in *The Menaechmi*.) Many of the early modern play's thematic elements encourage the audience to enjoy the play passively, but Shakespeare's borrowings from Roman theater reshape the space at the close, creating a visual allegory and an emphasis on the visual perception of time, represented by a hint of three-point perspective (something absent from—and indeed irrelevant to—the Roman play). The staging demanded by *The Comedy of Errors* thrust the watchers away from experience of the action; the visual tableau nudged them toward the necessity of actively interpreting the play's connection between recountal and recovery of the past.

The play's emphasis on the semiotics of the visual runs contrary to ruling assumptions about staging in the public theater and may have resulted from unusual conditions in the play's original staging. In our own recent past, London's recreation of the Globe Theater and the discovery of the remains of the Rose have driven certain basic assumptions about Shakespearean theater. Andrew Gurr, intimately involved with both projects, notes (along with Mariko Ichikawa) that the early modern theater audience's sense of where to place themselves was not structured primarily upon an expectation of tableaux:

> The modern use of the concept of a "front" to the stage reflects a basic change in audience thinking since 1601. . . . Hearing is possible all around a speaker, and it is natural for an audience listening to a speech to group themselves all around him. Spectacle by contrast presupposes a frontal view, and spectators expect to group themselves in front of the picture. Modern audiences are more properly spectators. . . . Elizabethans would not have positioned themselves anything like so readily at the "front" of the stage for a play.[18]

Gurr and Ichikawa suggest here that playgoers at early modern public theaters are more accurately defined as hearers, audience members, rather than watchers or spectators. Given the shape of the public theaters of early modern London, this comment makes perfect sense. We know that the thrust stage jutted out from the tiring-house into the yard where the groundlings stood; most were square, though the stage of the Rose was wider than it was long, thereby resembling the Roman stage.[19] The stage was about five feet above the yard level. Gurr and Ichikawa emphasize not only the spectators' proximity but also their field of vision: "Wherever you stood or sat, you were never more than thirty-five feet from the stage platform, and most people were much closer, but from every position you could see most of the other gazers and gapers on the far side of the stage platform. It was a self-conscious grouping."[20]

The Comedy of Errors, however, seems to have been constructed according to a different model of stagecraft. Whether or not the play was composed for the well-known Gray's Inn performance on December 28, 1594, is still debated.[21] The editor T. S. Dorsch discusses possible stagings of the play at the Great Hall of Gray's Inn; should this production have been the original one, it would have influenced later productions on the public stage. But even if the play premiered on the public stage (a possibility currently undocumented), it would have been affected by Shakespeare's Roman borrowings. Shakespeare's use of Roman theatrical conventions in *The Comedy of Errors* has led many critical commentators to emphasize similarities in the way *The Menaechmi* and *The Comedy of Errors* make use of space. The facts are these: *The Comedy of Errors* may be unique in Shakespeare's oeuvre in calling for three doorways on the rear wall of the stage, very likely a borrowing from the conventional setting of Roman comedy.[22] The effect would have rendered the frontal viewing of the stage more important than for most early modern dramatic productions on the public stage.[23] That full frontal view would probably have been the only view available at a Gray's Inn production. It would not have been the only perspective in the public theater; nonetheless, the demands of the play seem to call for it.

Staging Time with Space

In shaping this stage space to emphasize the pictorial, Shakespeare used a form of visual perspective to offer his audience a new way of seeing time—a concept more traditionally represented on the English stage by the use of an allegorical character. Many plays of the period (including Shakespeare's late play *The Winter's Tale*) represented time onstage by the use of an allegorical figure, often accoutred with his emblematic scythe, hourglass, and wings.[24] Such representations may be derived from medieval ways of thinking. The anthropologist Benjamin Whorf suggests that literacy has structured the currently more prevalent way of perceiving time: "Our objectified time puts before imagination something like a ribbon or scroll marked off into equal blank spaces, suggesting that each be filled with an entry. Writing has no doubt helped toward our linguistic treatment of time, even as the linguistic treatment has guided the uses of writing."[25] As the geographer Yi-fu Tuan points out,

> A characteristic of Indo-European languages is to spatialise time. Thus, time is "long" or "short," "thenafter" is "thereafter," and "alltimes" is "always." European languages lack special words to express duration, intensity, and tendency. They use explicit spatial metaphors of size, number (plurality), position, shape and motion. It is as though European speech tries to make time and feelings visible, to constrain them to possess spatial dimensions that can be pointed to.[26]

In this manner, the Antipholi characterize their experience in terms of movement, and though critics have often observed that Antipholus of Syracuse wanders as a manifestation of his sense of loss, we have seldom noted that the concept most frequently elided by the imagery is temporality—specifically, lost time. This theme emerges as a major concern in *The Comedy of Errors* in the second act, long before time and the possibility of its recovery are staged in the final scene.

Initially, Antipholus of Syracuse characterizes his source of grief in explicitly spatial terms: "I to the world am like a drop of water, / That in the ocean seeks another drop / Who, falling there to find his fellow forth / (Unseen, inquisitive), confounds himself" (1.2.35–38). His need is not expressed in terms of time at all; it is couched in terms of a present desire, not in terms of recovering lost time. Yet the larger implication of his desire to find his brother is to regain the past or, perhaps, to regain a part of his past life. While the Antipholi tend to characterize their problems in terms of spatial difficulties, the Dromios consistently allude to temporality instead. The Ephesian Dromio urges timeliness to a master concerned with concreteness: "'Tis dinner-time,' quoth I: 'My gold!' quoth he. / 'Your meat doth burn,' quoth I. 'My gold!' quoth he. / 'Will you come?' quoth I: 'My gold!' quoth he" (2.1.62–64). As Gamini Salgãdo comments, "[T]he series of pictures of disrupted time . . . are the first words uttered by E. Dromio."[27] Ironically, time *has* drawn the Syracusan Antipholus to travel across the seas; Egeon comments, "My youngest boy, and yet my eldest care / At eighteen years became inquisitive / After his brother; and importun'd me / That his attendant . . . / Might bear him company in the quest of him" (1.1.124–29). Yet in Ephesus this same Antipholus is unmoved by the demands of time. The power of time is stressed by the Syracusan Dromio when he argues wittily, "There's no time for a man to recover his hair that grows bald by nature" (2.2.72–73). Time cannot be commanded or manipulated, and the best response to the changes that time brings is the acknowledgement of Time's power. The Syracusan Antipholus is also correct, however, when he says that "there's a time for all things" (2.2.65). This play is built on the Syracusans' desire to restore lost time and to recapture the lost years when twins and parents were divided from one another. To do so, however, Egeon's family needs to recognize that their task *is* that of recovering time.

Time's capacity to steal from men is most clearly delineated in the Syracusan Dromio's comic turn late in the play, which I will quote in full:

> DRO. No, no, the bell, 'tis time that I were gone:
> It was two ere I left him, and now the clock strikes one.
> ADR. The hours come back! That did I never hear.
> DRO. O yes, if any hour meet a sergeant, 'a turns back for very fear.
> ADR. As if Time were in debt! How fondly dost thou reason!
> DRO. Time is a very bankrout and owes more than he's worth to season.
> Nay, he's a thief too: have you not heard men say,
> That Time comes stealing on by night and day?
> If 'a be in debt and theft, and a sergeant in the way,
> Hath he not reason to turn back an hour in a day? (4.2.53–62)

One point he makes is that time can reverse itself, a foolish assertion that becomes metaphorically true in Aemilia's terms. The other point is that time is a thief and a bankrupt: a thief because he creeps forward and steals opportunity away from people and a bankrupt because time is both static and progressive. The word "time" can refer either to the moment or to the passage of time, the flow of temporality. As Maurice Merleau-Ponty argues,

> If we separate the objective world from the finite perspectives which open upon it . . . we find everywhere in it only so many instances of "now." These instances of "now," moreover, not being present to anybody, have no temporal character and could not occur in sequence. The definition of time which is implicit in the comparisons undertaken by common sense, and which might be formulated as "a succession of instances of *now*" has not even the disadvantage of treating past and future as presents: it is inconsistent, since it destroys the very notion of "now," and that of succession.[28]

In other words, time, which is both a moment and an experience of movement forward into the future, is a paradox. When time moves, it annihilates itself as a moment. If a "now" exists, then past and present cannot. In Dromio's terms, time is his own creditor and, failing to pay himself, he turns backward.[29] Indeed, time fails to move forward for much of this play, as the arrival of the Syracusan Antipholus begins a circular movement wherein each twin prevents the other from accomplishing anything he intends. The slapstick is comic repetition, Henri Bergson's "mechanical encrusted upon the living";[30] no wonder that, for much of the twentieth century, the play was regarded as mechanical and simple, or as pure farce.

When Aemilia enters for the second time, bringing Antipholus and Dromio of Syracuse with her, most of the other characters believe at first that they are seeing another manipulation of space. Adriana perceives their presence as duplication: "I see two husbands, or mine eyes deceive me" (5.1.332). The Duke, more canny, suggests, "One of these men is genius to the other: / And so of these, which is the natural man, / And which the spirit? Who deciphers them?" (5.1.333–35). Each Dromio is convinced by this hypothesis and asks to have his spirit conjured away. What the characters themselves see—two Antipholi onstage simultaneously—is not sufficient to clarify the circumstances that have resulted in this tableau. The characters must treat the tableau as a semiotic field in order to make sense of the situation.

Aemilia questions not the twins but Egeon, asking him to confirm the story that he has already told about his experiences. The tableau begins to become readable: the Duke recognizes the significance of their exchange. He then reframes the presence of the Antipholi, acknowledging them as the missing twins. In a babble of voices, all the characters piece together the events of the day just past, reinterpreting events with their knowledge of two Antipholi. Their recountal turns the clock back to the day's beginning in an attempt to reorganize "the series of false starts, backtrackings, and collisions by means of which the main action is presented."[31] This brief experience of déjà vu, which clarifies rather than confuses the situation, nonetheless cannot mend the torn fabric of Egeon's family life. That task is left to Aemilia.

As I have said, throughout *The Comedy of Errors* the Antipholi seek spatial images to characterize their problems and spatial solutions to resolve those problems. But when Aemilia opens the door of the priory and steps out, the solution is revealed as another medium altogether: the medium of time. The door of the priory, which suggested, though it did not truly offer, the deep perspective of Renaissance interior paintings and famous sixteenth-century Italian theaters, gave the audience the sense of looking back and looking in.

Shakespeare's borrowings from Roman stage conventions reinforce the thematic significance of the third doorway (the Priory) as the dwelling of the deus ex machina figure, rendering this doorway the passage back to a unified family, bringing together brothers, father, mother, servants, and new wives. But to recognize how the original spectators would have understood what they were seeing, we have to consider carefully exactly what they were looking at (as James Wells says later in this volume). The question returns us to the various hypotheses of theater history: stage directions presumed original to Shakespeare do designate three houses, generally presumed to be the house of Antipholus, the house of the courtesan, and the priory.[32] How the houses were arranged relative to one another is a matter for debate.[33] Some scholars of Renaissance theatrical history suggest that the doorways were enhanced by booth-like architectural structures fixed to the wall; others assert that nothing more elaborate than curtained openings was used. Dorsch suggests that Sebastiano Serlio may have provided inspiration for the stage design. The possibility of some form of perspective design cannot be ruled out, and such a choice would have augmented the play's thematic emphases.

In the meaning he creates for the priory doorway, Shakespeare may have drawn on recent developments in perspective painting in order to offer the audience a visual representation of receding—but recoverable—time. Not only did the three doorways evoke a schema that urged the audience to "read" the scene allegorically, but they evoked a tradition that had already presented time in visual terms—specifically, the conventions of Dutch genre paintings. Karel van Mander's *Het schilder-boeck* (1604) uses the term *perspect* to characterize a vista in the context of an architectural setting, as when "a receding passageway or colonnade is viewed through an archway."[34] Through deep-space interior composition, *perspects* offered the painter an opportunity for dramatic revelation, narrative expansion, and commentary.[35] The art historian Martha Hollander comments, "While an opening in the picture space allows the eyes to 'plunge' into the picture, the 'small background figures and a distant landscape' inside it can be used to enhance the drama."[36] Hollander explains that these vistas can depict additional events in a story, "provid[ing] a narrative context," and she discusses in detail one painting where the *perspect* accomplishes that by illustrating an earlier moment in the story.[37] The relation of secondary to primary subject in the painting is also discussed by the seventeenth-century art theorist Gerard de Lairesse, who says in his *Groot schilderboek* (1707), "The outcome or ending of a story must always be set in the principal place in the composition, and the beginning of it in the background."[38] Hollander compares the deeper understanding a *perspect* provides to the viewer with the purpose of Erasmian *copia*: "variety as a tool of argument. Pictures use the same rhetorical strategies of comparison and opposition."[39] These compositional techniques seem more and more closely related to the uses of the memory-theater, and when we recall some of Erasmus's best-known adages—*Veritatem dies aperit* (Time brings the truth to light) and *Tempus omnia revelat* (Time reveals all things)—the evidence suggests that a curtained doorway containing the past may itself be a visual emblem of truth or coherence.[40]

In metaphorical terms as well in the presumed staging, Aemilia's emergence and her words gave the audience a sense of looking in and, in looking in, looking back in time: after emerging from the doorway, she offers characters the opportunity to examine the past in order to fill in the gaps of the present. As both Egeon's wife and a representative of the early Christian church, as both Aemilia and Ladie Abbesse (as she is named in the Folio), this figure serves as the missing piece whose presence finishes the puzzle. Unlike her offspring, she is not twinned, yet she manifests both a present and a past identity—a twinship not of presence but of disparate times. Whether her doorway originally stood center stage as some scholars suggest or off to one side, Aemilia's emergence from the priory—and, indeed, the priory itself—alters the shape of the stage space.[41]

While Antipholus resorts to the courtesan's house in act 3 as an alternative to his own, it is not until the final act that anyone either enters or emerges from the priory. This circumstance could have given the audience the impression that this was dead space, particularly since the courtesan's house does not play a major part in the action either. But if it was used effectively, the door to the priory could have attained an importance that only built as its use was delayed. As Abbess, Aemilia is a holy woman of Ephesus, seemingly energized with powers of Christian redemption specifically affiliated with St. Paul's epistle on Christian marriage. But she is also charged with the pagan powers of Time, turning the clock back to resolve events that have remained unresolved. The doorframe out of which Aemilia, emissary from the past, emerges offered a visual parallel to the frame story provided by Egeon at the play's opening and conclusion. This connection might have been further reinforced by staging that visually emphasized Egeon's plight, suggesting that the outcome of the comedy must integrate Egeon's story and offer a conclusion more profound than the slapstick that dominates much of the action.

The redemptive qualities of the *coup de théâtre* at the close of *The Comedy of Errors* derive in part from its relation to what has been called an "ideology of time." The perception of time as a concept (rather than a lived medium) was heavily inflected during the Renaissance by religious dogma; in discussing Augustine and his period, the historian Hans Blumenberg asserts "a new concept of human freedom [that lays] responsibility for the condition of the world as a challenge relating to the future, not as an original offense in the past."[42] By recapitulating the past, implicitly contained within the abbey, with her expanded family circle, Aemilia hopes to redeem the future, taking her family out of the confusion of human (and therefore faulty) temporal experience into a larger Christian cycle of time (represented by the 33 years she refers to). To recover the future, however, it is necessary to go backward in order to achieve the process of recovery that her words presage:

> Reverend Duke, vouchsafe to take the pains
> To go with us into the abbey here,
> And hear at large discoursed all our fortunes . . .
> And we shall make full satisfaction.
> Thirty-three years have I but gone in travail
> Of you, my sons, and till this present hour
> My heavy burthen ne'er delivered. (5.1.394–403)

Aemilia urges that all present go back through the door into the priory to hear not the recountal of that day alone but that of the last 33 years. Only by the family's shared recountal of the past can they recreate the family circle that existed before their odyssey began. Aemilia's doorway, I propose, represents a kind of "dark backward and abysm of time." Her promise to restore the past, which she characterizes as a birth process, suggests that we should see the doorway as representative of a passage, the woman's birth passage itself. But it is also a passage back to origins through the medium of memory.

The play's ability to convey the significance of time would depend on the audience's recognition of the need to read the scene allegorically, which is why the staging cues this recognition through the use of space. This new means of staging time would have given the spectators a foundation for how to judge the action and the significance of the conclusion. Moreover, it would direct the spectators to assess the action as the spectators of the medieval morality did, rather than encouraging them to identify with the characters, as in mimetic performance. Despite a radically different type of staging, the audiences of moralities were similarly nudged toward recognition of the responsibility to interpret the drama laid before them.[43]

Time progresses here by first moving backward in order to restore Egeon's family as the original family unit. Egeon redeems the time he has lost by paying it back not in the framework of the play itself—this drama of Aristotelian unities—but in the time of the abbey, receding into the past, where the audience cannot go. In Aemilia's characterization of the reunion, it is a new birth, from which point they can move forward to the present through the medium of the "gossip's feast" (the traditional celebration of a child's baptism) to the new family structure of two married sons presided over by matriarch and patriarch. Past time, or memory, shared among the characters of the play, brings resolution even beyond that shown to the audience. And for the audience, living in their own chronology, the collective memory that the characters piece together represents a closure all the more tantalizing because it is never revealed to them. The emphasis in *The Menaechmi* on the demands of community—and the play's inclusion of the audience as a community—seems to grow organically from the stage design. But the comical problems with time in *The Comedy of Errors* seem to be resolved by elements of the staging evident only when Aemilia emerges from the priory and offers an invitation that clearly *ex*cludes the theater audience, who must remain outside the priory door even as the characters onstage enter the imagined interior space.

The role of the audience is not merely shaped by the stage design; each play's themes generate a dramatic imperative for the audience as those themes become apparent to the watchers in the course of the performance. *The Menaechmi* is typical of Plautine drama in the interaction between actor and audience, yet the text suggests that the audience of the play developed a highly unusual relationship with Menaechmus of Syracuse. The audience of *The Comedy of Errors* was not a passive entity but began to fulfill its function at the moment when it was excluded from the action. The subject of community, which is so important to both plays, results in different expectations of the audience. In both plays, the audience receives a strong hint at the conclusion that the reunited families of this drama have come to substitute for the communities that were previously constituted onstage. The exclusion of the audience at the end becomes the very mark of closure, whether because observers have become redundant or because their exclusion makes of the family a smaller, tighter unit. While community may be the focal concern of Plautus's play, and the nuclear family that of Shakespeare's, both plots emphasize the completeness of the family circle at the conclusion of the dramas.

Notes

1. For David Bevington, one is farce and the other city comedy. David Bevington, "*The Comedy of Errors* in the Context of the Late 1580s and Early 1590s" in *The Comedy of Errors: Critical Essays*, ed. Robert S. Miola (New York: Garland, 1997), 341– 43. For Leo Salingar, on the other hand, Shakespeare's play is more clearly defined by medieval romance. L. G. Salingar, "Time and Art in Shakespeare's Romances," *Renaissance Drama* 9 (1966): 12–17.
2. For a treatment of this concept, see Keir Elam, *The Semiotics of Theatre and Drama* (New York: Routledge, 2002), 78–79.
3. Mary Thomas Crane, *Shakespeare's Brain: Reading with Cognitive Theory* (Princeton, NJ: Princeton University Press, 2001), 36–66; Amanda Piesse, "Space for the Self: Persona and Self-Projection in *The Comedy of Errors* and *Pericles*," in *Renaissance Configurations: Voices, Bodies, Spaces, 1580–1690*, ed. Gordon McMullan (New York: St. Martin's Press, 1998), 151–70.
4. Kathleen McCarthy, *Slaves, Masters, and the Art of Authority in Plautine Comedy* (Princeton, NJ: Princeton Univeristy Press, 2000), 37–38.
5. Cf. George E. Duckworth, *The Nature of Roman Comedy: A Study in Popular Entertainment* (Princeton, NJ: Princeton University Press, 1952), 82–85.
6. Ibid., 82. See also Richard C. Beacham, *The Roman Theatre and its Audience* (Cambridge, MA: Harvard University Press, 1992), 60.
7. Duckworth, *Roman Comedy*, 82–83.
8. Beacham, *Roman Theatre*, 60.
9. Ibid., 61.
10. Ibid., 63.
11. Plautus, *The Menaechmi*, ed. and trans. Lionel Casson (New York: Norton, 1971), 2.
12. Niall W. Slater, *Plautus in Performance: The Theater of the Mind* (Princeton, NJ: Princeton University Press, 1985), 16.
13. See ibid., 12, for detailed definitions of these terms.
14. Duckworth, *Roman Comedy*, 82–83.

15. All quotations from the works of William Shakespeare are from *The Riverside Shakespeare*, ed. G. Blakemore Evans (Boston: Houghton Mifflin, 1974) unless otherwise specified. Parenthetical citations refer to act, scene, and line.
16. All translations of *The Menaechmi* are from *Plautus*, trans. Paul Nixon (New York: Putnam, 1916) unless otherwise specified. Citations given are through-line numbers.
17. Martin Gardner offers the following comment on the philosophical dilemma posed by the King's dream: "The Tweedle brothers defined Bishop Berkeley's view that all material objects, including ourselves, as only 'sorts of things' in the mind of God. Alice takes the common-sense position of Samuel Johnson, who supposed that he refuted Berkeley by kicking a large stone. . . . The Berkeleyan theme troubled Carroll as it troubles all Platonists." Lewis Carroll, *The Annotated Alice*, ed. Martin Gardner (New York: Norton, 2000), 238.
18. Andrew Gurr and Mariko Ichikawa, *Staging in Shakespeare's Theatres* (Oxford: Oxford University Press, 2000), 18.
19. Ibid., 27.
20. Ibid., 4.
21. This debate is not new, of course; Sidney Thomas weighed in on the subject in 1956 ("The Date of *The Comedy of Errors*," *Shakespeare Quarterly* 7, no. 4 [1956]: 377–84). More recently, Charles Whitworth, editor of the Oxford edition of the play, said in 2002 that "[a] number of factors, not all of which are hard facts, converge to suggest further that the play, unique in the Shakespeare canon in several important respects, was composed expressly for that occasion, or at least for that Christmas season. . . . *The Comedy of Errors* looks like a new composition, purpose-written for the Christmas season, 1594." William Shakespeare, *The Comedy of Errors*, ed. Charles Whitworth (Oxford: Oxford University Press, 2002), 2–4. Yet T. S. Dorsch, editor of the New Cambridge Shakespeare edition of the play, said in 1988 that "it is now generally accepted that the date must be moved back to the first years of the 1590s." William Shakespeare, *The Comedy of Errors*, ed. T. S. Dorsch (Cambridge: Cambridge University Press, 1988), 1. Clearly, the date is still under debate.
22. While stage directions in F1 for *The Comedy of Errors* generally give only the names of the characters entering (e.g., "*Enter Adriana and Luciana*" [4.1.113 s.d.]), some stage directions do indicate a place from which characters are coming (e.g. "*Enter Dromio Sira. from the Bay*" [4.1.84 s.d.]). These and such directions as "*Exeunt to the Priorie*" (5.1.37 s.d.) and "*Enter Antipholus Ephes. Dromio from the Courtizans*" (4.1.13 s.d.) have provided strong evidence that Shakespeare is following Roman staging conventions. Two or three doors were common in Roman theater, and the painted boards used at the back could easily have been changed to suit the demands of the production. However, *The Menaechmi* calls for only two doors: one for Menaechmus's house and one for that of his mistress. The Folio references that specify "*the Courtizans*" and "*the Priorie*" lead Chambers to comment that "at the back of the stage three houses or doors represented to the right and left the Priory with some religious emblem over it, and the Courtesan's house with the sign of the Porpentine, and in the centre the house of Antipholus with the sign of the Phoenix." E. K. Chambers, *William Shakespeare: A Study of Facts and Problems* (Oxford:

Clarendon Press, 1930), 1:307, cited by R. A. Foakes, ed., *The Comedy of Errors*, The Arden Shakespeare, 2nd ser. (London: Methuen, 1968), xxxv. Foakes also cites "for accounts of the use of 'houses' on medieval and later stages" Allardyce Nicoll, *The Development of the Theatre* (New York: Harcourt Brace, 1952), 65–73, 82–85, 119. See Foakes, *Comedy of Errors*, xxxv.
23. George R. Kernodle considers in *From Art to Theatre* (Chicago: University of Chicago Press, 1944) how the demands of early modern plays with similar needs in staging might have been met (133, 160–63), cited in Foakes, *Comedy of Errors*, xxxv.
24. See Erwin Panofsky's *Studies in Iconology: Humanistic themes in the Art of the Renaissance* (New York: Harper, 1962), 69–91; see also Frederick Kiefer's *Shakespeare's Visual Theatre: Staging the Personified Characters* (Cambridge: Cambridge University Press, 2003), 159–68 for allegorical representations of time in such works as *The Winter's Tale, The Thracian Wonder, Corona Minervae, The Whore of Babylon,* and *The Trial of Treasure.*
25. Benjamin Whorf, "Relation of Thought and Behavior in Language," in *Collected Papers on Metalinguistics* (Washington, DC: Foreign Service Institute, 1952), 153.
26. Yi-fu Tuan, "Space and Place: Humanistic Perspective," in *Philosophy in Geography*, ed. Stephen Gale and Gunnar Olsson (Dordrecht, Netherlands: D. Reidel, 1979), 393.
27. Gamini Salgado, "'Time's Deformed Hand': Sequence, Consequence, and Inconsequence in *The Comedy of Errors*," *Shakespeare Survey* 25 (1972): 85.
28. Maurice Merleau-Ponty, *Phenomenology of Perception*, trans. Colin Smith (London: Routledge, 1962), 412.
29. Salgado reads the line quite differently:

> S. Dromio's cryptic line . . . has often been taken to mean "There is never enough time to do all that occasion offers" but it could equally easily, and with perhaps greater relevance, be understood as saying that time has so exhausted itself that it's more trouble than it's worth to set it straight ("season" neatly combining the two usual senses of "bring to maturity" and "make palatable or agreeable"). Alternatively, if we are not too snobbish to credit the lower orders with quasi-metaphysical intuitions, S. Dromio may be saying that time in itself is empty and owes all its powers and more to "season," the harmonious cyclical regularity of the natural world. In either case the involved and often—admittedly—tedious fooling does have an important bearing on the play's theme and structure.

See Salgado, "'Time's Deformed Hand,'" 89.
30. Henri Bergson, "Laughter," in *Comedy*, ed. Wylie Sypher (Baltimore, MD: Johns Hopkins University Press, 1980), 84.
31. Salgado, "'Time's Deformed Hand,'" 83.
32. Most critics have naturally associated this staging with its Roman antecedents. An exception, Arthur F. Kinney, asserts that "the forms and features of the mystery cycles are pervasive in *The Comedy of Errors*" and sees in the three buildings "the traditional stations of Hell, Earth, and Heaven of mystery and morality traditions." See Arthur F. Kinney, "Shakespeare's *Comedy of Errors* and the Nature of Kinds," in *The Comedy of Errors: Critical Essays*, ed. Robert S. Miola (New York: Garland,

1997), 168–69. While Kinney's Christian reading of the play seems plausible, it relies largely on a few key details such as Aemilia's statement, "Thirty-three years have I but gone in travail / Of you, my sons" (5.1.401–2).

33. E. K. Chambers suggests that Antipholus's own home was placed in the center; G. Blakemore Evans asserts that the Priory took center-stage; Arthur F. Kinney suggests that one doorway represented the Centaur, the inn where Antipholus of Syracuse stayed, while "the doorway of the priory . . . is the miraculously transformed doorway of the Porpentine (home of the courtesan)." See Kinney, "The Nature of Kinds," 170.
34. Martha Hollander, *An Entrance for the Eyes: Space and Meaning in Seventeenth-Century Dutch Art* (Berkeley: University of California Press, 2002), 9.
35. Ibid.
36. Ibid., 13.
37. Ibid., 14, 16. Hollander connects *perspects* and *doorsiens* to theatrical devices:

> Architectural structures in Renaissance paintings frequently imitate the three-part format of the stage. . . . The archway used in stage design was highly adaptable not only for different plays but also for different media. From the 1490s on this classical structure was used for assorted architectural fantasies. Serlio recommended it for windows, doors, gates, tombs, and altars. The three-part archway was also featured in pageants and triumphal entries. . . . It even became a popular format for book frontispieces, which expressed the author's intentions in diagrammatic form. The central archway revealed an important motif—a portrait of the author, or a scene, landscape, or symbolic image—flanked by allegorical personifications that were depicted as sculptures and separated from the central arch by columns. Thus stage design and emblems, frontispieces, book illustrations, and paintings incorporated the same organizing principle: partitioning an image into a main scene with one or more ancillary images.

Ibid., 33-34.
38. Qtd. in ibid., 46.
39. Hollander, *Entrance for the Eyes*, 17.
40. My reference to a curtained doorway assumes that the doorways were indicated with a minimum of actual structure, created with a minimum of effort. If, as I speculate, they were somewhat more elaborate, with either painted or actual architectural elements, then this effect would be enhanced much further.
41. As Mary Thomas Crane so concisely puts it, "There does seem to be some disagreement about the arrangement of the 'houses,' with some editors accepting Chambers's belief that Antipholus's house was in the center, and others . . . giving the central place to the Priory" (Crane, *Shakespeare's Brain*, 228). Dorsch confidently states in his introduction to the play, "In the centre the priory, the most important building, is marked with a cross or some other religious emblem." Dorsch, New Cambridge Shakespeare edition of *The Comedy of Errors*, 22–23. G. Blakemore Evans places the Phoenix in the center (*The Riverside Shakespeare*, 83), as does Richard Proudfoot. In Richard Proudfoot, ed. *The Comedy of Errors. The Arden Shakespeare Complete Works,* ed. Richard Proudfoot, Ann Thompson, David Scott Kastan (Walker-on-Thames: Arden, 1998), xxxv. Again, all we can do is conjec-

ture; here are my thoughts. If the players wanted to reproduce Plautus's antithesis of courtesan's dwelling versus wife's dwelling, placing the priory in the center would recreate the balance of the Plautine setting. Similarly, if, as Dorsch argues, the priory is the most important building, then it should be in the center. As the priory does provide the play's denouement, this argument is plausible. There is no problem with this hypothesis if all three houses were indicated by entries in the tiring-house wall. But if only the central *domus* was there and the other two were more elaborate structures elsewhere on the frame, then other considerations arise. As Proudfoot points out, "It is possible that an upper storey or gallery in the house of Antipholus was also used . . . but it is not essential to the play's action." Ibid., xxxiv–xxxv. If the upper story was used by Adriana and Antipholus of Syracuse while dining, then having the Phoenix in the center would have made the most sense. All these hypotheses are plausible, but it would be foolish to try to go beyond speculation in the matter.

42. Hans Blumenberg, *The Legitimacy of the Modern Age*, trans. Robert M. Wallace (Cambridge: Massachusetts Institute of Technology Press, 1983), 137.
43. Catherine Belsey, "Unity," in *The Subject of Tragedy: Identity and Difference in Renaissance Drama* (London: Methuen, 1985), 22–23.

CHAPTER 5

Audience as Witness in *Edward II*

Meg F. Pearson

Certain spectacular moments in plays recruit their audiences to transform: Lavinia, her hands cut off, her tongue cut out, and ravish'd; Hermione, "stone no more"; Richard II's improvised self-deposition. These instances—largely visual but in cooperation with dialogue—encourage audiences to change from spectators into witnesses. The audience witnesses in a basic sense any time they see a play. They are "present" as a spectator or auditor, seeing and hearing with their own senses.[1] What certain spectacles such as stage murders can do in such presence, however, is more profound. Onstage deaths, perhaps more than any other theatrical moment, contain the potential to engage or alienate an audience. To be a witness in these instances is to become "one who is called on, selected, or appointed to be present at a transaction, so as to be able to testify to its having taken place."[2] The members of the audience are enlisted by what they see and hear on stage in order that they might be made to interpret for themselves. To quote the prologue of Christopher Marlowe's *Tamburlaine the Great, Part I*, such witnessing audiences are compelled to "view but his picture in this tragic glass, / And then applaud his fortunes as you please" (7–8).[3] Applause signifies spectatorial judgment in Marlowe's phrasing. With the imperative "view," the prologue demands attention and then requests feedback. The audience has been appointed and is expected to testify.

While certainly inspired by assertions that early modern plays work to engage an audience's role as theatergoers and even fashion their subjectivity, this argument avers that playwrights summon their audiences intellectually at important junctures.[4] Rather than seeking to persuade (or subvert, to use the new historicist terminology), the playwrights call their audiences to attention and encourage them to judge for themselves. The summoning of a witnessing audience, I believe, may be imperative to the successful functioning of certain plays.

Onstage deaths can engage an audience in a number of ways, but the examples considered here will show how plays frequently undermine the pathetic appeal of certain deaths in favor of a distancing, grim humor. Alternatively, in the case of plays such as Marlowe's *Edward II*, the onstage murder of a king demands an emotional response of pity and horror. The overflow of emotion is a tool of the play, however, because it goes on to sabotage the spectacular scene that follows. Activating a play's audience results in competent witnesses who, in the case of Marlowe's history play, detect the contrived theatricality of the play's finale.

I employ the term "witness" in my discussion of the playhouse to assert the dynamic participatory role of the spectator in early modern drama. To term a spectator a witness is to draw attention to the moments in a play when the viewer engages not only with the play before them but with the contemporary discourses surrounding the judicial practices of the period and the lively debates surrounding the significance and credibility of vision and watching. The legal terminology intentionally reflects the comfort of early modern Londoners with lawyerly language and judicial discourse.[5] Witnessing and testimony, whether used in an explicitly legal setting or not, are inextricably entwined with conceptions of judgment and an awareness of how watching matters. Playwrights were arguably using "drama to create an alternative framework of judgment"; the language of witnessing participates in the same discourse.[6]

Witnessing History

In both its legal and evangelical valences, witnessing or being a witness carries considerable responsibility. Both fields support the witness's importance; their participation and thoughtful testimony was a matter of life or death, whether their own or the accused's. A medieval manual of customary law warns, for example, that the witness who wants to say "I know it for certain" cannot say this unless he also states "I was present and I saw it."[7] Knowledge and trustworthiness are linked to presence and spectatorial engagement and judicious watching. A nameless priest present at the execution of several Catholics, whose testimony is later printed, exemplifies this linkage between careful watching and trustworthiness. A witness to the events surrounding the execution of the Jesuit priest Edmund Campion, this "Catholike preist" is able to testify to the sights he has seen because the printer judged this churchman an excellent witness; he "apereth pressed to obserue & marke" the event clearly and the text's title page assures the reader that the priest was "present" at the time of the proceedings.[8] This text, attributed to Thomas Alfield, offers a Catholic reading of Campion's martyrdom and testifies to the visibility of truth in Campion's execution by providing illustrations of the process of martyrdom from rack to scaffold.[9] This attentive priest is an audience to martyrdom, which is in itself its own form of witnessing.

The best Christian witnesses testified for Christ by their public deaths, which were a battlefield of competing representations. In England, the state sought to execute the felons for treason rather than religion, while the martyrs themselves sought to engage their spectators and prove their godliness. Brad Gregory argues that "the sight of men and women going to their deaths willingly, and bearing extreme pain with extraordinary patience, could spark interest and even conversion" in eyewitnesses.[10] James Thompson, as he was climbing the ladder to his execution, called out to the viewers, "I pray and beseech you all to bear witness that I here die in the Catholic faith."[11] Both Catholic and Protestant reports of these executions are rich with attempts to read the messages of martyrdom: "[The careful watching of the felon's behavior] invested the smallest outward gesture on the gallows with a heightened spiritual significance, a fact that both sides tried to exploit to their own polemical advantage."[12] Reports of martyrs working to control the perception of their deaths are not uncommon, as when Protestant martyr Joyce Lewis consulted with friends in 1557 about the best way to die before the monarch, very aware that "public execution was the martyrs' climactic moment. . . . here selfless dependence on God was both most visible and most important."[13] These individuals testify, speaking and manifesting their religious truths to a watching public. The public for their part is activated by the intense social significance of these deaths and by the martyrs' attention to how their bodies and words communicate. Indeed, the spectators to these executions were engaged to the point of involvement.

A wide variety of audience participation could be found in the theater of the gallows, especially in these instances of Christian witnessing. Peter Lake and Michael Questier offer a brief list:

> John Nelson's Latin prayers and professions of his Catholic faith were interrupted by catcalls of "Away with thee and thy Catholic Romish faith." The refusal of Luke Kirby to pray in English drew shouts from the crowd of "Away with him" and William Sherwood's request only for the prayers of Catholics met cries of "Hang him, hang him, there be none here of his profession." In 1573 Thomas Woodhouse's defiant claim that rather than it being he who owed the Queen an apology she should ask pardon of the pope attracted cries from the crowd of "Hang him, hang him, this man is worse than [John] Story."[14]

The response of the crowd watching the execution could turn on a dime, influenced largely by the accused's words or gestures but also by what the audience deemed appropriate or fitting. Here we find instances of audiences who, when summoned to witness, testify their own pleasure or displeasure vocally. The men and women watching the execution are cued to action and encouraged to engage and judge by the behavior on the scaffold. The battle over perception in martyrdoms reflects the agendas of considerable numbers of plays in the same period. Playwrights, like the martyrs and their opponents, seek similarly communicative deaths that might engage and influence their watchers. Both expect close observation, and, as David M. Bergeron reminds us in Chapter 7 of this collection, both would prefer to guide and control their audiences.

Witnessing and Spectatorship

What might this potential witnessing portend for the early modern playhouse? This change from watcher to judger may be dynamic as well as dangerous, because once the spectator is successfully invoked, he or she thinks and judges for himself or herself. While the playgoers' testimony may be as explicit as their applause or their boos as the play successfully engages or alienates them, the testimony of a theatrical witness should be understood primarily as their interpretive analysis of the play before them and the conclusions that this interpretation enables.[15] Such a metamorphosis is, as we have seen, not unheard of in early modern audiences. The account of Anthony Babington's execution in Raphael Holinshed's *Chronicles*, for example, describes the audience attending this event "with earnest eie."[16] This report "positions the crowd as active participants in the event, rather than as passive recipients."[17] They are looking carefully and earnestly, seeking truth and making meaning from the events unfolding before them. This audience of real-life drama is not simply shown the tragedy; they look for it. This activation results in witnessing in an audience who engages directly with the stage with a critical eye. But it is not the eyes alone that matter. Both spectacle and language can "amaze indeed / the very faculties of eyes and ears," as that ever-perceptive Dane informed us (*Hamlet*, 2.2.565–66).[18] Together, the verbal and visual axes of interpretation in theater—particularly how and when they work together or do not—can offer the critic what may be called an affective taxonomy of spectacular function.[19]

Considering how the play seeks to interact with its audience enables us to examine the sensible discourses used by a playwright to call upon and challenge his spectators to become more involved. As Ruth Lunney has argued, "[T]he first impulse of an audience is to make sense of what is seen, to construct narratives and impose meaning."[20] The mechanisms by which playwrights both stimulate and subdue this impulse transcend the rhetorical. An investigation into this remarkable contract between artist and audience undertakes its own summoning: a call for new modes of interdisciplinary investigation that involves, in this case, the visual arts.[21]

To enquire fully into the mechanisms at work in this dynamic requires a shift in discipline. The activated spectator has received considerable attention in art history and, considering their terminology and findings, can illuminate the expectations playwrights seem to have had for their ideal audiences. In their discussion of Ernst Gombrich's views on the visual arts, Caroline van Eck and Edward Winters define a spectator's active observation not as an "isolated, private psychological act of perception by the painter or viewer, but a socially constructed act of recognition and interpretation."[22] The painter and his work, in other words, create an opportunity for spectatorial judgment that can be recognized and acted upon by a spectator. Renaissance art in particular, such historians argue, "directly implicat[es] the viewer and depend[s] upon his or her active participation to complete the meaning-making process."[23] For example, John Shearman distinguishes the casual and engaged spectators who stand before Donatello's *Tomb of Giovanni Pecci, Bishop of Grosseto* in Siena and argues that Donatello's floor slab, which features a full-length image of the bishop's body, is carved in a relief that may be viewed properly only by standing directly next to the slab, like a mourner: "The meaning for the disengaged or casual spectator—a bishop's floor slab—is quite different, then, from that which it holds for the engaged one, who is placed in the moment and position of witness at the bishop's funeral."[24] Donatello offers up several viewing experiences for his audience, but the slab functions most fully for the engaged spectator, who becomes a participant in the piece's meaningfulness. The work is a tomb, and the correct response of the spectator is to engage in mourning.

While Shearman suggests that artists anticipate different kinds of viewers, others argue for different kinds of interpretation. John Ward disputes the critical stance that Jan van Eyck used inscrutable or vague symbols in his paintings. Rather, Ward avers that ambiguity in painting may be seen as the artist engaging with his viewer and encouraging thoughtful consideration.[25] Van Eyck incorporated subtle systems of symbols in his painting for that "viewer who made a sustained effort to contemplate his pictures."[26] The artist sought "to invite the viewer to discover meaning at ever-deeper levels and to remain always in doubt whether the full meaning has been discovered," Ward continues. The painting offers up multiple alternatives of meaning to its viewer, transforming the viewing experience into one of dynamic skepticism. Considering these findings for early modern spectators and audiences may help us to harmonize our understanding of play and audience functions with the cultural expectations and optical expectations of the early modern period. The theories of art history may help critics of theater better comprehend the visuality of early modern England.[27] Renaissance works of art "assume and demand a more engaged spectator," argues Shearman, and the plays of the English Renaissance may be counted among those works.[28]

The demand for engaged spectatorship may also be linked to an early modern visuality best defined by its inconsistencies, an irony not lost upon the playwrights of the period. Whether we examine the discourses of witchcraft, painterly perspective, antitheatricalism, skepticism, or Reformation iconoclasm, we find a noteworthy distrust of ocular proof.[29] Stuart Clark notes in his recent work on early modern vision that, in addition to the number of scientific debates over optics and the trustworthiness of the eye, the early modern rediscovery of classical skepticism helped turn "every aspect of visual experience, correct and incorrect alike, into something relative, not absolute."[30] The doubt, however, serves a purpose in this discussion. The age's skepticism toward the seen may help generate better, more thorough viewers.

The skepticism associated with credulous watching increases the burden on the witness by compelling them to think carefully about what they do or do not see before them. Van Eyck may have seen his paintings as objects of contemplation and aids to meditation for this very reason. Their inherent ambiguity, which Ward argues would have been as noticeable in the fifteenth century as in the present, is either significant or distracting.[31] Such ambiguity potentially increases the quality of the witness. Marguerite Tassi has argued for Shakespeare's adherence to the "balance between the seen and unseen, belief and doubt, faith and reason." She continues, "[I]maginative conceptions are powerful in their own right and serve to heighten those embodiments of vision brought before our eyes in performance."[32] When the audience is cued to watch, they are also encouraged to examine their imaginations and memories to make sense of what they see. Consider Jack Falstaff coming upon Hotspur's body on the battlefield, for example, as he wonders worriedly whether he can trust the sight of Percy's dead body: "[H]ow, if he should counterfeit too and rise?" (5.4.121).[33] Falstaff makes Hotspur "sure" by stabbing him once more, but the audience to that scene would be undertaking a similar action by comparing the actions on stage to the facts and histories in their memory, testing them for surety.

Witnessing Murder

What cues these shifts, whether to summoning or to dismissal? How are certain embodiments heightened, to use Tassi's term, or deflated? Even in the case of onstage murder, this dynamism can wreak havoc on an audience's fears or deflate into comedy. Shakespeare's history plays are fertile ground for the strangely affecting onstage murder, deaths that encourage audiences' alienation from the victim.

Consider *Richard III*, in which Clarence is stabbed and drowned in malmsey (1.4.270).[34] Upon his waking in prison, Clarence calls for "a cup of wine" but is assured by his killers that "you shall have wine enough, my lord, anon" (1.4.164). A noticeable manic energy pervades the first half of this scene as the murderers waffle back and forth about the workings of conscience and the attraction of monetary reward. Even when they confront their victim, the murders rhyme and stammer. When Clarence reminds the First Murderer that the man is "not as I am, royal," the murderer completes the seven-beat couplet in his response: "Nor you as we are, loyal" (1.4.167–68). Once Clarence senses danger, he demands, "Wherefore do you come?" but the murderers respond only with "To, to, to—" (173–74), stuttering over the verb and seeming incapable of even articulating their task, let alone accomplishing their hired work.[35]

The stabbing is finally accomplished in spite of Clarence's eloquent pleas for his life, although the Second Murderer may attempt to save Clarence with the amateurish warning, "[L]ook behind you, my lord!" (1.4.267). The scene toys with the audience's historical awareness of Clarence's strange and boozy end through both his telling of his watery dream and the seemingly endless chattering between the murderers and the victim, which is ended by a blow that has the potential for slapstick. Even as the story and the scene stimulate the audience's cultural memory, the play simultaneously uses history's manifestation to push back their emotional engagement. Even at the scene's end, while the First Murderer is drowning Clarence in the malmsey butt offstage, the Second Murderer complicates the audience's engagement further by wishing that he could, "like Pilate," wash his hands of Clarence's murder (1.4.272). These quick shifts from comedy to tragedy unsettle any clear response to the murder. The death of noble Clarence is presented with grim humor and laughs, and the audience is cued to grieve only by the remorse of an ineffective murderer.

The potential pathos of Hotspur's death in *1 Henry IV* is likewise redirected by his abbreviated death speech and Falstaff's undermining appearance. Hotspur monologues throughout the play, often to the dismay of colleagues and family alike: "[D]runk with choler?" wonders Northumberland (1.3.129), while Worcester begs, "Peace, cousin, say no more" (1.3.187). Percy's death speech should be a work of staggering greatness given the fiery speeches preceding act 5. Instead, we have Hotspur cut off in words as he has been cut off in life. While this untimely cropping could produce regret or dismay from the audience—Hotspur charmingly steals scenes throughout the play, after all—his last line contains a surprising potential for audience amusement and, as a result, emotional distancing.

The staging of the battle at this point in the play places Percy on stage with Prince Harry, but it also presents Falstaff taking on the dangerous warrior Douglas. The stage directions tersely call for Douglas to enter, then "he fighteth with Falstaff, who falls down as if he were dead. The Prince killeth Percy" (5.4.75). As though intentionally undermining the importance of Hotspur's death, the play distracts the audience with the potential loss of the play's beloved clown. While Percy and Harry likely battle with talented and skilled swordplay, Falstaff's attempts to fend off Douglas near the rear of the stage are so ludicrously ineffective that he must play dead to escape with his life. Falstaff blusters that "you shall find no boy's play here, I can tell you," but his "playing possum" suggests that all the onstage deaths will be similarly counterfeit, like a neighborhood game of cowboys and Indians (5.4.73–74).

Exacerbating this distraction, Falstaff's "corpse" remains onstage while Percy attempts to die with dignity. Hotspur's eloquence is juxtaposed with a fat man playing dead, while the audience wonders worriedly if they have lost their favorite character. Even as later performances and familiarity with the play assured viewers that Falstaff would be fine, the potential for Falstaff to steal Percy's thunder remains. Depending on where he falls, Falstaff might improvise a running commentary with the groundlings watching with him at stage level. His inability to stay still, to be out of the spotlight, will likely make "dead" Falstaff the most restless and visible thing on stage.[36] The play confirms that the audience is not meant to feel for Percy by cutting off his words.

As he fades, Percy declares, "[N]o, Percy, thou art dust / And food for— *Dies*" (5.4.85–86). The beat that follows this line seems to demand a platea moment, one in which the audience considers along with the men on stage how best to end Hotspur's sentence.[37] One could even imagine Falstaff offering up several sotto voce suggestions from his side of the stage. After this undetermined pause, Hal replies, "For worms, brave Percy" and proceeds to deliver a moving eulogy to Hotspur's "great heart" (5.4.86). However, Falstaff follows on the heels of the Prince's poetry, popping up from the great beyond to remind us that an onstage death is the greatest counterfeit. "For he is but the counterfeit of a man who hath not the life of a man," he assures the audience (5.4.126). Falstaff turns his considerations on pretending into a metatheatrical commentary on how difficult it is to play dead when he pokes poor, dead Percy in the thigh before carrying him off stage.

Falstaff is able to come back from the dead because to pretend death in order to live is, to his thinking, the "true and perfect image of life indeed" (5.4.117–18). The most dangerous opponent he has, Falstaff acknowledges, is the too-attentive eyewitness who might see through his counterfeiting. As he explains, "[N]othing confutes me but eyes" (5.4.125). Falstaff finishes the thought in wonderful self-absorption, happily declaring that "nobody sees me" as he creates a set piece to garner favor using Hotspur's body (5.4.125). Hal picks up on this language of witnessing himself upon seeing Falstaff afoot, but the theatrical prince acknowledges that eyes can be fooled:

> I saw him dead,
> Breathless and bleeding on the ground. Art thou alive?
> Or is it fantasy that plays upon our eyesight?
> I prithee speak. We will not trust our eyes
> Without our ears. Thou art not what thou seem'st.
> (5.4.131–35)

Falstaff points to Hotspur's wound and assures Hal that their battle took place out of sight. Hotspur has fallen far in the space of one scene. The play not only denies him his dying words or a space of gravitas but implicates him as a counterfeit. As Falstaff says, "I grant you I was down, and out of breath, and so was he; but we both rose at an instant" (5.4.143–44). Hotspur is reduced to another actor, another liar like Falstaff, and then shrunk even further to become a prop.

As critics such as Kent Cartwright have argued, this distancing can have its own power for a play: "[T]he audience's sense of fiction and illusion, of blatant and even joyous theatricality, helps shape the effect of the dramatic action."[38] Laughing in the face of death, laughing transgressively, as the work of Thomas Cartelli and others has shown, possesses its own power to change the experience of a play. It is the alternative, however—the engaging death scene—that I would like to consider now in greater detail. For in this play we see an audience summoned powerfully, and their witnessing completes the play. Marlowe's *Edward II* offers up an emotional death scene—the murder of Edward in the sewers—and then juxtaposes this with the new king's considerably more stilted ceremonies, which end the play. The result may be an audience who is too alert to overlook the necessary contrivances of political spectacle.

Witnessing *Edward II*

Though the play brims over with images of metamorphosis, *Edward II*'s most potent change may take place offstage, in the audience.[39] "Marlowe's dramaturgy works through an assault on the audience's sensory perceptions," argues Janet Clare, and his history play in particular operates through both spectacle and language to summon its audience to action.[40] Several critics, including Christopher Pye, have averred that the history play relies on the person of the prince to galvanize attention. The audience may see the killing of the king as "conservative admonition or subversive fantasy," Pye argues, but only through the prince may the spectator understand his or her role in the playhouse and in the world outside the door.[41] In *Edward II*, however, we see that powerful charisma working and also malfunctioning. Rather than raptured by theatrical royalty, the audience members are made into witnesses, encouraged to judge for themselves the play's final scene of state show. This state funeral, deployed by one of those galvanizing princes, appears intentionally underwhelming after the movingly conflicted display of Edward's murder. Having shown the audience what was meant to be hidden by revealing Edward in the sewer, the play stokes its spectators' desire to understand and to make sense of what it has seen. Spectatorship becomes a compulsion and an obligation in *Edward II* as the audience changes into witnesses to history. Rather than seeing an audience being fashioned, we find a playwright "empowering . . . his contemporary audience."[42]

The plot of *Edward II* is thus: jealous and worried about the power of Piers Gaveston over their king, the English nobility turn against their feeble ruler, Edward II. Monarch and nobles only threaten to dismember one another at first, but then their language explodes into a civil war in which Gaveston is captured and decapitated. The noble Mortimer seizes both the throne and Edward's queen, conquers Edward II in battle, and takes the king to a hidden dungeon, where he is tortured and finally executed in a manner designed to leave no trace. After learning of his father's death, the young Edward III comes into his power and publicly punishes his father's killer using the scaffold and the traditional sentence for high treason. The play ends with a funeral ceremony and the display of the traitor's head by the new king.

The trajectory of the play encourages an expectation of peaceful resolution. Rather than witnessing the death of those who rebel against the king in act 5, however, we are presented with the torture and murder of the king himself. Although the dungeon scenes serve as an additional piece of evidence against Mortimer and lead the play toward a restoration of justice, the torturous execution of Edward II also creates an unexpected emotional eruption for the spectators. Placing this shocking scene directly before the anticipated conclusion of the play meddles with the audience's emotional barometer, prematurely arriving at catharsis. The viewer desires justice and a clear succession to the renowned able king, Edward III. Perhaps in a mild indictment of lazy spectatorship, the play turns sharply away from that vision of justice toward hidden criminality. The anticipation of violence meets the realization of murder, and the audience must reconfigure its ability to recognize and interpret what comes before it.

However well Lightborne the assassin follows the orders to keep Edward's death secret, Marlowe the playwright does not obey. As David Stymeist notes, "[D]espite the secretive manner of Edward's actual execution, Marlowe creates an admonitory show by reenacting the king's death in front of an audience."[43] Although Edward never sees the killing stroke, a hot poker in the fundament, the audience can see nothing else. Indeed, act 5, scene 5 proclaims its visibility with repeated references to vision, sight, and keeping one's eyes open.[44] After sharing an unpunctuated Latin letter with Edward's keepers, meant to order the king's death while appearing to say otherwise, Lightborne uses visual language that cues the audience to stay alert: "What eyes can refrain from shedding tears / To see a king in this most piteous state?" he wonders, inspiring Edward to say, "I looked not thus / when for [Isabel's] sake I ran at tilt in France" (5.5.49–50, 67–68). The exchange comes on the heels of several descriptions of Edward's sad appearance—his captors must shave away his beard "lest [he] be known and so be rescuèd" (5.3.32)—which turns the conversation into a command to behold what happens on stage. When Edward realizes Lightborne's intentions by recognizing that "these looks of thine can harbour nought but death. / O see my tragedy written in thy brows" (5.5.72–73), he begs him to "let me see the stroke before it comes" (5.5.76). Each of these demands to see and to look results in a particularly active audience, one that pays attention with eye and ear to see how the play handles this murder. The potency of this summoning appears in Lightborne's chillingly metatheatrical language when he reassures the nervous king, "[Y]ou're overwatched, my lord," and encourages him to close his eyes (5.5.91). He's correct: all eyes are turned toward the king.

Edward's is not a quick death, nor is it a silent one. In addition to the spitting that takes place on stage, the murder is aurally inescapable. Unlike Lightborne's previous jobs, which are described as quiet and subtle murders of unwitting victims, Edward resists to the very end. His agony is visible in his body trapped beneath the mattress and audible from his shrieks of terror and pain. As he is being tortured to death, the king cries out so loudly that Matrevis worries that "this cry will raise the town" (5.5.114).[45] Edward's death cries in the *Chronicles* were so evocative that those who heard them fell to their knees in prayer because "they vunderstood by his crie what the matter ment."[46] In the wooden theater where the Earl of Pembroke's Men performed this play, surely the very timbers would reverberate with the actor's screams.[47] William Kelly argues similarly that "Mortimer seeks to fix Edward as a bad king by almost literally pinning him, but Edward's scream foils the plan—it escapes the boundaries of the mapping that Mortimer had attempted."[48] These meaningful cries function as a sonic carryover lasting from act 5, scene 5 into act 5 scene 6. We are carried out of the dungeon to the palace, but we still hear Edward's cries. We share the keepers' discomfort as they nervously refer to Edward as "the king" even as act 5, scene 5 closes over his dead body; Matrevis wishes the deed "undone" in the next scene (5.6.2). The resonating spectacle and sound of Edward's death assure that the audience cannot transition into the next scene, featuring Edward III's revenge, without comparing the father's scene to the son's. Marlowe's juxtaposition of assassination and execution encourages the spectator to judge once more. We have witnessed Edward's death and now must continue our observation at a more politically significant show. However, this same comparative agenda also encourages the spectators to find the latter wanting.

The structure of a history play demands that attention be paid to succession and order. However, several critics have also noted how completely the play "provides a conventional moral frame while simultaneously undermining it."[49] Just as in the dungeon scene, when the audience is summoned to behold and see, "at the play's end, a king's body stands mute before us. We have to feel and judge its innocence. The sovereign cannot decree this innocence into being."[50] Indeed, we must judge for ourselves the innocence of the dead father and the newly crowned son. Both await the audience's sentence. Whether or not the succession is properly accepted rests on Edward III's performance of punishment and rule. Yet while the previous scene roils with naked emotions and shrieks of pain, the play's final set piece must necessarily be contrived and carefully planned. Ian McAdam worries, "[Edward III] handles the business so skillfully that doubts about the sincerity of his performance may begin to creep in."[51] The final scene appears to belong to the category of "too-tidy ending[s]" discussed by Jeremy Lopez in Chapter 10 of this collection. Even though history guarantees Edward III a strong future, a fact that may allow audiences to accept the necessity of this awkward transition, the scene offers few depths to plumb compared to the previous one. As a result, the chronicle play structure may work against itself by opening up the politically expedient and currently active modes of spectacularity to a spectator's judgment.

The language in act 5, scene 6 shifts the scene toward superficiality. When Queen Isabella intrudes on Mortimer's ruminations, she describes how Edward III responds to news of his father's death: "[H]e tears his hair and wrings his hands, / And vows to be revenged upon us both" (5.6.18–19). Mortimer disregards these signifiers, which correlate to the behaviors of the revenger figure in tragedies, but Edward III's mother recognizes the role and the play in which they now find themselves. As she declares, "Now, Mortimer, begins our tragedy" (5.6.23). While gesturing toward a *theatrum mundi* trope, this exchange also suggests the new level of attention that is being paid to the appearance of things. While the murder of Edward seems strangely spontaneous, with its sudden explosion of violence and screaming, the following scene scripts its shows more carefully.

The confrontation between young Edward III, his mother, and Mortimer resembles an older form of tragedy in its stately accusations and histrionic exclamations. Lunney notes the failure of language in the scene, declaring that the "words of the scene do not bear the weight of the action."[52] She attends especially to characters' reliance on titles and relationships like "mother," "father," and "traitor" in the scene to rationalize actions.[53] The result of this unnecessarily heavy-handed dialogue is a scene that borders on dumb show. Edward III brandishes the notorious unpointed letter in Mortimer's hand before he and Mortimer engage in a stilted stichomythia:

> MORT. 'Tis my hand; what gather you by this?
> ED III. That thither thou didst send a murderer.
> MORT. What murderer? Bring forth the man I sent.
> ED III. Ah, Mortimer, thou knowest that he is slain;
> And so shalt thou be too. (5.6.46–50)

Given the young king's apparent discomfort with appearing insincere that pervades this scene, these additional metatheatrical references can only emphasize the shallowness of the exchanges.[54]

In the scene that follows Edward's death, the new king, Edward III, attempts to punish secret assassination with the proven spectacle of state justice. However, the visual aspects of the scene present excessive possibilities for interpretation instead of the concise and didactic show accomplished by the execution of a traitor. Rather than accomplishing the inevitable decapitation of Mortimer offstage, as is done in previous scenes, Edward III orates the death sentence and then requests oracular proof that it has been done: "Bring him unto a hurdle, drag him forth; / Hang him, I say, and set his quarters up! / But bring his head back presently to me" (5.6.51–53). To be especially clear, he notifies Mortimer and his on- and off-stage audiences of the same:

> My father's murdered through thy treachery,
> And thou shalt die, and on his mournful hearse
> Thy hateful and accursed head shall lie,
> To witness to the world that by thy means
> His kingly body was too soon interred. (5.6.28–32)

Edward seeks to present a show that could conceivably cleanse his father's death, one that can "witness to the world" Mortimer's criminal intent. However, even when he has access to the visible indicators of state justice, such as when he brings forth Mortimer's severed head, Edward III seems to doubt their efficacy. He does not release the head to the crowd but has it brought back to the throne room.

The methodologies of execution were largely standardized in early modern England.[55] The traitor would be drawn on a hurdle to the site of execution, where he would be hanged until dead, if lucky, and then mutilated before being decapitated and dismembered. The deterrent effect on potential traitors was then augmented by displaying the quarters of the traitor's body and the head—which were parboiled or tarred to preserve them—at locations where the treason had been hatched, where the traitor had found support, or at public sites like London Bridge and the other gates of the city.[56] Corporal and capital penalties need not indicate an increased taste for violence but a need for visible legitimacy. Elaborately choreographed dismemberments were performed on raised scaffolds in market squares; state-sanctioned punishment and retribution were meant to be seen. Presenting dismemberment before the public signals its legitimacy—open proceedings and spectacular maimings suggest that the legal system has nothing to hide and that the accused is rightly punished before God and man. Ironically, the very visibility that was supposed to guarantee legitimacy at Tyburn can instigate doubt in the theater. Edward III, for example, does not call for Mortimer's head to be staked on London Bridge. Rather, he presents the head to the only witnesses who matter: the theater audience.

Seemingly in an attempt to ensure that the head is a legible sign, Edward places the traitor's head on top of Edward II's hearse, the centerpiece of his private funeral procession. The spectacles are combined to create a visual equation between the crime and the punishment. This spectacular stacking seems to communicate as it is intended; one critic asserts that "the final tableau of the play, Edward standing next to his father's hearse with Mortimer's head in hand, is too powerful to be ignored."[57] The danger with such emblematic tableaux, however, is the inherent ambiguity of emblems, which was "an essential element of the rhetorical decorum of the emblems as [the audience] attempted to grasp the deep meaning of political actions, their complexity and, consequently, their contradictions."[58] Just as Edward's horrific spitting could conceivably summon competing images of hell-bound sodomites or carnival meat, the tableau created by Edward III has an unstable potentiality.

A hearse and a head flanked by a boy in funeral robes, meant to embody the price of wrongdoing and the power of a king, no matter how young, also offers visual alternatives. Metatheatrical intertextuality may again cue a theater audience to alternative interpretations of this scene. The props-heavy tableau could remind a well-heeled audience of other, older plays featuring dumb shows and emblematic displays of this kind, such as *Gorboduc* or *Cambyses*. In the same way, the boy dressed as a king could hearken to the boy companies such as the Children of Paul's. In both instances, Edward III's tableau looks so theatrical that its contrivedness could work against its political effectiveness. Alternatively, the multiple emblems of head, mourning, hearse, and boy—left to stand without their pithy explanation—could stand for the inevitability of death. Even though the king has taken action against those who wronged his father, his future is naturally limited. Such melancholy musings could lead the audience to consider the monarchy's ever-tenuous succession, a particular concern given the aged queen on the throne at the play's debut. The tightly choreographed ceremony reveals far more ambiguous meanings than it intends. The young king shows his worth, however, by recognizing his shaky ground, and he works diligently to reinforce his visual message with a spoken interpretive guide.

Edward III attempts to infuse and stabilize his own show with emotion by offering his tears as proof of his grief. As he stands with Mortimer's severed head, Edward III asks his audience to "let these tears distilling from mine eyes / Be witness of my grief and innocence" (5.6.100–102). Though he calls the audience to witness for him, Edward's performance is not an activated moment of punishment like the spectacle of his father's death. The scene's procedural efficiency and his own well-timed tears appear staged and false, especially compared to the deep pathos and spectacular power of his father's murder. The young king's request to "help me to mourn" further suggests that the show before us is difficult to hold together and challenging to play (5.6.97).

Having been summoned, the audience engages with Edward III's spectacle and finds it wanting. If not for the preceding emotional eruption, the funeral and punishment may have been acceptable. Indeed, juxtaposing the murder with its punishment would appear an intuitive pairing. However, by staging the murder in a manner that involves the audience as witnesses rather than as consumers of images, Marlowe sabotages his finale. The witnessing audience concludes that state spectacles such as Edward III's may be politically expedient, but the unsatisfying experience of the finale reveals the emptiness of the show. History must march on, the play avers, yet it compels its audience to remember Edward instead of gazing hopefully upon his far more capable son.

Notes

1. *Oxford English Dictionary, OED Online*, 2009, s.v. "witness," (*n.*, def. 4), http://dictionary.oed.com.
2. Ibid., (*n.*, def. 5a). This particular definition dates back to the twelfth century.
3. Christopher Marlowe, *Tamburline the Great, Part I*, in *Doctor Faustus and Other Plays*, eds. David Bevington and Eric Rasmussen (Oxford: Oxford University Press, 1995).
4. Cf. Christopher Pye, *The Regal Phantasm: Shakespeare and the Politics of Spectacle* (London: Routledge, 1990), 3–6.
5. Other scholars have asserted a widespread familiarity with judicial and legal practices during the period. Subha Mukherji notes the law backgrounds of many English Renaissance dramatists, who had studied law at the Inns of Court, and the theater audience itself, which contained lawyers and law-students. Additionally, "the jury system that replaced older forms of trial in England reinforces, in this period, the role of people's representatives in independently evaluating evidence, including witness testimony." *Law and Representation in Early Modern Drama* (Cambridge: Cambridge University Press, 2006), 2–4. Similarly, Lorna Hutson avers that "the strongly participatory structures of English criminal justice, which depended on unpaid officers of the peace and on the institution of jury trial, ensured that these evidential concepts, which were transforming legal practice, were not part of some esoteric professional doctrine, but were relatively widely diffused throughout society." *The Invention of Suspicion: Law and Mimesis in Shakespeare and Renaissance Drama* (Oxford: Oxford University Press, 2007), 3.
6. Mukherji, *Law and Representation*, 4.
7. See Philippe de Beaumanoir's thirteenth-century manual, *Coutumes de Beauvaisis* (1283), quoted in Andrea Frisch, *The Invention of the Eyewitness: Witnessing and Testimony in Early Modern France* (Chapel Hill : University of North Carolina Press, 2004), 13. The modern translation most frequently cited is *Coutumes de Beauvaisis*, vols. 1 and 2, ed. Amédée Salmon (Paris: Picard, 1899–1900) and the English translation by F. R. P. Akehurst (Philadelphia: University of Pennsylvania Press, 1992), but Frisch does not note a translation.
8. Thomas Alfield, "To the Reader," in *A true reporte of the death and martyrdome of M. Campion Iesuite and preiste, and M. Sherwin, and M. Bryan preistes, at Tiborne*

the first of December 1581 Observid and written by a Catholike preist, which was present therat Wheruuto [sic] is annexid certayne verses made by sundrie persons (London: printed by R. Rowlands or Verstegan, 1582), Av1.
9. Elizabeth Hanson, "Torture and Truth in Renaissance England," *Representations* 34 (Spring 1991): 83.
10. Brad S. Gregory, *Salvation at Stake: Christian Martyrdom in Early Modern Europe* (Cambridge, MA: Harvard University Press, 1999), 7.
11. Thomas Alfield, *A True Report of the Death and Martyrdom and M. Campion* (London, 1591), unpaginated, quoted in Peter Lake and Michael Questier, *The Antichrist's Lewd Hat: Protestants, Papists and Players and Post-Reformation England* (New Haven, CT: Yale University Press, 2002), 246.
12. Lake and Questier, *Antichrist*, 241.
13. Gregory, *Salvation*, 135.
14. Lake and Questier, *Antichrist*, 270.
15. In her kind considerations of this paper in its early stages, Kara Northway posed the question, "What action does the audience perform exactly that indicates witnessing?" The responses may range, I believe, but the Marlovian order to "view . . . And then [respond or take action] as you please" strikes me as a place to begin. Witnessing includes the twofold actions of viewing and responding. Those responses may be as banal as applause but they also include the subtle cognitive shifts in awareness—brought on by allusion, by language, by spectacle, by actors' bodies, and by staging—which create spectatorial engagement. Kara Northway, email message to author, March 23, 2009.
16. Raphael Holinshed, *Chronicles of England, Scotland and Ireland*, 2nd ed. (London, 1587), 4:914–16, quoted in Margaret E. Owens, *Stages of Dismemberment: The Fragmented Body in Late Medieval and Early Modern Drama* (Newark: University of Delaware Press, 2005), 122.
17. Owens, *Stages*, 122.
18. *The Tragical History of Hamlet Prince of Denmark*, in *The Complete Pelican Shakespeare*, ed. Stephen Orgel and A. R. Braunmuller (New York: Penguin Putnam, 2002).
19. Thanks to Paul Yachnin and Steven Mullaney for their conversations with me about this terminology.
20. Ruth Lunney, "Marlowe's *Edward II* and the Early Playhouse Audience," in *Placing the Plays of Christopher Marlowe: Fresh Cultural Contexts*, ed. Sara Munson Deats and Robert A. Logan (Aldershot: Ashgate, 2008), 27.
21. Critics such as Erika Lin have noted how considerations of the dynamics of the performance medium, including "the circulation of cultural attitudes and practices" on stage can strengthen cultural history and literary criticism as well as performance scholarship and theater history. Erika T. Lin, "Performance Practice and Theatrical Privilege: Rethinking Weimann's Concepts of Locus and Platea," *New Theatre Quarterly* 22, no. 3 (2006): 283–84.
22. Caroline van Eck and Edward Winters, eds., *Dealing with the Visual: Art History, Aesthetics, and Visual Culture*, Histories of Vision (Aldershot, UK: Ashgate, 2005), 2.
23. John K. G. Shearman and National Gallery of Art (US), *Only Connect: Art and the Spectator in the Italian Renaissance* (Princeton, NJ: Princeton University Press, 1992), 2. See also Rudolf Arnheim, *Art and Visual Perception: A Psychology of the*

Creative Eye, The New Version (Berkeley: University of California Press, 1974); Norman Bryson, *Vision and Painting: The Logic of the Gaze* (New Haven, CT: Yale University Press, 1983); Thomas Frangenberg and Robert Williams, eds., *The Beholder: The Experience of Art in Early Modern Europe*, Histories of Vision (Aldershot, UK: Ashgate, 2006); Norman E. Land, *The Viewer as Poet: The Renaissance Response to Art* (University Park: Pennsylvania State University Press, 1994); and Jules David Prown, *Art as Evidence: Writings on Art and Material Culture* (New Haven, CT: Yale University Press, 2001).
24. Shearman, *Only Connect*, 14.
25. John Ward, "Disguised Symbolism as Enactive Symbolism in Van Eyck's Paintings," *Artibus et Historiae* 15, no. 29 (1994): 13.
26. Ibid., 12.
27. The New Art History argues that "whereas vision is a physical act, an operation of the organ of sight, visuality is a social construction." Van Eck, *Dealing with the Visual*, 3. See also Marcus Nordlund, who argues for "transitional nature of early modern visuality," suggesting that early modern audiences were not completely clear about how vision functioned biologically, psychologically, or spiritually. Marcus Nordlund, *The Dark Lantern: A Historical Study of Sight in Shakespeare, Webster, and Middleton*, Gothenburg Studies in English 77 (Goteborg, Sweden: Acta Universitatis Gothoburgensis, 1999), iii. Stuart Clark's most recent cultural history addresses this issue as well. See Stuart Clark, *Vanities of the Eye: Vision in Early Modern European Culture* (Oxford: Oxford University Press, 2007).
28. Shearman, *Only Connect*, 17.
29. Stuart Clark's latest work, *Vanities of the Eye*, is the most recent book to attend to this shift. He organizes his text around demonology, perspective, Reformation theology, and the resurgence of Pyrrhonian skepticism. See also Suzannah Biernoff, *Sight and Embodiment in the Middle Ages* (Basingstoke, UK: Palgrave Macmillan, 2002); A. C. Crombie, *Science, Optics, and Music in Medieval and Early Modern Thought* (London: Hambledon Press, 1990); Clifford Davidson and Ann Eljenholm Nichols, eds., *Iconoclasm vs. Art and Drama*, (Kalamazoo: Medieval Institute Publications, Western Michigan University, 1989); Huston Diehl, *Staging Reform, Reforming the Stage: Protestantism and Popular Theater in Early Modern England* (Ithaca, NY: Cornell University Press, 1997); Judith Dundas, "'To See Feelingly': The Language of the Senses and the Language of the Heart," *Comparative Drama* 19, no. 1 (1985): 49–57; Lucy Gent, "The Self-Cozening Eye," *Review of English Studies* 34, no. 136 (November 1983): 419–28.
30. Clark, *Vanities of the Eye*, 4.
31. Ward, "Disguised," 14.
32. Marguerite A. Tassi, *The Scandal of Images: Iconoclasm, Eroticism, and Painting in Early Modern English Drama* (Selinsgrove, PA: Susquehanna University Press, 2005), 214–15.
33. Shakespeare, *The First Part of King Henry the Fourth*, in *The Complete Pelican Shakespeare*, ed. Stephen Orgel and A. R. Braunmuller (New York: Penguin Putnam, 2002), 1039–79. All quotations from *1 Henry IV* taken from this edition, unless otherwise noted. Parenthetical citations refer to act, scene, and lines.
34. Shakespeare, *The Tragedy of King Richard the Third*, in *The Complete Pelican Shakespeare*, ed. Stephen Orgel and A. R. Braunmuller (New York: Penguin Putnam,

2002), 904–57. All quotations from *Richard III* taken from this edition, unless otherwise noted. Parenthetical citations refer to act, scene, and lines.

35. This repeated "to" could represent the men's coy stammering, but the "to, to, to" could as easily be an example of *epizeuxis*, the repetition of a word for emphasis. If the latter, the bumbling idiots may here transform into conscience-burdened hired hands whose disinclination to murder Clarence is manifested in their hesitation to name the deed.

36. My thanks to Ralph Alan Cohen for his helpful comments to me about Falstaff's importance in this scene.

37. In the theatrical moments that exemplify this summoning to witness, the performance penetrates from the stage into the audience's awareness in a manner comparable to that described by Robert Weimann in his discussion of platea. Summoning, to continue Weimann's theoretical geographies, occurs in the region termed platea. However, the platea is redefined for my purpose as a region of theatrical attention rather than the physical place nearest the spectator. It is neither solely spectacular nor linguistic, but it is distinguished by its cueing of the audience to behold and see in a particular manner that includes interpretation. Certain plays rely on their audiences to finish the scene for themselves, in other words. While Weimann works with these concepts in several books, the terms are discussed at length in Robert Weimann, *Shakespeare and the Popular Tradition in the Theater: Studies in the Social Dimension of Dramatic Form and Function*, ed. Robert Schwartz (Baltimore, MD: Johns Hopkins University Press, 1978). Both Erika Lin and Jennifer Low have made similar arguments for Weimann-inspired conceptions of how stage space may function for the audience. Lin suggests that "regardless of who is socially privileged within the world of the play and regardless of what is privileged, thematically or otherwise, in a text-based analysis, moments in these plays that foregrounded the process by which elements presented onstage came to signify within the represented fiction were theatrically privileged." Lin, "Performance Practice," 294–95. Low also recognizes the connection between theatrical space and audience awareness: "Further, in moving from locus to platea, an actor not only penetrates an empty stage but also steps into and above space that the audience would experience as their own." "'Bodied Forth': Spectator, Stage and Actor in the Early Modern Theater," *Comparative Drama* 39, no. 1 (Spring 2005): 1–29.

38. Kent Cartwright, preface to *Shakespearean Tragedy and Its Double: The Rhythms of Audience Response* (University Park: Pennsylvania State University Press, 1991), ix.

39. Gaveston's famous speech about his plans for masque comes to mind, but references to Ovid (particularly Actaeon) and transformation abound in the play. See Sara Munson Deats, "Myth and Metamorphosis in Marlowe's *Edward II*," *Texas Studies in Literature and Language: A Journal of the Humanities* 22 (1980): 315.

40. Janet Clare, "Marlowe's 'Theatre of Cruelty,'" in *Constructing Christopher Marlowe* (Cambridge: Cambridge University Press, 2000), 87.

41. Pye, *Regal*, 3.

42. Lunney, "Marlowe's *Edward II*," 27.

43. David Stymeist, "Status, Sodomy, and the Theater in Marlowe's *Edward II*," *Studies in English Literature 1500–1900* 44, no. 2 (2004): 245.

44. Christopher Marlowe, *Edward the Second*, in *Doctor Faustus and Other Plays*, ed. David Bevington and Eric Rasmussen (Oxford: Oxford University Press, 1995),

323–402. All quotations from *Edward II* taken from this edition unless otherwise noted. Parenthetical citations refer to act, scene, and lines.

45. This line draws upon the famous scream in Holinshed: "His crie did mooue manie within the castell and towne of Berkley to compassion, plainelie hearing hum vtter a wailefull noise, as the tormentors were about to murther him, so that diuerse being awakened therewith (as they themselues confessed) praied heartilie to God to receiue his soule, when they vunderstood by his crie what the matter ment." Holinshed, *Chronicles of England, Scotlande, and Irelande*, 2nd ed. (London, 1587), 3:341.
46. Holinshed, *Chronicles*, lines 693–726.
47. Knutson suggests that, although Marlowe seems to have written the role of Edward II with Alleyn in mind, because Pembroke's men premiered the play, Burbage would have had the role. See Roslyn L. Knutson, "Marlowe, Company Ownership, and the Role of Edward II," *Medieval and Renaissance Drama in England* 18 (2005): 37–48.
48. William B. Kelly, "Mapping Subjects in Marlowe's *Edward II*," *South Atlantic Review* 63, no. 1 (Winter 1998): 16.
49. Clare, "'Theatre of Cruelty,'" 81.
50. Anthony DiMatteo, "Identifying Marlowe's Radicalism: A Response to Christopher Wessman," *Connotations: A Journal for Critical Debate* 9, no. 3 (1999): 238.
51. Ian McAdam, "*Edward II* and the Illusion of Integrity," *Studies in Philology* 92, no. 2 (Spring 1995): 203.
52. Ruth Lunney, "Marlowe's *Edward II*," 40.
53. Ibid.
54. DiMatteo, "Identifying Marlowe's Radicalism," 236.
55. While the executions themselves could feature lively debates between the accused and the crowd, bloodthirsty calls for pain, or displeased observations about the righteousness of the sentence, the ceremony itself was highly ritualized. In addition, many pamphlets circulated fictionalized versions of the deceased's "final words" to stabilize the intended meaning of the execution for the state. John Bellamy, *The Tudor Law of Treason* (London: Routledge, 1979), 198; and Lake and Questier, *Antichrist*, esp. chapter 7.
56. For example, the quarters of the Gunpowder Plot conspirators were deliberately placed: Fawkes and the other leaders' heads were placed on London Bridge, but the two men who died before capture—Robert Catesby and Thomas Percy—were exhumed, decapitated, and their heads placed on stakes atop Parliament, the building they sought to destroy. Antonia Fraser, *Faith and Treason: The Story of the Gunpowder Plot* (New York: Doubleday, 1996), 195; and Eric N. Simons, *The Devil of the Vault: A Life of Guy Fawkes* (London: Frederick Muller Limited, 1963), 209.
57. Carla Coleman Prichard, "'Learn Then to Rule Us Better and the Realm': Restoration of Order and the Boy King in Marlowe's *Edward II*," *Renaissance Papers* (1998): 30.
58. Manuel Gomez Lara, "Ambiguous Devices: The Use of Dramatic Emblems in Marlowe's *Edward II* (1592)," *Sederi* 15 (2005): 103.

CHAPTER 6

"Lord of thy presence"
Bodies, Performance, and Audience Interpretation in Shakespeare's *King John*
Erika T. Lin

In Shakespeare's *Cymbeline*, when Imogen wakes up next to the decapitated Cloten, she is horrified to discover what she assumes is her husband's corpse:

> [IMO.] A headlesse man? The Garments of *Posthumus*?
> I know the shape of's Legge: this is his Hand:
> His Foote Mercuriall: his martiall Thigh
> The brawnes of *Hercules*: but his Iouiall face—
> Murther in heauen? How? 'tis gone. (TLN 2630–34; 4.2.308–12)[1]

Imogen misidentifies the body because it is dressed in "The Garments of *Posthumus*," perhaps even that "mean'st Garment" (TLN 1111; 2.4.133) that earlier in the play she emphatically swore to value more than Cloten. The irony of the moment depends on the power of clothing as a marker of identity: dressed properly as a prince, Cloten's body would presumably have been easily recognized. Yet the scene also implies that sartorial signifiers can be deceptive in more than one way: because the corpse's "Iouiall face" is missing, Imogen places too much stock in the clothes he wears and ends up misreading the body. Pointing to his leg, hand, foot, thigh, and "brawnes"—a term referring to arms, calves, or buttocks, as well as more generally to rounded muscles[2]—she insists that she recognizes the signs of her husband's flesh. Both clothes and body parts here fail to function properly as markers of identity; a mistake in one semiotic system occasions the breakdown of the other.

Exchangeable Bodies

The episode in *Cymbeline* highlights the potential for slippage between two different strategies through which audiences made sense of what they saw on the early modern stage. On the one hand, in a repertory system where doubling of roles was common, costumes were crucial semiotic markers through which playgoers identified characters.[3] For such a system to work, spectators had to ignore the actor's body and instead pay attention to his dress. On the other hand, actors were the physical incarnations of characters. Their corporeal presence was required in order to represent persons within the fictional world of the play. When Imogen misidentifies the corpse, both semiotic systems are imagined as dangerously—and amusingly—unstable. Bodies, like clothes, can apparently be exchanged. The humor in this episode is made all the more pointed by the fact that early modern playgoers themselves risked making precisely the same mistake as Imogen. By staging the misinterpretation of the very signifiers that audiences themselves used to decode performance, the play calls attention to gaps and fissures in theater's own semiotic practices. Spectators are admonished to remember that both kinds of identity markers can be read in multiple ways.

The instability of signifiers in *Cymbeline* might be understood as one of the more undesirable end results of the historical process that Hans Belting traces in his influential book *Likeness and Presence*.[4] Belting argues that, over the *longue durée* from Antiquity to the Renaissance, a fundamental change took place in European mimetic practices: visual images that had previously been understood as divine embodiments were increasingly viewed as aesthetic objects. Stripped of spiritual efficacy, objects became mere matter, debased matter, their former ritual functions replaced by the power of representation. Although this is rather an oversimplified account of Belting's more nuanced argument, its general outlines nevertheless highlight a problem central to early modern theater: if physical matter is to be understood as likeness, not presence, then the human body itself becomes a representational signifier. But how exactly do bodies signify? The episode in *Cymbeline* stages this difficulty taken to its logical conclusion: the representational body fails as a signifying object because bodies are themselves as changeable as clothes. Not only are bodies not presences, they are not even very good likenesses.

In this essay I explore early modern understandings of bodies as signifiers by analyzing how questions of likeness and presence intersected with theater's own representational practices. Scholars have often noted that Shakespeare's original spectators would have treated costumes as essential visual markers of characters' identities. This essay interrogates that assumption by examining early modern cultural beliefs about the body as itself a signifier of identity. Thomas Heywood described early modern spectators at "our domesticke hystories" as responding to actors "as if the Personator were the man Personated."⁵ In distinguishing performer from role, Heywood underscores the distance between theatrical presentation and dramatic representation; at the same time, the parallelism inherent in his syntax and diction reveals an overlap between signifier and signified at the site of the actor-character's embodied "person." Such semiotic dynamics complicated the interpretive practices of early modern audiences. Spectators had to determine which characteristics of the actor's body counted as interpretable information, signifying something about the character, and which could be disregarded as irrelevant background noise. Ambiguity about when and how playgoers should, to borrow Keir Elam's terminology, "disattend" bodies onstage resulted in greater fluidity in the "transactional conventions" between performer and spectator that defined the boundaries of the representational frame.⁶

To explore the multilayered implications of the semiotics of the body onstage, this essay centers on Shakespeare's *King John*, a play that offers two competing notions of bodies as signifiers. On the one hand, physical resemblance is treated as a sign of patrilineage within traditional theological-political discourses of identity as based on land and title. On the other hand, embodied presence is viewed as the foundation for the self within emergent sociotheatrical discourses of identity as performatively produced through actions. These overlapping belief systems, I contend, are not only thematized in the play but also enacted onstage. Because both patrilineage and theater are modes of identity construction in which individuals take up roles that then become constitutive of their selves, theatrical representations of patrilineage as marked on the body produce a complex interplay between the character's imaginary body and the actor's actual one. When these dynamics are brought into dialogue with performative notions of identity as grounded in individual bodies, the resulting contradictions, I argue, implicate theatrical audiences in the cultural discourses enacted within the dramatic fiction: as characters within the play negotiate different notions of identity, spectators in the playhouse must learn to cope with multiple ways of reading actors' bodies. Previous scholarship on Shakespeare's *King John* has emphasized issues of legitimacy, especially in relation to gender and monarchy.⁷ Combining historicist analysis with a materialist examination of early modern performance, I demonstrate how such issues are imbricated in theater's own semiotics. Situating the play in relation to questions of audience interpretation allows us to see more clearly how stage performance reshaped traditional notions of authority found in texts such as Holinshed's *Chronicles*. Discourses of political legitimacy, I argue, were not merely disseminated through theater but actively revised by the medium of performance itself.

Signifying Legitimacy

Shakespeare's *King John* opens with an altercation between two brothers over who is to inherit the property of their recently deceased father. Although Philip Faulconbridge is the eldest son, his younger brother, Robert, claims that Philip is illegitimate and must therefore relinquish his claim. As the two men debate the issue, Queen Elinor, John's mother, notices a curious resemblance between the older sibling and her own deceased son, Richard the Lionheart. Philip, she says, "hath a tricke of *Cordelions* face," and "The accent of his tongue affecteth him" (TLN 93–94; 1.1.85–86). King John agrees: "Mine eye hath well examined his parts," he says, "And findes them perfect *Richard*" (TLN 97–98; 1.1.89–90). Elinor offers the man a choice:

> ELI. Whether hadst thou rather be a *Faulconbridge*,
> And like thy brother, to enioy thy land:
> Or the reputed sonne of *Cordelion*,
> Lord of thy presence, and no land beside. (TLN 142–45; 1.1.134–37)

Seeing advantage in the switch, Philip promptly renounces his estate and becomes known henceforth as the bastard son of Coeur-de-Lion.

At the heart of this scene lies the issue of how the body signifies identity. Because Philip possesses physical features similar to Richard the Lionheart, he receives a new name (Sir Richard), a new status (the Bastard), and perhaps even a new coat of arms for his costume.[8] His body declares his noble heritage, "The very spirit of *Plantaginet*" (TLN 176; 1.1.167). Robert Faulconbridge, by contrast, has an unattractive "half-face" (TLN 100; 1.1.92), his "legs . . . two such riding rods" (TLN 148; 1.1.140), and his "armes, such eele-skins stuft" (TLN 149; 1.1.141)—all characteristics of old Faulconbridge. Because Robert has inherited his father's body, he also gets his father's name and property; or, as the Bastard puts it, "Your face hath got fiue hundred pound a yeere" (TLN 160; 1.1.152). The opening sequence of the play thus trains audiences to regard verbal descriptions of characters' physical features as meaningful theatrical signifiers. Playgoers are taught to disattend the real bodies of actors in favor of verbal assertions of likeness put forward within the dramatic representation. Moreover, the play affirms that patrilineage hinges on that bodily likeness. Faces, we are told, speak true—and what they speak is legitimacy and inheritance.

This interplay of bodies, lineage, and legitimacy returns to the foreground in act 2, when King John and King Philip of France argue before the gates of Angiers. Philip points out to John that young Prince Arthur's body declares his parentage and, thus, his right to the crown: "Looke heere vpon thy brother *Geffreyes* face, / These eyes, these browes, were moulded out of his; / . . . England was *Geffreys* right, . . . / How comes it then that thou art call'd a King . . . ?" (TLN 396–97, 402, and 404; 2.1.99–100, 105, and 107). Just as the man who bears Cordelion's face is understood to be his son, Arthur's physical similarity to Geffrey is here presented as evidence of his royal authority. Later in the same scene, when Elinor accuses Constance of having been unfaithful to Geffrey's bed and of trying to foist a bastard on the throne, Constance defends her child's legitimacy by insisting that he is "Liker in feature to his father *Geffrey* / Then thou and *Iohn*" (TLN 423–24; 2.1.126–27). Arthur's royal lineage, like the Bastard's in act 1, is traced in the outlines of his body. The episode at Angiers foregrounds questions similar to those that earlier animated the argument between the brothers Faulconbridge. In both cases, playgoers are asked to imagine the son's physical similarity to a royal father who never actually appears onstage. In the earlier sequence, however, when Elinor asks the Bastard to choose whether he wants to "be a *Faulconbridge* . . . Or the reputed sonne of *Cordelion*," her offer explicitly lays out patrilineal inheritance and bodily resemblance as two competing systems for regulating identity. The Bastard can possess either "land" or "presence," but not both simultaneously. By contrast, Arthur's body serves as straightforward justification of both his royal descent and his kingly inheritance. The notion that the body is the warrant of patrilineage breaks down at the point of bastardy: physical resemblance becomes a marker of identity that destabilizes those other markers of identity, names and claims to property.

Even as the play teaches audience members to disattend the actor's body as theatrical signifier, then, it also underscores the notion that physical features are crucially significant: within the dramatic representation, bodily resemblance to the imagined body of Richard the Lionheart is what ultimately alters Philip Faulconbridge's identity. For early modern readers of the Folio, this change would have been made visible by a shift in speech tags and stage directions. Initially designated "*Philip.*" or "*Phil.*," the character's prefix changes to "*Bast.*" immediately after Elinor presents her offer, and all subsequent speech tags and stage directions refer to him as "*Bastard*" or "*Bast.*" As Randall McLeod has convincingly shown, such variations in speech prefixes not only articulate broader cultural investment in fluid notions of subjectivity but also register the many kinds of identities that were assigned to characters.[9] Here, in addition to being recast as the "reputed sonne of *Cordelion*," the former Faulconbridge also adopts a new identity *type*. These two kinds of renaming are, on the one hand, at odds with each other: renaming Philip as the Bastard type destabilizes his claims to lineage and property. On the other hand, these two acts of renaming work in the same direction in that both serve to construct identity as something inherently changeable. Identity is fixed in terms of neither legitimacy nor lineage; it changes both within the dramatic fiction and in the textual apparatus through which the narrative is conveyed.

Bodily resemblance further interrupts traditional patrilineal inheritance in the onstage knighting of Philip Faulconbridge:

> K. IOHN. What is thy name?
> BAST. *Philip* my Liege, so is my name begun,
> *Philip*, good old Sir *Roberts* wiues eldest sonne.
> K. IOHN. From henceforth beare his name
> Whose forme thou bearest:
> Kneele thou downe *Philip*, but rise more great,
> Arise Sir *Richard*, and *Plantagenet*. (TLN 165–71; 1.1.157–62)

As A. R. Braunmuller points out, "dubbing ceremonies in Shakespeare's time and for centuries before include[d] a recitation of the new knight's ancestry"; renaming, however, was not a part of the standard ritual.[10] For early modern audience members familiar with such ceremonies, then, this scene may well have highlighted the substitution of a new name for traditional genealogy. Indeed, traditional notions of naming are imagined as inadequate. The only lineage that can be determined for certain is the mother's: Philip is "Sir *Roberts* wiues eldest sonne." In order to base name on ancestry, one must resort to the body—first, to the mother, or *mater* (etymologically linked to the word *matter*),[11] from whom the Bastard's origin is certain, and only then to his father's "forme." That form, which early modern audiences would have understood as being stamped upon the matter provided by the mother, serves to give Philip a new identity grounded in a new genealogy.[12]

However, matrilineage here interrupts systems of patrilineal inheritance. The Bastard's new title, "Sir Richard," is not a warrant for the transfer of property; instead the title divests him of it. Traditional inheritance laws ignored whether an heir was adulterously conceived, as John explains to the dismayed Robert Faulconbridge:

> K. IOHN. Sirra, your brother is Legittimate,
> Your fathers wife did after wedlocke beare him:
> And if she did play false, the fault was hers,
> Which fault lyes on the hazards of all husbands
> That marry wiues: tell me, how if my brother [i.e., Richard]
> Who as you say, tooke paines to get this sonne [i.e., the Bastard],
> Had of your father claim'd this sonne for his,
> Insooth, good friend, your father might haue kept
> This Calfe, bred from his Cow from all the world:
> Insooth he might: then if he were my brothers,

My brother might not claime him, nor your father
Being none of his, refuse him: this concludes,
My mothers sonne did get your fathers heyre,
Your fathers heyre must haue your fathers land. (TLN 124–37; 1.1.116–29)

In a traditional system of patrilineage where the body is irrelevant, physical resemblance does not interfere with the smooth transfer of property. In a revised system where bodily appearance indicates lineage, however, mother/matter's wayward tendencies to record women's illegitimate sexual partners undermines the proper functioning of protocols for distributing land. Shakespeare's play thus imagines two different ways bodies mark identity: physical likeness is the legacy of the father, but it is the bodily presence of the mother that enables such resemblances to complicate matters of inheritance. The two semiotic systems through which audiences read actors' bodies onstage are here gendered and mapped onto cultural discourses of lineage.

Royal Presences

Tension between likeness and presence can be seen also in the argument between King John and King Philip of France before the gates of Angiers. The renaming of the Bastard in act 1 portrays identity as something that demands choice and privileges individual agency. The notion that identity can be voluntarily selected also animates this episode in act 2. In this scene, the citizens of Angiers are asked not simply to declare their allegiance but to decide who shall be England's rightful king:

> *Fra.* Speeke Citizens for England, whose your king?
> *Hub.* The king of England, when we know the king.
> *Fra.* Know him in vs, that heere hold vp his right.
> *Iohn.* In Vs, that are our owne great Deputie,
> And beare possession of our Person heere,
> Lord of our presence[,] Angiers, and of you. (TLN 676–81; 2.1.362–67)[13]

Identity is here a matter of choice. Who shall be the king of England is not preordained but is subject to the agency of ordinary citizens. The same tension between patrilineage and the body that we saw in the opening sequence of the play is here embodied in the two monarchs. Philip of France stands in for young Arthur, whom he believes to be the rightful heir by patrilineal descent. John, by contrast, asserts that he is his "owne great Deputie." His royal authority, he contends, rests in the fact that he is *not* a substitute for the king—and is, therefore, presumably, the king himself.

The phrase "Lord of our presence," which John deploys here, seems to be particularly significant because it echoes Elinor's earlier comment to the Bastard. One of the *Oxford English Dictionary's* (*OED*) definitions for the word *presence* is the following: "With possessive: a person's self or embodied personality."[14] Of the examples used to substantiate this meaning, the *OED* includes one from *King John*: when the Bastard urges France and England to join together to defeat Angiers, he insists, "Your Royall presences be rul'd by mee" (TLN 691; 2.1.377). The *OED* definition emphasizes the conflation of bodily presence, royal authority, and personal identity. According to this definition, to be "Lord of our presence" would be to have legitimate royal authority over a self that is defined and bounded by the body.[15] Yet when we look to Shakespeare's play, this phrase is not deployed in quite the same way in act 1 as it is in act 2. In the first instance, Elinor suggests that Philip Faulconbridge, if he chooses to become the bastard son of Richard Cordelion, will be "Lord of [his] presence, [but] no land beside"; that is, he will have his body, but he will have nothing else. The body is the thing that both indicates his patrilineage and divests him of his inheritance.

In act 2, when John stakes his right to Angiers, the phrase "Lord of our presence" is used to emphasize that John is here in his own "Person," in his own royal flesh. Whereas in act 1 presence and land are imagined as mutually exclusive, here John's bodily presence *is* his claim. Moreover, the term "presence" signifies in two different ways. First, John describes himself as the embodied agent of divine authority on and over the earth, here specifically England and Angiers. By using the royal "we"—which King Philip also uses, though only to refer to his own French throne, not to England's, which he views as Arthur's—John performs his monarchical identity while also invoking the concept of the king's two bodies. Combined with the assertion that he is his "owne great Deputie," John's comments call to mind divine right notions of kingship, which saw earthly rulers as the agents of God and, thus, embodied extensions of the deity's authority.[16] John here invokes traditional concepts of identity as grounded both in lineage and in land. The true monarch has his roots in God, and the kingdom is his body. John's deployment of "presence" in this sense corresponds to what David Bergeron, in his essay for this collection, refers to as Elizabeth I's "lineal charisma," a divinely sanctioned covenant that is nevertheless dependent on genealogy. As Bergeron shows, royal authority of this sort is produced through actions, such as gift-giving, that supposedly demonstrate subjects' voluntary and willing submission to a loving monarch. In this sense, John's declaration of his "presence" functions as a claim to legitimacy in the *old* system, in the system of lineage.

In contrast to this notion of king-as-deputy, however, the phrase "Lord of our presence" also refers to the king-as-individual. John does, after all, rule by "borrowed Maiesty" (TLN 9; 1.1.5), by bodily might, not inherited right. Because, according to patrilineal descent, the crown actually belongs to Arthur, the invocation of "presence" is meant as an assertion of the king's "other" body, his physical presence as an individual. Indeed, it is only because John's claim by patrilineage is not clear that he must declare his right to the throne as coextensive with his "Person." As Elinor points out earlier in the play, John rules by "strong possession much more then your right" (TLN 46; 1.1.39). Here, that notion of "possession" gets reiterated and expanded: to "beare possession of our Person," John insists, is parallel—both grammatically and figuratively—to possession of Angiers and, by extension, England. Yet, in invoking such terms to substantiate his authority, John simultaneously undermines his claim by drawing the audience's attention to the body of the actor. The "presence" and "Person" materially present on the stage are precisely that which playgoers must disattend in order to imagine John as king.

Performing Bodily Deception

In acts 1 and 2, then, physical resemblance and bodily presence are repeatedly invoked to undergird traditional notions of patrilineal identity, yet the play also undoes its own premises by portraying the body as that which destabilizes identities bound up in titles and in land. In acts 3 and 4, the body itself becomes an unreliable signifier, and the play extends the problematizing of identity into the realm of the audience. In the scenes surrounding Arthur's death, bodies are repeatedly imagined as texts that resist proper interpretation both by characters within the play and by actual playgoers. When young Arthur attempts to escape and accidentally jumps to his death from the prison walls, the fact that he is "disguis'd" in "Ship-boyes semblance" (TLN 2000; 4.3.4) does not deceive Salisbury for even an instant. He immediately centers in on the body beneath the clothes and identifies the corpse correctly as the prince. However, Salisbury mistakenly concludes that the prince was murdered:

> SAL. Sir Richard, what thinke you? you haue beheld,
> Or haue you read, or heard, or could you thinke?
> Or do you almost thinke, although you see,
> That you do see? Could thought, without this obiect
> Forme such another? This is the very top,
> The heighth, the Crest: or Crest vnto the Crest,
> Of murthers Armes: This is the bloodiest shame,
> The wildest Sauagery, the vildest stroke
> That euer wall-ey'd wrath, or staring rage
> Presented to the teares of soft remorse. (TLN 2040–49; 4.3.41–50)

As spectator-interpreter of the dead body, Salisbury serves as playgoers' onstage counterpart. His language draws attention to what it means to "beh[o]ld," "read," "hear," "thinke," and "see"—the same perceptual and interpretive practices that theater audiences used to make sense of performance. When Salisbury asks, "Could thought, without this obiect / Forme such another?" his words emphasize that, in fact, early modern spectators relied on the actor's body ("this obiect") to give "Forme" to their "thought[s]."

Yet those outward forms might well be deceptive. In asserting that there is only one possible reading of the body, Salisbury ironically highlights the fact that his interpretation is mistaken. Salisbury insists that the spectacle of death before him is so extreme that it admits to only one explanation: "This is the very top, / The heighth, the Crest: or Crest vnto the Crest, / Of murthers Armes." Salisbury's word choice foregrounds the relationship between (mis)interpretation, patrilineage, and the body. Arthur's corpse here serves as the "Crest" of "murthers Armes," as if the prince were a heraldic emblem. The phrase personifies Murder by positing an imaginary noble lineage, which Arthur's body certifies. That murder is to be understood as a person, not merely a concept, is reinforced by the allusions to "wrath" and "rage" as allegorical figures that "Present" Arthur to "the teares of soft remorse." In referring to the affective response Arthur's death invokes ("teares") *as* the audience "to" which the spectacle is presented, the play likens Salisbury's own emotional reaction to that of offstage spectators. Yet if actual playgoers did shed "teares of soft remorse" when faced with the spectacle of the boy's body, their reaction would have mirrored Salisbury's despite the fact that he has clearly mistaken the cause of death. The play here implies that such emotional responses proceed from the "obiect" of the actor's body on display. The cause, the root—indeed, what we might call the "lineage"—of that response is deceptive performance. Bodily resemblance is thus complicated by corporeal presence in the theater: just as, within the dramatic representation, the appearance of Arthur's body deceives onstage spectators, in the actual playhouse, appearance necessarily belies lineage because onstage bodies are never actually who they purport to be. Arthur does not look like Geffrey; the Bastard does not look like Cordelion. Bodies onstage are no more warrants of patrilineage than live actors are dead. In performance, the play suggests, the presence of the actor's body both demands and effects the audience's voluntary disavowal of physical resemblance as a sign of lineage.

This emphasis on theater's problematic relation to bodies as signifiers is reiterated when Pembroke concurs that Arthur's body is the epitome of murder:

> PEM. All murthers past, do stand excus'd in this:
> And this so sole, and so vnmatcheable,
> Shall giue a holinesse, a puritie,
> To the yet vnbegotten sinne of times;
> And proue a deadly blood-shed, but a iest,
> Exampled by this heynous spectacle. (TLN 2050–56; 4.3.51–56)

The "deadly blood-shed" to which Pembroke refers is, of course, the crime of the future, which will seem innocent in comparison to "this heynous spectacle" of Arthur's death. However, the terms in which Pembroke couches his statement extends the question of how to interpret the body into the realm of the audience. The notion that all future murders will seem "but a iest" compared to this one foregrounds the fact that playgoers are, in fact, there specifically to see death enacted. To them, it *is* jest.[17] In referring to the stage business as "this heynous spectacle," the play further calls attention to the theatricality of death onstage. Rather than naturalizing the convention that actors stand in for corpses, the episode highlights it.[18] Doing so deconstructs the semiotic system that audiences used to decode performance. Bodies onstage, the play suggests, are not transparent signifiers but must be carefully interpreted.

This attention to the semiotics of bodies, here not only represented within the play but also woven into the presentational dynamics of audience interpretation, reflects broader cultural emphasis on the epistemological difficulties of interpreting material evidence. Such concerns can be seen especially clearly in extratheatrical accounts of murder. Early modern murder pamphlets frequently adopt a providential narrative that murder will always be revealed. In *The Horrible Murther of a Young Boy of Three Yeres of Age*, for example, a girl has her tongue cut out to prevent her from disclosing the names of her brother's murderers. When she miraculously recovers the ability to speak and testifies against the criminals, the author insists that clearly "with God nothing is impossible."[19] In another pamphlet, *The Cry and Reuenge of Blood*, when a disfigured corpse is finally identified after much difficulty, the revelation leads the author to declare, "See the wisedome of God herein: all outward tokens might seeme to fayle, yet one remayned."[20] The trope that "blood will out" likewise informs the discovery of Arthur's corpse in Shakespeare's play. When the prince's body is found, Pembroke declares that "The earth had not a hole to hide this deede" (TLN 2035; 4.3.36). Salisbury agrees: "Murther, as hating what himselfe hath done, / Doth lay it open to vrge on reuenge" (TLN 2036–37; 4.3.37–38). The notion that murder will inevitably be revealed is here tied to the physical body, which cries out from beyond the grave.

Early modern murder pamphlets evince a similar emphasis on bodies as signs that must be searched and interpreted. In *The Cry and Reuenge of Blood*, the fact that the corpse was "high of stature, sixe foote long" is taken as a "token" of his identity.[21] The victim's name is confirmed when his mother recalls "that her sonne Iohn had two teeth broken out of his vpper iaw, and the scull being searched approues the same; and so both markes concurring vpon the same carcase, the length and iaw marke: hereby vndoubted conclusion was made, that, that carcase was her sonne Iohns."[22] In another pamphlet, *The Crying Murther*, a dismembered corpse is identified when neighbors search the body for special signs and discover that "in all likelihood it was Mr. *Trat* their olde Curate that was murthered, there being one of his fingers knowne by a secret marke vnto them."[23] Such accounts treat corpses as texts through which the "marke[s]" of their identity might be read. In Shakespeare's play, when Salisbury describes Arthur's body, he takes on a role similar to that of the lay investigators described in murder pamphlets.[24] However, he is unable to interpret the evidence properly.

When Hubert is blamed for the young prince's death, the notion that viewers might misread bodies is highlighted in yet a different way. Suborned by John to kill the prince, Hubert supposedly reveals his murderous nature in the outlines of his face. Pembroke asserts that "The image of a wicked heynous fault / Liues in his [i.e., Hubert's] eye: that close aspect of his, / Do shew the mood of a much troubled brest" (TLN 1789–91; 4.2.71–73). King John likewise declares that Hubert's "aspect" is a sure sign of villainy:

> [*Ioh.*] Had'st not thou beene by,
> A fellow by the hand of Nature mark'd,
> Quoted, and sign'd to do a deede of shame,
> This murther had not come into my minde.
> But taking note of thy abhorr'd Aspect,
> Finding thee fit for bloody villainie:
> Apt, liable to be employ'd in danger,
> I faintly broke with thee of *Arthurs* death:
> And thou, to be endeered to a King,
> Made it no conscience to destroy a Prince. (TLN 1945–54; 4.2.220–29)

By using the words "mark'd," "Quoted," and "sign'd," all terms having to do with the permanency of writing and their resultant legal force, John describes faces as if they were texts—texts that are written specifically by "Nature" and understood to be permanently binding. His rhetoric here resembles that found not only in early modern murder pamphlets but also in physiognomic treatises. The earliest of the much reprinted English version of Bartolommeo della Rocca Cocles's *A Brief and Most Pleasau[n]t Epitomye of the Whole Art of Phisiognomie*, for example, specifically uses the term "marked" to describe faces.[25] Moreover, as in Shakespeare's play, it is "nature" that does the marking.[26] A man's character, the author declares, is "marked by nature in the proporcion and liniamentes of mans body . . . and specially in the face and handes."[27] Cocles's view is typical of many early modern physiognomists. In these texts, as Juliana Schiesari puts it, "Facial features occur as a kind of graphism of writing which in turn is in need of the systematic decoding that physiognomy can provide."[28] When John treats

Hubert's face as an indication of his predisposition toward murder, his rhetoric calls to mind such early modern systems for interpreting the physical body.

However, the reliability of such interpretive mechanisms is undermined by the fact that Hubert has not actually killed Arthur. Bodies, the play again insists, cannot be taken at face value. As Hubert puts it, John has "slander'd Nature in my forme, / Which howsoeuer rude exteriorly, / Is yet the couer of a fayrer minde" (TLN 1981–83; 4.2.256–58). This emphasis on Hubert's "rude exterior" and "abhorr'd Aspect" is ironic given that such rhetoric mirrors the very terms Constance uses to justify Arthur's royal inheritance. In act 3, when she reiterates the notion that the young prince's face bespeaks his paternal heritage and, therefore, his right to the crown, she also asserts that it is only because he is not ugly that she has urged his claim:

> CON. If thou that bidst me be content, wert grim
> Vgly, and slandrous to thy Mothers wombe,
> Full of vnpleasing blots, and sightlesse staines,
> Lame, foolish, crooked, swart, prodigious,
> Patch'd with foule Moles, and eye-offending markes,
> I would not care, I then would be content,
> For then I should not loue thee: no, nor thou
> Become thy great birth, nor deserue a Crowne.
> But thou art faire, and at thy birth (deere boy),
> Nature and Fortune ioyn'd to make thee great. (TLN 964–73; 3.1.43–52)

Whereas Hubert's face, "by the hand of Nature mark'd," hides his "fayrer minde," Arthur's face lacks these "eye-offending markes," and his visible "faire"-ness reveals that "Nature and Fortune ioyn'd to make [him] great." Likewise, Hubert's unattractive features lead John to "slander . . . Nature in his forme"; but Arthur's "natiue beauty" (TLN 1468; 3.4.83) renders him not "slandrous to [his] Mothers wombe." Patrilineage is here tied to the body's aesthetic qualities. Arthur's good looks, as much as his resemblance to his father, justify his claim to the crown.

Constance's speech recalls the opening sequence in act 1, in which Robert Faulconbridge's unattractive appearance is read as a sign of his patrilineage. Here we see the flip side of the coin: just as the Bastard's pleasant appearance signifies his lineage as a Plantagenet, Arthur's beauty defines royal authority. The *mis*reading of Hubert's ugly face is thus tied into the questions of legitimacy that animate the play. It undermines the discourse of how beauty signifies moral righteousness and rightful inheritance. This destabilization extends from the interpretive practices of characters to those of the audience, whose assessment of the identity of the rightful king is complicated by the difficulty of determining, based on outward form, the truth of the people within. The contradiction between Hubert's external appearance and his true character foregrounds the intersection of morality and politics. Legitimacy, in this play, is tied to tensions between divine right and Machiavellian notions of kingship, but in such a universe, the play suggests, having an accurate semiotic system is not enough. The possibility that spectators, onstage and off, might misinterpret what they see is presented as a matter with serious consequences.

A similar concern with the potential for misreading bodies can be found in early modern physiognomic treatises. These texts suggest that, even though the signs of a person's face could—with skill and practice—be accurately read, correct interpretation of the signs was ultimately only by the grace of God. As Cocles puts it,

> although a man may perfitly by Phisiognomy declare the natural inclinacions of any man, yet may he not perfectly iudge hym except he know whether he haue grace or no. And the lacke of thys consideraunce hath brought thys science to be thought false because grace brydeleth or vseth wel the naturall inclinacions of man.[29]

Cocles here suggests that the problem is not simply an inaccurate reading of the bodily text; *that* can be remedied by reading Cocles's book and by learning physiognomy. Rather, the problem is reading the wrong bodily signs altogether. It is only the grace of God, he asserts, that allows one to accurately see the face in the first place. Such a view is echoed in the opening epistle to Joannes ab Indagine's *Briefe Introductions . . . vnto the Art of Chiromancy, or Manuel Diuination, and Physiognomy*:

> I wold wishe & desire yt al men which shal read or take any frute of this smal treatise: to vse such moderativn in perusyng of the same, that they do not by and by take in hand to geue iudgment, eyther of theyr owne, or of other mens estates or natiuityes, without diligent circumspection and taking hede. Wayinge & considering how many wayes a man maye be deceyued, as by the prouidence & discretion of the man in whom thou geuest iudgement. Also the dispensation of God, and oure fallible and vncertaine speculation.[30]

The "fallible" nature of human "speculation"—a term that collapses the act of seeing with the act of interpreting—is a problem; it is only "the dispensation of God" that can discover the truth within. Like Shakespeare's play, these physiognomic treatises suggest that human senses are easily deceived. Proper interpretation of the body rests on a shaky foundation because visual signifiers are themselves unreliable.

This ambivalence about perception is also manifested in *King John* through references to the malleability of sight and the changeability of the body, a dynamic that parallels the play's emphasis on identity as something that can be altered. When John apologizes to Hubert, he says,

> [IOHN.] Forgiue the Comment that my passion made
> Vpon thy feature, for my rage was blinde,
> And foule immaginarie eyes of blood
> Presented thee more hideous then thou art. (TLN 1988–91; 4.2.263–66)

In this passage John does not say that there is no connection between outward form and internal character. Instead he argues that his rage made him "blinde," that Hubert was merely not as ugly as he had thought. Faces still signify correctly; John has simply not *seen* the right face. His comments echo those of Arthur himself in act 4, scene 1. When Hubert decides not to go through with the murder, Arthur exclaims, "O now you looke like *Hubert*. All this while / You were disguis'd" (TLN 1705–6; 4.1.125–26). Constance, too, asserts that Salisbury's appearance is altered by his unwelcome report of the alliance between Blanche and the Dauphin: "Fellow be gone: I cannot brooke thy sight," she says, "This newes hath made thee a most vgly man" (TLN 957–58; 3.1.36–37). All these instances suggest that the difficulty in reading bodies is not just that they signify incorrectly. Rather, bodies themselves are subject to change, and, indeed, the very act of seeing is called into question.[31]

Pulling the Body Apart

By highlighting the interpretive practices spectators use to understand performance, then, the second half of Shakespeare's play unsettles the semiotic reliability of the body that it previously established as a signifier of identity. The Bastard's statement that "I am I, how ere I was begot" (TLN 184; 1.1.175) is thus potentially misleading: although he invokes a notion of self that is independent of patrilineage, the new identity he adopts is neither inherently stable nor quite as distinct from the old one as it might appear. It is, moreover, specifically *not* some sort of straightforward precursor to the bourgeois subject.[32] The implied singularity and cohesion of the assertion that "I am I" is repeatedly undermined by the presentational dynamics of theater. When Pandulph breaks the union by marriage between England and France, then, it is especially appropriate that Blanche uses a metaphor of dismemberment to describe her torn allegiances:

> [BLA.] Which is the side I must goe withall?
> I am with both, each Army hath a hand,
> And in their rage, I hauing hold of both,
> They whurle a-sunder, and dismember mee. (TLN 1260–63; 3.1.327–30)

In the tug-of-war over Blanche's body, physical and interpretive conflicts are enacted both literally and symbolically. The dissolution of the body politic within the fictional world of the play not only is thematized at this moment but also may have been enacted onstage as actors each took hold of one of Blanche's hands.[33] Moreover, the onstage physical action serves as commentary on the audience's interpretive challenges. The semiotic systems through which they have been asked to read bodies are problematically fractured. Just as the character is pulled in multiple directions, so, too, is the spectator.

If we return to the scene before the gates of Angiers, then, we can see that the audience is put in a difficult position not only in acts 3 and 4 but in the opening acts as well. Immediately after King John's reference to being "Lord of our presence," the Bastard interrupts the exchange between John and Philip. He explicitly compares the townsmen to playhouse spectators:

> BAST. By heauen, these scroyles of Angiers flout you kings,
> And stand securely on their battelments,
> As in a Theater, whence they gape and point
> At your industrious Scenes and acts of death. (TLN 687–90; 2.1.373–76)

In invoking this metatheatrical figure, the Bastard dismembers the audience even as he incorporates them into a unified whole. Playgoers are split, as it were, into two bodies: one that is their own and the other inhabited by their counterparts onstage. At the same time, they are integrated into the body politic: like the citizens of Angiers, they must assess the relative legitimacy of the varied claims to the throne. In this sense, the audience experiences what Paul Menzer, in his essay for this collection, describes as a form of "crowd control": playgoers are trained into proper subjectivity, in the Althusserian sense of the word, by watching the behavior modeled for them by the citizens of Angiers.

Yet Shakespeare's play completely deconstructs the grounds on which actual spectators might make the choice demanded of their onstage counterparts. Standing in for Arthur, Philip embodies a principle of likeness: he asks to be treated *as if* he were Arthur because he upholds the young prince's right. However, in asserting right by proxy, Philip ironically highlights the fact that the actor is also a substitute, one who takes the part of the king but is not the king himself. Similarly, when John invokes physical "presence" as the basis for his claim, he draws attention to his material substance; yet in doing so, he directs the audience's attention to the body of the actor, who cannot actually embody real royal authority. The space of the playhouse converges with the fictional world of the play. As in the Bastard's comparison of the "battelments" of Angiers to a "Theater," when John says that he "bear[s] possession of our person here," the word "here" refers not only to the gates of Angiers but also to the "here" of the theater. Ascribing royal authority either to Philip or to John requires that the audience privilege either likeness or presence not only within the representational narrative but also in the actual playhouse.

In the interplay between dramatic representation and theatrical presentation, then, Shakespeare's *King John* highlights the tension between two different conceptions of identity that undergird disparate visions of legitimate monarchy. In early modern pageants, progresses, and civic entries, as in the public playhouses, royal authority was traditionally tied to the use of sartorial markers. The crown, the scepter, the "enter-tissued Robe of Gold and Pearle" (TLN 2112; 4.1.262), as Henry V puts it—all these material objects composed the "Ceremonie" (*Henry V*, TLN 2089; 4.1.239) that performatively produced the king. In *King John*, however, such objects fail to certify royal authority. The question "Doth not the Crowne of England, prooue the King?" (TLN 579–80; 2.1.273) is repeatedly answered in the negative. Unlike the 1577 edition of Holinshed's *Chronicles*, in which the same woodcut of a king was reused to illustrate different rulers, where the crown of England *did* prove the king as far as the illustrations were concerned, here the traditional legitimators of patrilineal inheritance—names that signify land or power, objects such as a crown—do not signify in any trustworthy way.[34] Comparing Shakespeare's play to this edition of Holinshed points out the difference that genre and medium make. Chronicle history is not history play, nor is printed text the same as performance. Holinshed's *Chronicles* adopts a theological-political logic, in which identity is patrilineal and divinely ordained, and assumes not simply resemblance but equivalence, not simply likeness but presence. Less than two decades later, Shakespeare's play undermines these premises; in their place, it offers the unstable alterations of performance, in which identity and/as meaning is constantly up for grabs. Yet it is this very instability, this opening up for audience interpretation, that is the legitimacy that the theater offers and affords. The play presents identity as grounded in a body that possesses both likeness and presence and that requires the interpretation of spectators. This presence is of a very different kind than that which Hans Belting describes, and the authority and efficacy it enables is of a different register. But this shift in understandings of the body is the precondition for the phenomenology of the modern theater, where it is only through likeness that actors can become characters. We are, as it were, in a postlapsarian theater where it is only through resemblance that we can achieve transcendence.

Notes

My thanks to Marissa Greenberg, Jennifer Low, Nova Myhill, Phyllis Rackin, and Tamara Sears for their very helpful feedback on earlier versions of this essay.

1. Italics in original. Quotations from Shakespeare's plays are taken from Charlton Hinman, ed., *The First Folio of Shakespeare*, 2nd ed. (New York: Norton, 1996) with through-line numbers (TLN) followed by act, scene, and line numbers from G. Blakemore Evans et al., eds., *The Riverside Shakespeare*, 2nd ed. (Boston: Houghton Mifflin, 1997).
2. *Oxford English Dictionary* (*OED*), 2nd ed., s.v. "brawn" (*n.*, defs. 1a and 1b).
3. On clothing's implications for theatrical semiotics, see my discussion of livery in "Popular Festivity and the Early Modern Stage: The Case of *George a Greene*," *Theatre Journal* 61 (2009): 271–97. On costuming conventions, see G. K. Hunter, "Flatcaps and Bluecoats: Visual Signals on the Elizabethan Stage," *Essays and Studies*, n.s., 33 (1980): 16–47; and Jean MacIntyre, *Costumes and Scripts in the Elizabethan Theatres* (Edmonton, Canada: University of Alberta Press, 1992). On the cultural valences of clothing practices, see Amanda Bailey, *Flaunting: Style and the Subversive Male Body in Renaissance England* (Toronto, Canada: University of Toronto Press, 2007); and Ann Rosalind Jones and Peter Stallybrass, *Renaissance Clothing and the Materials of Memory* (Cambridge: Cambridge University Press, 2000).
4. Hans Belting, *Likeness and Presence: A History of the Image Before the Era of Art*, trans. Edmund Jephcott (Chicago: University of Chicago Press, 1994).
5. Thomas Heywood, *An apology for actors Containing three briefe treatises. 1 Their antiquity. 2 Their ancient dignity. 3 The true vse of their quality* (London, 1612), B4r. See also Andrew Gurr, *The Shakespearean Stage, 1574–1642*, 3rd ed. (Cambridge: Cambridge University Press, 1992), 99–100.
6. On disattendance and/as transactional convention, see Keir Elam, *The Semiotics of Theatre and Drama*, 2nd ed. (London: Routledge, 2002), 79–81.
7. Phyllis Rackin notes that, "Although legitimacy is always the issue in Shakespeare's history plays, it is nowhere else so central as it is in *King John*. The entire action hangs on the unanswerable question: 'Who is the legitimate heir of Coeur-delion?'; and the presiding spirit of this play is not the king who gives it its name but the embodiment of every kind of illegitimacy, the Bastard." *Stages of History: Shakespeare's English Chronicles* (Ithaca, NY: Cornell University Press, 1990), 186. On legitimacy, gender, and authority as central concerns of *King John*, see also Gina Bloom, *Voice in Motion: Staging Gender, Shaping Sound in Early Modern England* (Philadelphia: University of Pennsylvania Press, 2007), 66–110; Deborah T. Curren-Aquino, ed., *King John: New Perspectives* (Newark: University of Delaware Press, 1989); Juliet Dusinberre, "*King John* and Embarrassing Women," *Shakespeare Survey* 42 (1990): 37–52; Barbara Hodgdon, *The End Crowns All: Closure and Contradiction in Shakespeare's History* (Princeton, NJ: Princeton University Press, 1991), 22–43; Jean E. Howard and Phyllis Rackin, *Engendering a Nation: A Feminist Account of Shakespeare's English Histories* (London: Routledge, 1997), 119–33; Ken Jackson, "'Is It God or the Sovereign Exception?': Giorgio Agamben's *Homo Sacer* and Shakespeare's *King John*," *Religion and Literature* 38 (2006): 85–100; Kathryn Schwarz, "A Tragedy of Good Intentions: Maternal Agency in *3 Henry VI* and *King John*," *Renaissance Drama* 32 (2003): 225–54; Robert Weimann and Douglas Bruster, *Shakespeare and the Power of Performance: Stage and Page in the Elizabethan Theatre* (Cambridge: Cambridge University Press, 2008),

57–76; and Peter Womack, "Imagining Communities: Theatres and the English Nation in the Sixteenth Century," in *Culture and History, 1350–1600: Essays on English Communities, Identities and Writing*, ed. David Aers (Detroit: Wayne State University Press, 1992), 91–145.
8. As Alison Findlay notes in *Illegitimate Power: Bastards in Renaissance Drama* (Manchester, UK: Manchester University Press, 1994), "bastards who were publicly acknowledged by kings or aristocrats . . . were allowed to bear the family arms, provided it was distinguished with a mark to indicate illegitimacy—the band azure or band sinister" (41).
9. Random Cloud [Randall McLeod], "'The very names of the Persons': Editing and the Invention of Dramatick Character," in *Staging the Renaissance: Reinterpretations of Elizabethan and Jacobean Drama*, ed. David Scott Kastan and Peter Stallybrass (New York: Routledge, 1991), 88–96.
10. A. R. Braunmuller, ed., *King John*, The Oxford Shakespeare (Oxford: Clarendon Press, 1988), 67.
11. *Oxford English Dictionary*, Draft Revision March 2010, s.v. "mother" (*n.1* and *int.*) and "matter" (*n.1*); *Oxford English Dictionary*, Draft Revision September 2009, s.v. "mater" (*n.1*).
12. On the wide discursive currency of early modern notions of reproduction as the imprinting of the father's form upon the mother's matter, see Douglas A. Brooks, ed., *Printing and Parenting in Early Modern England* (Aldershot, UK: Ashgate, 2005).
13. Despite differences in characterization, the citizen in this sequence is apparently the same Hubert who appears later in the play. Arden editor E. A. J. Honigmann notes that the speech prefix for "the Citizen of Angiers is *Cit.* from II.i.201 to II.i.281, and from II.i.325 is *Hubert*, and so on." E. A. J. Honigmann, ed., introduction to *King John*, 4th ed., The Arden Shakespeare, 2nd ser. (London: Methuen, 1965), xxxiv.
14. *Oxford English Dictionary*, Draft Revision March 2010, s.v. "presence" (*n.*, def. 4a).
15. Editors have explained the phrase "Lord of our presence" in a variety of ways. A. R. Braunmuller stresses its corporeal connotations, glossing the phrase as "'demeanour' or 'carriage' (5) mixed with 'immediate vicinity, the space you occupy' (2)." E. A. J. Honigmann offers no strong opinions of his own, but records J. D. Wilson's suggestion that the words "imply feudal supremacy. Arthur does not bear possession of his person, is not lord of his presence." Braunmuller, ed., *King John*, 1.1.137n; Honigmann, ed., *King John*, 2.1.366n.
16. On early modern notions of agents as deputies invested with the authority of those whom they serve, see Katherine Rowe, *Dead Hands: Fictions of Agency, Renaissance to Modern* (Stanford, CA: Stanford University Press, 1999).
17. On notions of "jest" and "earnest," see V. A. Kolve, *The Play Called Corpus Christi* (Stanford, CA: Stanford University Press, 1966); and Alan C. Dessen, *Recovering Shakespeare's Theatrical Vocabulary* (Cambridge: Cambridge University Press, 1995), 127–49, esp. 129–34.
18. On staging options that accentuate or undermine the verisimilitude of Arthur's death, see Alan Armstrong, "Arthur's Fall," *Shakespeare Bulletin* 24 (2006): 1–10.

19. *The horrible murther of a young boy of three yeres of age, whose sister had her tongue cut out and how it pleased God to reueale the offendors, by giuing speech to the tongueles childe. Which offendors were executed at Hartford the 4. of August. 1606* (London, 1606), B2r.
20. Thomas Cooper, *The cry and reuenge of blood Expressing the nature and haynousnesse of wilfull murther. Exemplified in a most lamentable history thereof, committed at Halsworth in High Suffolk, and lately conuicted at Bury assize, 1620* (London, 1620), G2r.
21. Ibid.
22. Ibid.
23. C. W., *The crying murther Contayning the cruell and most horrible bu[tchery] of Mr. Trat, curate of old Cleaue; who was first mu[rthered] as he trauailed vpon the high way, then was brought home to hi[s house] and there was quartered and imboweld: his quarters and bowels b[eing af]terwards perboyled and salted vp, in a most strange and fearefull manner. For thi[s] the iudgement of my Lord chiefe Baron Tanfield, young Peter Smethwi[cke, An]drew Baker, Cyrill Austen, and Alice Walker, were executed this last sum[mer] Assizes, the. 24. of July, at Stone Gallowes, neere Taunton in Summersetshire* (London, 1624), B4r.
24. On "searchers" of murder victims' bodies and their forensic techniques, see Malcolm Gaskill, *Crime and Mentalities in Early Modern England* (Cambridge: Cambridge University Press, 2000), 254–61. On the use of lay investigators, see Lorna Hutson, "Rethinking the 'Spectacle of the Scaffold': Juridical Epistemologies and English Revenge Tragedy," *Representations* 89 (2005): 30–58.
25. Bartolommeo della Rocca Cocles, *A brief and most pleasau[n]t epitomye of the whole art of phisiognomie, gathered out of Aristotle, Rasis, Formica, Loxius, Phylemo[n], Palemo[n], Consiliator, Morbeth the Cardinal and others many moe*, trans. Thomas Hill (London, 1556), "The Preface to the Reader." This document begins with A1r only after the prefatory material; I have accordingly cited by section heading only.
26. Ibid.
27. Ibid.
28. Juliana Schiesari, "The Face of Domestication: Physiognomy, Gender Politics, and Humanism's Others," in *Women, 'Race,' and Writing in the Early Modern Period*, ed. Margo Hendricks and Patricia Parker (London: Routledge, 1994), 55–70, esp. 57. On early modern physiognomy, see also Martin Porter, *Windows of the Soul: Physiognomy in European Culture, 1470–1780* (Oxford: Clarendon Press, 2005); and Michael Torrey, "'The Plain Devil and Dissembling Looks': Ambivalent Physiognomy and Shakespeare's *Richard III*," *English Literary Renaissance* 30 (2000): 123–53.
29. Cocles, *Brief and most pleasau[n]t*, preface.
30. Johannes ab Indagine, *Briefe introductions, both naturall, pleasaunte, and also delectable vnto the art of chiromancy, or manuel diuination, and physiognomy with circumstances vpon the faces of the signes. Also certain canons or rules vpon diseases and sickenesse. Whereunto is also annexed aswel the artificiall, as naturall astrologye, with the nature of the planets*, trans. Fabian Withers (London, 1558), Sig. †4v.

31. On early modern notions of vision as potentially deceptive, see Stuart Clark, *Vanities of the Eye: Vision in Early Modern European Culture* (Oxford: Oxford University Press, 2007).
32. I use this term in the sense offered in Catherine Belsey, *The Subject of Tragedy: Identity and Difference in Renaissance Drama* (London: Methuen, 1985).
33. In *King John*, Shakespeare in Performance (Manchester, UK: Manchester University Press, 1994), Geraldine Cousin notes that, in the 1984 BBC production directed by David Giles, Blanche's speech takes place "as the various factions swirled round her preparing themselves for the coming battle" before "form[ing] . . . themselves into opposed groups leaving her in the centre" (91). In Deborah Warner's 1988–89 RSC production, Blanche knelt for her speech, then exited while being "pulled away from centre, one hand firmly joined to that of Lewis, the other reaching out to John" (114).
34. Raphael Holinshed, *The firste [laste] volume of the chronicles of England, Scotlande, and Irelande conteyning the description and chronicles of England, from the first inhabiting vnto the conquest : the description and chronicles of Scotland, from the first originall of the Scottes nation till the yeare of our Lorde 1571 : the description and chronicles of Yrelande, likewise from the first originall of that nation untill the yeare 1571* (London, 1577).

CHAPTER 7

Charismatic Audience
A 1559 Pageant
David M. Bergeron

Ben Jonson's *Bartholomew Fair* begins curiously with an Induction that immediately raises the question of the audience's position and prerogatives. In this Induction, the Scrivener, following the Stage-keeper and Book-holder, reads the "Articles of agreement" between the playwright and audience, the "spectators or hearers."[1] These "articles" clearly derive from the author's pen; the Scrivener has but inscribed them and serves as the conduit between author and audience. "It is covenanted and agreed, by and between the parties above-said" (66–67), the Scrivener says as he reads from this quasi-legal document. "Covenant" becomes one of the recurring words meant to indicate a mutual arrangement between playwright and audience. Jonson dictates the terms that he has already thought through. Having already paid their money and thereby entered into a kind of bargain (covenant), the audience can now confirm this agreement by their applause. Jonson wins.

However we consider the play's Induction, we conclude that this extraordinary document has no equal in the drama of the period. Jonson fulfills a fantasy: a seemingly actual agreement with his audience, whose rebuke he has felt intensely (see *Sejanus*). Obviously, Jonson only creates a metatheatrical fantasy, but one that suits his general idea of the relative merits of author versus audience. I have argued elsewhere that Jonson fulfills this desire in another way: by writing epistles dedicatory and addresses to readers, which allow him to imagine intelligent readers correctly reading his drama.[2] In *Bartholomew Fair*, Jonson constructs a covenant that he wishes for all his plays; that is, a means to guide and control the audience. I have a sneaking suspicion that Jonson may be responding to Francis Beaumont's *Knight of the Burning Pestle*, whose fiction wreaks havoc on audience response—a nightmarish metatheatrical experience, which Jonson wants to avoid. What if an audience simply took over? That's Beaumont's premise; but even he suffered the indignity of an unfavorable theater audience response, an audience that incredibly missed the "privy mark of irony" in the play, according to the play's publisher, Walter Burre.[3]

Jonson's play with its unusual Induction compels us to consider what we know about theater audiences in Shakespeare's time: their behavior, social makeup, and dramatic preferences. Alfred Harbage and Ann Jennalie Cook, to cite two prominent scholars, have taken opposing positions on the social and economic background of the public theaters' spectators. In a nutshell, Harbage argues for a socially diverse audience with plenty of room for the lower economic class, and Cook suggests that the theaters attracted a higher social and economic class.[4] Subsequent scholars have wrestled with these competing views. Andrew Gurr has written extensively about the public theater and its audiences in his *Shakespearean Stage, 1574–1642*, and *Playgoing in Shakespeare's London*.[5] In the latter book, Gurr tackles all the basic issues about audience makeup and preferences. But he focuses exclusively on the public theaters of Shakespeare's time, ignoring the court and the thousands of people who lined London's streets for civic pageants.

To offer a partial remedy to Gurr's neglect, I turn away from the public theater to the public streets, where another kind of covenant emerges, one that engages the audience in a charismatic response—one that Jonson might have envied. I take as my cue and sanction Stephen Orgel's dictum: "Festivals, pageants, and masques are probably a better index to the complex nature of Renaissance theater than drama is."[6] Eventually the major playwrights get involved with pageants, writing and designing Lord Mayor's Shows and royal entry pageants, partly because of the substantial financial reward. These civic pageants, a special genre of street theater, attracted thousands of spectators and the industry of architects, musicians, designers, artisans, and well-known actors (including Richard Burbage).[7] When the pageants involve the sovereign, they, in the words of Clifford Geertz, "locate the society's center and affirm its connection with transcendent things by stamping a territory with ritual signs of dominance."[8]

For just such a moment, I intend in this essay to focus on Queen Elizabeth's royal entry pageant on January 14, 1559, the day before her coronation, as she moved from the Tower through the City of London toward Westminster, where her coronation would take place the next day. Elizabeth served as recipient of the audience's adulation even as she performed her role as actor and audience. Partly fiction, partly myth-making, and fully political reality, the pageant explores and exploits the audience's function, one that the audience carried out instinctively. They needed no Jonsonian covenant. Robert Weimann reminds us, "The relationship between actor and audience is, therefore, not only a constituent element of dramaturgy, but of dramatic meaning as well."⁹ He adds, "The proximity of actor and audience was not only a physical condition, it was at once the foundation and the expression of a specific artistic endeavor."¹⁰ Although Weimann writes of the public playhouse, the observations pertain to the street theater as well. Elizabeth was in this instance, Geertz suggests, the "center of the center," whose charisma grew because of her willingness "to stand proxy, not for God, but for the virtues he ordained. . . . It was allegory that lent her magic, and allegory repeated that sustained it."¹¹ By its reaction, the audience confirmed and endorsed Elizabeth's position as their sovereign, thereby assisting charisma, that is, the interdependence of sovereign and subject so necessary to successful rule, a covenantal relationship of profound spiritual and emotional significance.

My ideas about charisma derive in part from Raphael Falco's important book *Charismatic Authority in Early Modern English Tragedy*.¹² Falco notes the Christian idea of charisma (from the Greek *charism*, meaning "gift") found in St. Paul's first letter to the church in Corinth, where the apostle discusses the various "gifts" that believers have. He asks, "Have all the gifts of healing? do all speak with tongues? do all interpret? / But covet earnestly the best gifts: and yet shew I unto you a more excellent way" (1 Cor 12: 30–31, KJV). The Catholic Church eventually developed the concept of nine official charisms. Falco emphasizes a basic paradox of charismatic response: namely, the interplay and interdependence of group and individual. He writes, "[C]harisma is therefore a shared experience," and he adds that "no charismatic authority can be sustained in the absence of an interdependent relation between it and a group."¹³ While we most often think of personal magnetism when we think of charisma, the concept clearly has other resonances. In discussing Shakespeare's *Richard II*, Falco develops the idea of lineal charisma, that is, the strength and position that come from a sovereign's lineage. Clearly Queen Elizabeth enjoyed a lineal charisma, even if some doubted her claim to the throne. This royal entry pageant of 1559 does in fact underscore the queen's legitimacy. In terms of audience, I will be focusing on the interdependent quality of charisma, this *group* responding to the *individual* monarch.

These pageants, first cousins to the more-often discussed court masques, bear as well an analogous relationship to plays in the public theaters. They contain actors, speeches, costumes, action, spectacle, and of course audience. But they differ significantly because they occur as *real* events; thus their fiction battens onto an actual, historical occasion. The texts, typically in the past tense, always come as reports after the fact, and they seek to fulfill multiple functions. Unlike texts of regular plays, the pageant ones occasionally include some account of audience responses. Thus the real Queen Elizabeth moved through the streets of London as both participant in and recipient of the entertainment in the midst of a world created for the day, full of allegorical, biblical, historical, and symbolic action and characters. We modern-day readers of the text need not blanch at Elizabeth's encounter in London's streets with Time and Truth any more than the sixteenth-century audience did. One might say that the more Elizabeth responded, the more charisma emerged, that is, an intensifying of the interaction between the individual and the group, or what Falco might call the "systemic structure of mutuality."[14]

The compiler of the text for this 1559 pageant, Richard Mulcaster (according to records of the Corporation of London), writes, "So that if a man should say well, he could not better tearme the citie of London that time, than a stage wherin was shewed the wonderfull spectacle, of a noble hearted princesse toward her most loving people, and the peoples excading comfort in beholding so worthy a soveraign."[15] As King James himself would note later in *Basilicon Doron*, a sovereign is as one set on a stage. But in London's streets, the concept of "stage" resonated beyond metaphor. The queen processed through an urban stage, made up of the ancient city's meandering streets, and she traversed them, surrounded by the audience of citizens. Not only was the city a stage, it also contained actual stages (scaffolds, arches) erected by the pageant's devisers, which stood on these streets, and on these stages dramatic tableaux unfolded in the queen's presence. The audience thus witnessed several stages, literally and figuratively, as spectators appropriated the richness of the occasion, the speeches, action, decorations, and the queen's reaction.

Elizabeth herself seems to have gone a step beyond that familiar theater metaphor/reality. Two documents, found in the papers of Sir Thomas Cawarden, Master of the Revels, and preserved in the Loseley Manuscripts in the Folger Shakespeare Library, reveal the queen's interest and determination to make the pageant as striking and spectacular as possible. She thus ordered Cawarden to lend garments and costumes to the city authorities for their use in the pageant.[16] Therefore, Elizabeth's charism, her gift to the city, is not only her presence but also a practical loan of costumes from the Revels office. This gesture assures a charismatic as well as spectacular theatrical event. Such concern underscored the queen's astute awareness of the necessity and possibility of self-fashioning, which she seems to have taken literally in 1559.

I have no evidence that any audience member coming to the Globe Theater arrived in costume, but we do find evidence for such in the 1559 pageant. I refer to the members of London's guilds, who beginning at Fenchurch stretched through the streets to the Little Conduit in Cheapside. They stood, Mulcaster writes, "well apparelled with many ryche furres and theyr livery whodes upon theyr shoulders in comely and semely maner, having before them sondry persones well apparelled in silkes and chaines of golde" (44–45). In addition to their self-conscious apparel, these guildsmen had been responsible for decorations along the pageant route: "Out at the windowes and penthouses of everie house, did hange a number of ryche and costlye banners and streamers." These members of London's livery companies participated in the show by their authenticating presence, even as they served as audience; by their mute garments, they nevertheless provided a gift of color and spectacle and thereby responded to the theatrical occasion.

Beyond expecting to be entertained, drink some ale, and possibly make assignations for later, theatergoers at the Globe arrived typically with little or no concept of what the play might contain and represent. If the audience member learned that, say, *Othello* or *Love's Labor's Lost* would be performed that afternoon, he or she probably did not know what to expect but went eagerly to be entertained. Perhaps the spectators would have more informed ideas about some of the English history plays—perhaps. On the other hand, rushing to find a spot along London's streets for the 1559 pageant on that snowy January afternoon, one would have some clear ideas; that is, the audience knew that they would see much spectacle, hear some speeches, and catch a glimpse of their new queen. Mulcaster puts the matter succinctly: "This her graces loving behaviour preconceived in the peoples heades upon these consideracions was then throughly confirmed, and indede emplanted a woonderfull hope in them touching her woorthie government in the rest of her reygne" (28). The pageant thus confirmed "preconceived" ideas about the performance and about the queen, whose charismatic responses implanted great hope in the audience for the possibilities of her "worthy government."

The pageant text reinforces the "dual," interdependent nature of this dramatic experience from its earliest pages. Referring to Elizabeth's reception, Mulcaster writes that she "was of the people received merveylous entierly, as appeared by thassemblie, prayers, wisshes, welcomminges, cryes, tender woordes, and all other signes, whiche argue a wonderfull earnest love of most obedient subjectes towarde theyr soveraygne" (27). The audience thus demonstrated its love by these various signs—no passive audience here. "And on thother side," Mulcaster observes, "her grace by holding up her handes, and merie countenaunce to such as stoode farre of[f], and most tender and gentle language to those that stode nigh to her grace, did declare her selfe no lesse thankefullye to receive her peoples good wille." In Mulcaster's formulation, this pageant has two sides; these correspond to audience and actor. These "sides" confirm the function of charisma, the reaction and integration of queen and spectators; and they underscore how incomplete the pageant would be without these two sides. Mulcaster continues, "So that on eyther side ther was nothing but gladnes, nothing but prayer, nothing but comfort" (27–28). Gladness, prayer, and comfort define the mutual gifts that the queen and audience exchange—the "best gifts" to which St. Paul refers.

The "dialectic" that Mulcaster offers rings true but incomplete, I think. He presupposes fixed boundaries between queen and audience, but the text encourages the idea that these boundaries shifted and did not remain static. For example, at various moments in the pageant, the queen became an "actor" and not simply an audience to which the entertainment pointed, although obviously she never completely surrendered that function, either. The citizens as audience by their active engagement slipped across the static idea of their position. The parallel "sides" that Mulcaster imagines and documents also intersect. In other words, the legal and political boundaries between sovereign and citizen did remain fixed, but the boundaries of dramatic entertainment became permeable. In addition, to be accurate, one would have to refer to multiple audiences; that is, since the queen moved in procession through the city, she would have encountered different groups at the various stages.

The "sides," we might suggest, existed inside a large circle (literally the city itself), another way of imagining the exchanges that took place. We can posit a movement that flows from the dramatic representation itself to the queen, the honored guest, to her response, to the audience's response both to her and to her reaction, and back finally to the queen, who occasionally reacted to the audience's response. As Elizabeth stood or paused in front of the scaffolds or arches, she and the audience existed in a kind of perpendicular relationship to the structure, as I have discussed elsewhere.[17] Indeed, the vertical arch that punctuated the horizontal streets created just such an arrangement. I write, "The sign of the triumphal arch becomes manifest in its dramatic scene. The spectators see multiple signs because their gaze fixes also on the sovereign, seeing in him or her the sign and manifestation of power and rule. The fiction of the scaffold stages joins the reality of the streets to create a theatrical scene that presents and re-presents a joyous people honoring its sovereign."[18] The various means of accounting for what transpired between the queen and the audience all underscore a circular exchange and thereby highlight the *charisma* that emerged in this dynamic relationship.

The queen moved from the Tower through London, making various stops at which she confronted pageant devices, typically arranged on some kind of scaffold. She stopped first at Fenchurch. The text describes the scene: "[T]he people on *eche syde* joyouslye beholding the viewe of so gracious a Ladie their quene, and her grace no lesse gladlye noting and observynge thesame" (29, my emphasis). The scaffold at Fenchurch contained a "noyes of instrumentes, and a child in costly apparel," who had the task of welcoming Elizabeth on behalf of the whole city. The child stepped forth and spoke:

O pereles soveraygne quene, behold what this thy town
Hath thee presented with at thy fyrst entraunce here: . . .

> Behold with what two gyftes she [city] comforteth thy chere.
> The first is blessing tongues, which many a welcome say
> Which pray thou maist do wel. . . .
> The second is true hertes, which love thee from their roote. . . . (29)

In response, the people "gave a great shout, wishing with one assent as the childe had said" (30). The queen also responded by thanking the city for its reception and these gifts of their tongues and hearts, which, she notes, "confirm" the city's goodwill—a sure sign of charisma. Mulcaster notes a "marvelous change" in Elizabeth's appearance as she absorbed the child's message: "[T]he childes wordes touched either her person or the peoples tonges and hertes" (30). He continues, "So that she with rejoysing visage did evidently declare that the woordes tooke no lesse place in her mynde, than they were moste heartelye pronounced by the chylde, as from all the heartes of her most heartie citizeins" (30).

In addition to observing the queen's visage, Mulcaster had earlier noted that merely hearing the queen's voice "set thenemie on fyre" but "could not but enflame her naturall, obedient, and most lovyng people" (28–29). What an extraordinary occasion it must have been for this audience, scattered along London's streets, to *hear* the queen speak—an experience that they would ordinarily not have. This is not some actor on a stage impersonating a queen but the real person being observed as one might an actor. Not only her mere presence stirred the audience but also her voice sounding in grateful response. Small wonder that the audience felt "enflamed," stirred, and impassioned by the experience—an exceptional reaction from any audience at a theatrical event. This small event at Fenchurch reinforces the point of Elizabeth as "actor"; it also implies the circularity of the episode, as she, also a kind of audience for the dramatic representations, nevertheless responded.[19] Then the larger audience responded to her, and so the circulation goes—on all sides!

The queen got a much-desired dose of "lineage charisma" at the arch located at Gracechurch Street. Here an arch stretched across the street, containing three stages in degrees: the first represented Henry VII and his wife Elizabeth "sitting under one cloth of estate in their seates," Henry enclosed in a red rose and Elizabeth, in a white rose. On the platform above sat child actors representing Henry VIII and his wife Anne Boleyn with appropriate signs of their office. On the uppermost stage sat a representation of the current Queen Elizabeth, "crowned and apparelled as thother prynces were" (32). The devisers had garnished the whole scaffold with red and white roses, denoting the union of the Lancaster and York houses by the first Tudor king and queen, from whose line Elizabeth descends. Various "sentences" hung from the arch, all referring to unity. The strategy of representation in this pageant (and many others) included *resemblance* and *recall*; that is, the arch looked retrospectively to the foundation of the Tudor house and "resembled" it by the presentation of these figures made to resemble the precursors and founders of the royal line.[20] The audience looked at a representation of Elizabeth on the arch while also seeing the real queen standing in their midst.

The queen had some trouble seeing and hearing the speaker, so she had her chariot moved to a more advantageous place, and someone interpreted the scene for her. After she had understood the meaning of this device, "she thanked the citie, praised the fairenes of the worke, and promised, that she would doe her whole endevour for the continuall preservacion of concorde" (34). At this arch Elizabeth saw her heritage, which this device confirms, erasing whatever doubts might linger. The queen looking at a representation of herself must have provided the audience with an unusual perspective: the real queen looking at an image of herself—another instance of circulation. The audience exchanged this gift of lineage for the queen's promise; the dramatic scene thus stirred recollection and commitment, as group and individual coalesced.

The pageant device in Cornhill represented the "seat of worthie governance," which includes another representation of Elizabeth, imperially crowned, surrounded on the arch by allegorical virtues that help sustain good government: Pure Religion, Love of subjects, Wisdom, and Justice. These qualities tread on their opposing vices; for example, Pure Religion steps on Superstition and Ignorance. The emblematic costumes and names affixed to these characters assist in understanding what they represent. The queen "caused her charyot to be drawen nyghe thereunto, that her grace might heare the childes oration" (39). The speaker closes, "Now all thy subjectes hertes, O prince of perles fame / Do trust these vertues shall maintain up thy throne, / And vice be kept down still, the wicked put to shame" (39). Elizabeth responded to the pageant by giving the city thanks for it and promising "her good endevour for the maintenance of the sayde vertues, and suppression of vyces" (41). Having at the previous arch established Elizabeth's genealogy, the deviser of the Cornhill show extended this by presenting an allegory of state in which virtues battle vices. The street audience eagerly awaited the queen's response.

Elizabeth, in effect looking at herself in these two pageant devices, underscores the tension between the real event and the fictional representations at the arches. The audience looked at the queen gazing at representations of herself, all standing in London's very real streets. This axis of fiction-reality received another twist in the queen's encounter with the Recorder of the City of London, Ranulph Cholmley, whom she met in the upper end of Cheapside. No allegorical or historical figure, the Recorder "presented to the Quenes majestie a purse of crimosin sattin richly wrought with gold, wherin the citie gave unto the Quenes majestie a thousand markes in gold" (45). He explained that "the Lord mayor, hys brethren, and comminaltie of the citie, to declare their gladnes and good wille towards the Quenes majestie, did present her grace with that gold." Mulcaster records Elizabeth's response: "I thanke my lord mayor, his brethren, and you all. . . . I wil be as good unto you, as ever quene was to her people. No wille in me can lacke, neither doe I trust shall ther lacke any power. . . . for the safetie and quietnes of you all, I will not spare, if nede be to spend my blood" (46). This answer "moved a mervaylous showte and rejoysing" from the audience. This mutual exchange interrupted the unfolding fictional drama, as this audience supported the queen in yet another way: a concrete gift from the city to which she responds graciously, writing her own script. This tangible sign of the city's symbolic goodwill reinforced the charismatic nature of this moment in Cheapside. The queen acknowledged the support of the group by pledging nothing less than to "spend" her own blood, if needed, for the country's safety and tranquility.

Sometimes as the queen moved through the streets and confronted the arches, she had to request silence from the audience. At Soper Lane End, the city had erected an arch containing eight persons who represented the Eight Beatitudes from the fifth chapter of St. Matthew's gospel. These beatitudes, which Elizabeth should embody, demonstrated "the promises and blessinges of almightie god made to his people" (42), in effect *charisms* of God. The child speaker made the link between these virtues and the queen, in a sense creating another series of "gifts" that the queen receives and dispenses—the blessings that she should exercise. Elizabeth moved closer to the scaffold so that she might hear more clearly, "the Quenes majestie geving most attentive eare, and requiring that the peoples noyse might be stayde." She quieted the audience, but after the speech, they erupted with praise for her, wishing for her the blessings found in scripture. As Mulcaster indicates, "When these woordes were spoken, all the people wished, that as the child had spoken, so god woulde strengthen her grace against all her adversaries, whom the Quenes majestie did most gently thanke for their so loving wishe" (43).

Elizabeth made a similar request for quiet at the Fleet Street arch, which contained a representation of Deborah, who had served as judge of Israel for forty years. The child speaker likened Elizabeth to Deborah, who served as a "worthie president, O worthie Queene, thou hast, / A worthie woman judge, a woman sent for staie" (54). The queen had her chariot draw nearer "that she might plainlie heare the childe speake," and she "required silence" from the audience. Thus Old and New Testaments provided suitable and indeed compelling models for Elizabeth, and, not wanting to miss a word, she moved close to the arches and asked her exuberant audience for silence—but only for a moment. To certify the charismatic experience, both parties needed to respond in some way, confirming their interdependence.

Stretching across the area at the Little Conduit in Cheapside, an elaborate device contained two hills: one on the north side symbolized a dying commonwealth, and the south hill depicted a flourishing commonwealth. Every decaying item on the north hill met its opposite on the south hill, including a barren tree and a vibrant one, from which sentences hung enumerating the causes of either a dying commonwealth or a flourishing one. Clearly the northern hill referred to the past (with a nod to Mary's recent reign) and the southern one to the present and future. Between these hills a cave stood "with doore and locke enclosed," out of which, at the queen's arrival, "issued one personage whose name was Tyme, apparaylled as an olde man with a Sythe in his hande" (47). He led his daughter Truth, "all cladde in whyte silke." The two together met the queen, and Truth gave her the word of Truth, the English Bible. Learning beforehand about this intended gift, Elizabeth had ordered John Parrat "to goe before and to receive the booke. But learning that it should be delivered unto her grace downe by a silken lace, she caused him to staye" (44). Sensitive to her role, Elizabeth wisely waited to fulfill her role in the allegorical fiction. The speaker at the arch urged, "We trust O worthy quene, thou wilt this truth embrace" (48). After the speech, Elizabeth responded: "[s]he as soone as she had received the booke, kyssed it, and with both her handes held up the same, and so laid it upon her brest, with great thankes to the citie therfore" (48–49). The child speaker reminded the queen that Truth "doth present to thee the same, O worthy Queene, / For that, that wordes do flye, but wryting doth remayn." In the audience's view, no greater gift could have been offered the queen than the English Bible. And she, although the recipient and therefore "audience," nevertheless responded with great skill and imagination—not to mention theatrical flair. Apparently impressed by Elizabeth's response to the Bible, Mulcaster returns to the event at the end of his text, recounting again the queen's gracious action "to the great comfort of the lookers on. God will undoubtedly preserve so worthy a prince" (64).[21]

At St. Paul's, the queen heard a Latin oration from one of the children of St. Paul's school, which the "Queenes majestie most attentively harkened unto. And when the childe had pronounced he did kisse the oration which he had there faire written in paper, and delivered it unto the Quenes majestie" (52). Elizabeth "gently" received the paper. The text does not note an English translation of the oration; therefore, clearly the speaker intended rather exclusively for the queen to be the audience for this presentation. Throughout the pageant, Latin sayings and mottoes appear regularly, restricting the audience. At such moments, most spectators had to be content with the presence of the queen and the overall spectacle. Using Latin certainly complimented the queen's well-regarded learning and facility with languages. The focus shifted to Elizabeth's response, not unlike the situation of audiences in a number of plays that include foreign languages.

As the queen made her way past St. Paul's toward Ludgate, a person near her commented on the considerable expense and effort that the City had made for this pageant and "[h]er grace answered that she did well consider the same, and that it should be remembered" (53). Mulcaster interprets this response in what amounts to a kind of definition of "charisma": "An honorable answere, worthie a noble prince, which may comfort all her subjectes, considering there can be no point of gentlenes, or obedient love shewed towarde her grace, which she doth not most tenderlie accept, and graciously waye [weigh]" (53). With "the people on either side rejoysing," Elizabeth made her way on to Fleet Street. The queen's understanding and the city's gracious generosity assured the interdependence, characteristic of charisma. The audience's rejoicing on "either side" surrounded the queen and enveloped her in the mutual exchange.

The queen sought a different kind of response at her final stop before exiting the City. On the south side of Temple Bar, she found a "noyse of singing children, and one child richely attyred as a Poet," who addressed the queen by summarizing what she had seen (58). The Poet began by referring to the "tonges and heartes" that the audience offered her, the hope that they invested in her, and the wish that she protect them by rooting out error and restoring truth (a veiled reference to the change in religion from Mary to Elizabeth). Mulcaster writes, "While these wordes were in saieng, and certeine wishes therein repeted for maintenaunce of truthe and rooting out of errour, she now and then helde up her handes to heaven warde, and willed the people to say, Amen" (59). Elizabeth willed the appropriate response from the audience, not unlike the function of numerous epilogues in plays. We might recall several from Shakespeare alone, such as the comments by Puck at the end of *A Midsummer Night's Dream*, in which he commands bluntly, "Give me your hands" (5.1.429); or Rosalind's at the end of *As You Like It*; or the expansive epilogue at the end of *2 Henry IV*, in which the speaker promises another play from the playwright, and it will include Sir John and Katherine of France, that is, *Henry V*. The most haunting epilogue may be Prospero's at the end of *The Tempest*. Here Prospero asks explicitly for two reactions from the audience: "But release me from my bands / With the help of your good hands" (9–10); and, "As you from crimes would pardoned be, / Let your indulgence set me free" (19–20).[22] The queen willed a suitable reaction, a punctuation mark on the ideas spoken of by the Poet, asking the audience to release her from this event by their responses, to set her free for tomorrow's coronation.

This charismatic interaction continued as she left the city: "At which saieng her grace departed forth through temple barre towarde Westminster with no lesse shooting [shouting] and crieng of the people," a response that Mulcaster likens to the firing of cannons as Elizabeth left the Tower earlier in the afternoon.

Although the pageant officially ended as the queen exited the City, Mulcaster continues his text with recollections of what he calls "[c]ertain notes of the quenes majesties great mercie, clemencie, and wisdom used in this passage" (61). In a sense, we can see Mulcaster as another kind of audience, even though we cannot prove that he functioned as an eyewitness. But his "I/eye of the beholder" *allows* us through recollection to participate in the events of that January pageant.[23] We can view Mulcaster's loving care in offering these final comments as his "gift," his active participation in the charismatic audience of this street entertainment. The events continue to resonate in his remembrance as he puts together the text, published on January 23. Mulcaster responds to Elizabeth and to the audiences' reactions. He may thereby seem at moments like the ideal reader whom Jonson so desired.

Mulcaster recounts how the queen answered the report of one of her knights who had noted a certain citizen who had turned his back and wept in Cheapside. "The quenes majestie hearde him, and said, I warrant you it is for gladnes. A gracious interpretation of a noble courage," Mulcaster adds (61). So pleased at the queen's notice and kindness, this gentleman's tears flowed more fully for joy. An unexpected smile by Elizabeth along the route prompted her to explain "she had heard one say, Remember old king Henry theight. A naturall child, which at the verie remembraunce of her fathers name toke so great a joy." Augmenting what Mulcaster had earlier reported about the queen's comments after the presentation of the gift by the Recorder, he claims that her answer melted the hearts of the audience; and Mulcaster adds, "so may the reader therof conceive what kinde of stomacke and courage pronounced thesame" (62). The simple gift of rosemary from a poor woman along the streets Elizabeth accepted and carried in her chariot all the way to Westminster. Out of these actions and exchanges Mulcaster concludes that Elizabeth "passed through a cittie that most entierlie loved her, so she at her last departing, as it were bownd her selfe by promes to continue good ladie and governor unto that citie which by outward declaracion did open their love, to their so loving and noble prince" (63). The city declared its love, and the queen countered by being bound by promises to its citizens, the audience in London's streets. Such charismatic circularity defines the covenant symbolically agreed upon on January 14, 1559.

At the conclusion of the description of the arch at Soper Lane and its representation of the Beatitudes, Mulcaster observes, "Besides these [verses], every voide place in the pageant was furnished with sentences touching the matter and ground of the said pageant" (43). The devisers of the pageant left no void places. The queen also contributed many sentences that fruitfully occupy a meaningful space. And the audience, through its response, completed the queen's sentences, punctuating her thoughts with charismatic identification: "As a visible sign moving through the streets of London, Elizabeth accumulates unto herself the representations of herself, the images, and the speeches; and she returns these to the city in her truthful gestures and words, signifying everything."[24] The queen thus left the city full of hope and confirmation—no void spaces. On the next day, she would experience the rich panoply and ceremony of coronation, with the intertwining of religious, institutional, and political forces. But she first passed through the City, as if needing this public display and affirmation before arriving at Westminster. The citizens of London covenanted with her in ways far richer than the Scrivener understood in *Bartholomew Fair*.

In *Bartholomew Fair*, Jonson, decades later, assumes an adversarial relationship between actor and audience, author and audience. Thus, he seeks to control the audience's reaction through the Induction, in which he creates an idea, a fiction of a covenant between stage and audience—one that the author deliberately imposes. The playwright hopes for assent, but he cannot determine it. In a word, the charisma here remains only potential. Mulcaster's text reveals to us something radically different in London's streets in the 1559 pageant. We could argue that the pageant fulfills the covenantal agreement that Jonson could later only dream about. The audience in 1559 affirmed and assisted with charisma by its responses to the queen and the dramatic action. The spectators arrived predisposed, of course, to a favorable reaction. Elizabeth's actions enflamed the audience's passion of support and brought "great comfort" to all, underscoring the shared experience—this "systemic structure of mutuality," to use Falco's words. In response to this queen who was willing to "spend" her blood to protect them, who greeted every "point of gentleness" offered to her with gracious acceptance, the audience reciprocated with shouts of joy and support. In the theatrical space of London's streets, Elizabeth bound herself to the spectators, who embraced and surrounded her with loving hearts and tongues. She may have passed through the city, but she left behind a residue of charismatic interdependence that temporarily, at least, dissolved boundaries.

Notes

1. Ben Jonson, *Ben Jonson: Three Comedies*, ed. Michael Jamieson (Baltimore, MD: Penguin, 1966). All quotations from the play derive from this edition and are cited by line numbers.
2. David M. Bergeron, *Textual Patronage in English Drama, 1570–1640* (Aldershot, UK: Ashgate, 2006), 119–39.
3. For a discussion of Burre's dedication of the play to Robert Keysar, see David Bergeron, *Textual Patronage*, 32. For additional consideration of the Beaumont text see David Bergeron, "Paratexts in Francis Beaumont's *The Knight of the Burning Pestle*," *Studies in Philology* 106 (2009): 456–67.

4. Alfred Harbage, *Shakespeare and the Rival Traditions* (New York: Macmillan, 1952); Ann Jennalie Cook, *The Privileged Playgoers of Shakespeare's London, 1576–1642* (Princeton, NJ: Princeton University Press, 1981).
5. Andrew Gurr, *The Shakespearean Stage, 1574–1642*, 3rd ed. (Cambridge: Cambridge University Press, 1992); Andrew Gurr, *Playgoing in Shakespeare's London* (Cambridge: Cambridge University Press, 1987). With quite a different approach is Charles Whitney's *Early Responses to Renaissance Drama* (Cambridge: Cambridge University Press, 2006), which looks at specific spectators and their reactions, such as Simon Forman, documented by Whitney on 147–60. Also, Jennifer A. Low, "'Bodied Forth': Spectator, Stage, and Actor in the Early Modern Theater," *Comparative Drama* 39 (2005): 1–29, comes at the issue of "audience" in terms of its social space in the theater. Low discusses also the spectator reaction to certain plays, for example, quite tellingly in the analysis of *'Tis Pity She's a Whore*.
6. Stephen Orgel, "Reading Occasions," *Renaissance Drama* 34 (2006): 37. This provocative essay appears on 31–45.
7. See David Bergeron, *English Civic Pageantry 1558–1642*, rev. ed. (Tempe: Arizona State Medieval and Renaissance Studies, 2003), originally published in 1971.
8. Clifford Geertz, "Centers, Kings, and Charisma: Reflections on the Symbolics of Power," in *Local Knowledge: Further Essays in Interpretive Anthropology* (New York: Basic Books, 1983), 125. This essay appears on 121–46.
9. Robert Weimann, *Shakespeare and the Popular Tradition in the Theater: Studies in the Social Dimension of Dramatic Form and Function*, ed. Robert Schwartz (Baltimore, MD: Johns Hopkins University Press, 1978), 7.
10. Ibid., 212–13.
11. Geertz, "Centers, Kings," 129.
12. Raphael Falco, *Charismatic Authority in Early Modern English Tragedy* (Baltimore, MD: Johns Hopkins University Press, 2000), esp. 1–25. Falco himself builds on the work of Max Weber in *Economy and Society* (1956).
13. Falco, *Charismatic Authority*, 2–3.
14. Ibid., 11.
15. Richard Mulcaster, *The Quenes Maiesties Passage through the Citie of London*, ed. James M. Osborn (1558; repr., New Haven, CT: Yale University Press, 1960), 28. I have modernized slightly some of the quotations.
16. I have discussed and transcribed these documents in David Bergeron, "Elizabeth's Coronation Entry (1559): New Manuscript Evidence," in *Practicing Renaissance Scholarship* (Pittsburgh, PA: Duquesne University Press, 2000), 36–42. This article originally appeared in *English Literary Renaissance* 8 (1978): 3–8, plus plates.
17. See David Bergeron, "Representation in Renaissance English Civic Pageants," *Theatre Journal* 40 (1988): 319–31.
18. Ibid., 322.
19. Emma Rhatigan's essay in this volume addresses some of the same issues in her discussion of the Gray's Inn Christmas revels of 1594, an indoor entertainment that blurred the boundaries between actor and audience, compounded by the performance by professional actors of *Comedy of Errors*. As Rhatigan observes, several audiences filled the hall on that evening. Watching the Prince constituted part of the attraction of the evening, even as spectators in London's streets a few decades

earlier had focused on Queen Elizabeth and noted her reaction to the drama. Matters of social identity run through the Gray's Inn entertainment as they also permeate *The Comedy of Errors*. One can make a similar point about the 1559 street pageant.
20. See Bergeron, "Representation in English Civic Pageants," 319–31 for further discussion of this technique.
21. A new, different kind of audience confronted this scene when Thomas Dekker duplicated it, with slight changes, in his *The Whore of Babylon* (1607), the opening dumb show. In this scene Time and Truth greet Titania, the Faerie Queene, and present her with a "book," which she accepts and kisses. Thomas Heywood also nods in this direction in the closing scene of *If You Know Not Me, You Know Nobody*, part 1 (1605), in which the Lord Mayor presents a Bible to Elizabeth, who in her speech says that she must first kiss this book.
22. All quotations come from Shakespeare, *The Complete Pelican Shakespeare*, ed. Stephen Orgel and A. R. Braunmuller (New York: Penguin, 2002).
23. For additional insight into this concept, see David Bergeron, "The 'I' of the Beholder: Thomas Churchyard and the 1578 Norwich Pageant," in *The Progresses, Pageants, and Entertainments of Queen Elizabeth I*, ed. Jayne Elisabeth Archer, Elizabeth Goldring, and Sarah Knight (Oxford: Oxford University Press, 2007), 142–59.
24. Bergeron, "Representation in English Civic Pageants," 325.

CHAPTER 8

Audience, Actors, and "Taking Part" in the Revels

Emma K. Rhatigan

On January 28, 1594, the Gray's Inn Christmas revels hit a snag. An evening of entertainment put on by the prince of Purpoole to entertain his guest, Frederick Templarius, the ambassador from the Inner Temple, dissolved into chaos. Put simply, the audience refused to stay in their seats. The account of the revels describes the following:

> When the Ambassador was placed, as aforesaid, [beside the prince of Purpoole] and that there was something to be performed for the Delight of the Beholders, there arose such a disordered Tumult and Crowd upon the Stage that there was no Opportunity to effect that which was intended.[1]

Such, we learn, was the "multitude of Beholders" that "there was no convenient room for those that were Actors" (29). Unimpressed by the chaos, the ambassador and his train departed "discontented and displeased" and the revellers were left to contemplate the consequent "Discouragement and Disparagement to [the] whole State" (31–32).

Up until this point events had gone to plan. The Christmas revels usually lasted from just before Christmas until Candlemas (February 2), during which time the governing body of the inn, the benchers, would relinquish their authority to the students.[2] In most years this period would be marked by activities such as dancing, music, feasting, and gaming. Occasionally, however, these revels would be more elaborate, and the students would set up a temporary mock state, governed by a Christmas prince. The prince's reign would be marked by a series of ceremonies such as the conferring of knighthoods and a declaration of laws, in addition to entertainments such as dancing, masques, and plays. The 1594–95 Gray's Inn revels were some of the most elaborate of the period and were recorded in the anonymous account *Gesta Grayorum*, first printed in 1688.[3] From this account we learn that the students elected one Henry Helmes as their prince on December 12 and assigned him a privy council, officers of state, and a household. There was then a period of fund-raising, before Helmes was officially crowned the prince of Purpoole (Purpoole referring to the parish of Portpool in which Gray's Inn was situated) on December 20 and the following days set aside for further entertainments. These festivities were extremely successful. So successful, indeed, that word spread. The account tells us that "the common Report amongst all Strangers was so great, and the Expectation of our Proceedings so extraordinary, that it urged us to take upon us a greater State than was at the first intended" (28). This seems to have been where the problems on Innocents' Night started. The prince and his court were victims of their own success, with the number of external guests seeking to attend the evening's entertainments turning out to be far beyond what they had anticipated—hence the debacle with the seating arrangements.

In the event, the night did not prove to be the catastrophe the revellers feared it might. Eventually the "Throngs and Tumults" were appeased, the audience returned to their seats, and the students were able to proceed with "Dancing and Revelling with Gentlewomen" (31–32). By the end of the evening, order was sufficiently restored for the night to conclude with a performance of *The Comedy of Errors* by a group of professional actors. The confusion that occurred on Innocents' Night does, however, remain puzzling. Amid the multiple stages, audiences, and embedded performances within performances, including the "something to be performed" that was intended for the ambassador, the performance of *The Comedy of Errors*, and, of course, the overall performance of the revels, it is hard to establish not only which stage became so crowded but also which audience was watching which performance. In a manner analogous to other entertainments such as the masque or, as David Bergeron describes in Chapter 7 in this volume, city pageants, the events of Innocents' Night, and indeed, the revels more generally challenge the categories of actor and audience; the audience's temporary occupation of the stage points to more complex issues surrounding participation in the revels. My purpose here is to assess what it meant to "take part" in the revels.[4] I will start by surveying the various audiences in the Gray's Inn Hall on Innocents' Night, analyzing the nature of their engagement with the performance of the revels as both actors and audiences. I wish then to focus on the professional players' performance of *The Comedy of Errors*. As a play that is itself underpinned by an exploration of identity formation, I want to suggest that the staging of this particular comedy within the specific institutional context of the *Gesta Grayorum* would have foregrounded precisely those concerns with "taking part," which permeated the performance of the revels.

Taking Part in the Revels

The questions surrounding the staging of the 1594 Gray's Inn revels have been resolved, as nearly as possible, by the work of Margaret Knapp and Michal Kobialka.[5] The revels took place, for the most part, in the Great Hall. At the west end of the hall was the dais, and it was on this that the prince took his throne, surrounded by his counsellors and great lords. It would have been here that the ambassador and his companions were seated. Knapp and Kobialka estimate that there would have been approximately 70 people on the dais with additional members of the prince's household seated at a table just below. The east end of the hall would usually have been filled with the students' tables, but for the revels these seem to have been removed and replaced with scaffolds positioned on the sides of the walls, leaving the central space clear for dancing. These scaffolds provided temporary seating for the "Strangers" and members of the inn not directly partaking in the revels. The stage was situated directly in front of the dais, and this would have been the performance space both for the revellers who were performing entertainments for the prince and the ambassador and for the professional actors who performed *The Comedy of Errors*. Thus on the chaotic evening in question, the crowd of external guests, unable to find space on the dais, had pushed forward onto the stage just in front. The disorder, then, arose not just from the audience failing to stay in their allocated seats on the scaffolds but from two distinct audiences, the revellers and the guests, becoming confused.

Unusually for theatrical performances of this period, at least one of these audiences—the one seated on the dais—can be identified reasonably accurately, since the account of the revels published in 1688 lists everyone who participated. The majority of those named are not mentioned in the Gray's Inn records, suggesting they were never called to the bar and did not go on to pursue a legal career. These, then, were most likely young students who were treating Gray's Inn as a finishing school not only picking up some knowledge of the law but also using their time in London to take classes in dancing, fencing, and music and to orient themselves in the social and political cultures of the capital. The only such students who are named in surviving records are those who committed some infraction of the society's rules, such as the six revel participants who were put out of commons in 1590 "for their abuse in outrageous manner com[m]itted the 3rd of Februarii about 2 or 3 of the clock in the morning of the same day."[6] Approximately 28 of the named participants, however, did go on to be called to the bar, of which up to nine were then called to the bench and made members of the governing body of the inn. There is even the possibility that some of those who participated were already practicing barristers. For example, one "Crew" listed as being the "Lord Chief Justice of the Prince's

Bench" (12) could be Thomas Crew, who had been called to the bar in 1590. Equally, the "Johnson" listed as "Lord Chancellor" could be William Johnson, who as a member of the "grand company," would also have been called to the bar (13).[7] It would certainly be appropriate if these two men, who were among the most senior participants, were allocated two of the most senior offices in the prince's court.

The list of participants, then, enables us to add to what we already know about the Inns of Court audience. It does not, however, offer us the detailed biographical information about which theater historians fantasize, and the fact that most of these men passed through Gray's Inn without leaving any trace in the society's records means that attempts to glean further information are likely to be met with frustration. But arguably, to pursue this line of inquiry is to read this evidence in the wrong context. For what the list of participants is intended to offer us is not a list of audience members but rather a cast list. And this, perhaps, is what is most interesting about the audience on the dais: they were not only observers but also actors. Undoubtedly the "Strangers" who pressed into Gray's Inn Hall on Innocents' Night were an enthusiastic audience for the professional players who performed *The Comedy of Errors*, but their primary objective in attending was to see the revellers. As the account tells us, it was "Expectation of our Proceedings" that drew them in, and part of the purpose of the evening was "for the Entertainment of Strangers to our Pass-times and Sports" (28–29). Moreover, this external audience was most likely keen to see not only those revellers who were to present the "notable Performance" (29) but also those revellers who were the audience to such entertainment. Watching the prince watching the entertainment was surely a considerable part of the attraction.

The notion of audiences engaging in their own "performances" is, of course, not new. Critics of early modern performance have frequently noted the porous nature of the roles of actor and audience. In Chapter 7 of this volume, Bergeron describes the participation and "authenticating presence" of the "costumed" guildsmen attending Elizabeth I's royal entry, and there is an equally clear parallel with the private playhouses in which the gentry who took stools on the stage functioned not only as an audience but as a part of the spectacle itself. As Tiffany Stern writes of the Blackfriars theater, it was a space that "collectively created a theatrical event of which the play was an element."[8] The challenge of such an observation, though, lies in differentiating between the different ways in which actors and audience members might be taking part in a theatrical event; this question is foregrounded by the cast list of the revels.[9] Stern and Simon Palfrey have emphasized the close relationship between an early modern actor and the parts written for him, an intimacy facilitated by the fact that playwrights would frequently be writing a part for a specific actor. As they describe, actors were cast according to personality "type"; in other words, although an actor would play a range of characters, these would always be determined by his "type," his particular body and "humour." The actor John Sincler, for example, always played thin and melancholy parts, such as Cassius in *Julius Caesar* or Andrew Aguecheek in *Twelfth Night*. In *The Comedy of Errors* he thus probably took the part of Pinch, "a hungry lean-faced villain . . . A needy, hollowed-eyed, sharp-looking wretch."[10] Indeed, as Palfrey and Stern go on to argue, what was most prized in early modern actors was the ability to "internalize a part fully, and to elide the barrier between performance and identity," a notion of characterization captured by the early modern term "personation," which, as Andrew Gurr demonstrates, was just coming into use in the early seventeenth century.[11]

The cast list of the Gray's Inn revels implies, however, that the revellers would have had a series of quite different relationships with their parts. Obviously to some extent this stems from the nature of the parts themselves; a part in the revels differed from a part in a play in that it lacked the sense of coherence that the larger narrative of a play gave to a character. Important too, however, is the nature of the participation in the revels demanded by these parts. Specifically, the extent to which the parts necessitated "personation," inhabiting a completely new character, varied. For example, at one end of the spectrum there are listed "Gentlemen for Entertainment, three Couples" (11). For these gentlemen there was clearly very little, if any, acting involved; their dancing, although certainly a performance, would not have necessitated the impersonation of any new identity. Equally, while parts such as the "Master of the Revels" or the "Cup-bearer" were certainly more prestigious, it is debatable whether the students were really acting these either. Lambert, for example, who took the part of the "Master of Revels," would presumably have actually been involved in the onerous task of supervising the revels.[12] Indeed, there seem to have been occasions when the revellers would actually take on the authority of their parts. Thus on January 6, 1594, Henry Helmes used his authority as the prince of Purpoole to admit the Lord Mayor, Sir John Spenser, into the society. As Desmond Bland explains, in signing the admissions register in record of this, Helmes was conspicuously usurping the role of the treasurer.[13] Equally, Philip Finkelpearl draws our attention to an entry in the Parliament of the Middle Temple in 1589 where it states the following:

> The order set down in the buttery book by the Christmas lord and Utter Barristers then in commons for removing Henry Poole, the Steward, from his office for ill provision of victual and other abuses, is revoked, as the makers of the order had no sufficient authority, but his misdemeanours and evil usage of the Butlers and other officers is referred to the Treasurer and two others of the Bench.[14]

Although the Christmas prince's authority here is deemed insufficient actually to sack the steward, the complaint is clearly being taken seriously. The order makes clear, moreover, the very real domestic duties undertaken by members of the prince's household. Lambert was not acting when he had to supervise the meals of over a hundred revellers.[15] Other parts, however, such as the prince's attorney and solicitor required more thespian, not to mention oratorical, expertise. Both the attorney (Holt) and the solicitor (Dunne) made important contributions to the prince's mock court. On the first day, for example, the Attorney made a "Speech of Gratulation" (15) to the prince. This sort of participation is clearly different from that of the "Master of Revels" in that these men were *pretending* to perform legal offices in a way that the "Master of Revels," burdened with organizing events, could not afford to do.

The extent to which these men were acting also needs to be complicated by the fact that these were parts to which they could well have been aspiring. If, for example, the "Holt" who took the part of the attorney was William Holt, then he was actively pursuing a legal career; twenty years later, in 1615, he would become a bencher of Gray's Inn.[16] For this young lawyer to play the part of attorney, one of the country's top legal offices, must to some extent have been an experiment in wish fulfillment. Indeed, providing the students with an opportunity to hone their legal, rhetorical, and courtly accomplishments and, quite literally, to try out public roles was one of the main objects of the revels, which were meant to facilitate not just recreation but also the opportunity for self-creation.[17] As a 1540 report on the inns by Nicholas Bacon explained, the students took up offices mimicking real ones "onely to the intent that they should in time to come know how to use themselves."[18] In other words, the participants were meant to have a relationship to their part that was not only imaginative but also aspirant. This aspect of the part must have been particularly resonant when the revels went "on tour," staging entertainments at the Lord Mayor's House and before the court at Greenwich. Performing before the queen, the part of aspirant courtier must have become indistinguishable from the part of real courtier. Of course, the assigning of individuals to roles to which they were particularly suited or in which they had a particular investment created scope for precisely the sort of in-jokes that the revels thrived on and celebrated. The part of the archbishop of St. Andrews in Holborn, for example, is given to one "Bush." The only Bush listed in the index to the Gray's Inn records is Paul Bush, the society's chaplain. The joke of (very likely) placing the chaplain in the role of bishop, and a made-up bishopric at that, seems entirely in keeping with the witty, self-conscious mood of the revels.[19] Such congruence between actor and part is clearly reminiscent of the casting according to type that governed the professional theater. Indeed, the joke of giving Bush the part of a bishop is comparable with the self-conscious intertexual reference to *Julius Caesar* in *Hamlet*, when Polonius (played by the actor who would have played Caesar) tells Hamlet (played by the actor who would have played Brutus), "I did enact Julius Caesar. I was killed i'th' Capitol. Brutus killed me."[20] This allusion, which of course becomes yet further pertinent when two scenes later Hamlet stabs Polonius, relies on the audience's appreciation of the relationship between an actor and his parts.[21] At the same time, however, it remains important to distinguish between the personal investment in a part that governed the casting of the *Gesta Grayorum* and the "personation," the eliding of self and part, that the revellers would have seen in the actors who performed *The Comedy of Errors*.

Participating in the revels was not, moreover, limited to those students who had a specific part. The very act of entering the Great Hall and acknowledging the prince of Purpoole necessitated engaging with and taking part in the make-believe and in effect becoming a member of the prince's court. Consequently, the audience of students seated on the scaffold were in many ways just as important as those seated on the dais. Indeed, the only way a member of the society could not take part in the events was not to enter the inn. Hence the reference in the prince's pardon to

> All Fugitives, Failers and Flinchers that, with Shame and Discredit are fled and vanished out of the Prince's Dominons of *Purpoole*, and especially from his Court at *Graya*, this time of *Christmas*, to withdraw themselves from his Honour's Service and Attendance. (27)

Although the pardon is clearly humorous, participation in the revels was taken extremely seriously. Students were ordered to attend, and those who did not were subject to fines.[22] As Michelle O'Callaghan has argued, because the inns had no formal legal existence as a corporation, "their corporate identity resided in acts of living and working together as a professional fraternity, and relied on rituals and cultural fictions to bind individuals into a voluntary contract."[23] The revels are a crucial example of just such a cultural fiction. One of their main objects was to foster and reinforce the institutional bonds that bound the society's members. Thus, just as the prince's titles of "prince of Purpoole" and "Arch-Duke of Stapulia and Bernardia" celebrated the distinct geographic space of the society by evoking the parish of Portpool in which Gray's Inn was situated and Staple's and Barnard's Inns (the Inns of Chancery over which it had jurisdiction), so too the self-conscious parody, in-jokes, and learned play that constituted the revels worked, again in O'Callaghan's words, to incorporate both "performers and audience into a humanist community whose primary bonds of association were those of education and intellect."[24] As both actors and spectators, then, the students' participation in the revels was not only an important means of exploring new, aspirant, individual identities but also a means of creating a shared institutional, fraternal identity.

Finally, of course, even those troublesome "worshipful Personages" (31) who crammed onto the stage were, by virtue of their presence in the prince's "court," taking part. Indeed, what is striking about the revels is the willingness of nonmembers of Gray's Inn to play along with the fiction. The prince's guests include practically all the great and good of London. Thus on January 31, the prince's court was augmented by "the Right Honourable the Lord Keeper, the Earls of *Shrewsbury, Cumberland, Northumberland, Southampton*, and *Essex*, the Lords *Buckhurst, Windsor, Mountjoy, Sheffield, Compton, Rich, Burleygh, Mounteagle*, and the Lord *Thomas Howard*; Sir *Thomas Henneage*, Sir *Robert Cecill*; with a great number of Knights, Ladies and very worshipful Personages" (35). The climax of the revels came when Elizabeth I invited the prince and his followers to Greenwich and commended their performances, thus providing their invented state a peculiar degree of legitimacy.

Taking Part in *The Comedy of Errors*

It was before this peculiarly incorporated audience, bound by their shared identity not only as an audience but also as participants in a wider imaginative enterprise, that the professional players concluded the night's entertainment with *The Comedy of Errors*. There is much to be said about the congruence of *The Comedy of Errors* and the audience of Inns of Court revellers. It is, after all, a play that starts with the declaration of a legal sentence, when the Duke, despite his sympathy for Egeon insists, "I am not partial to infringe our laws" (1.1.4) and culminates with the Duke determining two cases: Adriana's appeal and Egeon's suspended death penalty.[25] Structurally, the pattern of the play in which a period of confusion and social disorder is resolved, is precisely that of the *Gesta Grayorum*, in which the prince of Purpoole's rule is eventually terminated and the Christmas festivities give way to the start of the new legal term. What other audience, moreover, would be so alert to the play's engagement with its Plautine source? It was the Inns of Court that had produced the first English adaptation of a Greek tragedy, *Jocasta*, and the first prose comedy, a translation of Ariosto's *I Suppositi* as *Supposes* (1599), both by George Gascoigne. And it is surely no coincidence that the one comment on the content of the play that makes it into the *Gesta Grayorum* is that it is "like to *Plautus* his *Menechmus*" (32). Finally, the play also melds with the linguistic tenor of the revels. Eamon Grennan has noted how *The Comedy of Errors* holds in tension both conventional and ordered language, as exemplified in formal set speeches such as Adriana's defense of marriage and the threat of "linguistic anarchy" as embodied in the Dromios' wordplay and punning.[26] Not only would the rhetorically trained Inns of Court students relish such linguistic games, but the revels themselves are constituted by precisely this sort of rhetorical exuberance, juxtaposing virtuoso oratorical set pieces, such as six counsellors' speeches advising the prince, and extended parodies of rhetorical and legal forms.

For some critics such thematic and stylistic affinities provide convincing evidence that the play was commissioned and written specifically for the revels.[27] While such lines of argument are certainly engaging, however, the argument I want to make here is not predicated on (although it equally does not preclude) a predetermined relationship between the play and the *Gesta Grayorum*. Rather, the particular resonances between Shakespeare's comedy and the students' revels that I want to explore, namely their shared interest in identity creation, would, I believe, have emerged out of the staging of the play as part of the revels.[28] In other words, the audience's simultaneous status as "actors," invested in the performance of the revels even as they were watching the play, would have made them particularly attuned to Shakespeare's dramatization of the processes of "taking part."

Antipholus of Syracuse's arrival in Ephesus is marked by a profound sense of displacement. Telling Dromio "I will go lose myself, / And wander up and down to view the city" (1.2.30–31), he indicates a disorientation that is both geographic and psychic. Ironically, his attempt to find his brother and reintegrate himself into his family has resulted not only in further isolation but also in a forfeiting of the self. As he tells us,

> I to the world am like a drop of water
> That in the ocean seeks another drop,
> Who, failing there to find his fellow forth
> Unseen, inquisitive, confounds himself.
> So I, to find a mother and a brother,
> In quest of them unhappy, lose myself. (1.2.35–40)

He is, we might say, lacking a part. The confusion that immediately follows from the simultaneous presence of two sets of identical twins in the same city, unbeknown to either themselves or anyone else, means however, that Antipholus of Syracuse is not long without a role. Given that everyone who encounters him assumes that he is his brother, Antipholus of Ephesus, Antipholus of Syracuse is very quickly offered a whole series of new parts, as husband to Adriana, master to Luce, and business associate to Angelo and Balthasar. Despite being completely in the dark as to what these relationships entail, Antipholus shows himself, to begin with at least, willing to play along, improvising his part until events become clearer. Thus on being accosted by Adriana he responds, "Until I know this sure uncertainty, / I'll entertain the offered fallacy" (2.2.188–89). Indeed, with a striking, perhaps even disarming, versatility, Antipholus of Syracuse is willing to suspend his identity in order to explore new ones:

> Am I in earth, in heaven, or in hell?
> Sleeping or waking? Mad or well advised?
> Known unto these, and to myself disguised?

I'll say as they say, and persever so,
And in this mist at all adventures go. (2.2.215–19)

Like all good actors both Antipholus and Dromio of Syracuse are willing to be "transformed":

Dromio of Syracuse: I am transformèd, master, am not I?
Antipholus of Syracuse: I think thou art in mind, and so am I. (2.2.198)

In a manner comparable to the participants in the revels, then, the master and servant from Syracuse are open to experimenting with unfamiliar roles.

While Antipholus of Syracuse thus experiences a series of liberating encounters with new parts, for Antipholus of Ephesus, by contrast, the action of the play consists of increasingly desperate attempts to keep hold of his identities of husband, master, and businessman. Indeed, it is arguably the tension between Antipholus of Syracuse's opportunist appropriation of these parts and Antipholus of Ephesus's bewildered refusal to surrender them that constitutes the heart of the comedy. This struggle reaches a climax in one of the most comic episodes in the play, the lockout scene (3.1). Arriving home for dinner accompanied by his two business associates, Antipholus of Ephesus is denied entry into his own house. His wife, sister-in-law, and servants, quite simply refuse to acknowledge him as husband and master, and locked outside, both Antipholus and Dromio of Ephesus are effectively transformed from actors to audience, forced to step aside while Antipholus and Dromio of Syracuse usurp their places:

Antipholus of Ephesus. What art thou that keep'st me out from the house I owe?
Dromio of Syracuse. The porter for this time, sir, and my name is Dromio.
Dromio of Ephesus. O villain, thou hast stol'n both mine office and my name!
   (3.1.42–44)

While Dromio of Syracuse embraces his new, temporary part as porter with apparent ease, Dromio of Ephesus is unable to improvise, clinging tenaciously to his "office." Antipholus of Ephesus too refuses to relinquish his role as head of the household and is prepared to gain entry by force: "I'll break ope the gate" (3.1.74). It is notable, moreover, that Balthasar only succeeds in dissuading him from this course by warning him of the possible detriment to his social standing:

If by strong hand you offer to break in
Now in the stirring passage of the day,
A vulgar comment will be made of it,

And that supposèd by the common rout
Against your yet ungalled estimation,
That may with foul intrusion enter in
And dwell upon your grave when you are dead. (3.1.99–105)

It is only because it might jeopardize his social identity that Antipholus of Ephesus is persuaded to surrender temporarily his role as husband and master. This dramatization of exclusion would arguably have carried particular potency in the highly competitive atmosphere of the Inns of Court in which many of the gentleman students were struggling to gain preferment. As already discussed, the desire for social and professional advancement was one of the students' central motivations for participating in the revels. But, as Arthur Marotti describes, these men were seeking employment in a world in which "the rewards were genuine, but the opportunities few," and many were left frustrated and disappointed.[29] Indeed, Antipholus of Ephesus's resort to violence is perhaps reminiscent of the disruption caused by those revellers who were unable to gain a suitably prestigious place on the dais. Relegated from the dais to the scaffold, these students were, like Antipholus of Ephesus, being denied the parts they coveted, reduced from actors to audience members.

In act 5, of course, the confusion is resolved and the characters reassigned their correct parts:

ADRIANA. Are you not my husband?
ANTIPHOLUS of Syracuse. No, I say nay to that. (5.1.372–73)

The resolution of the play reveals, however, that it is only those characters who were willing and able to try on a new identity who discover new relationships and are successfully reintegrated into the community. Thus Antipholus of Syracuse's growing love for Luciana is expressed in terms of a re-creation of the self. He tells Luciana,

Are you a god? Would you create me new?
Transform me, then, and to your power I'll yield. (3.2.39–40)

Although galvanized by the heady experience of falling in love at first sight, this openness to transformation is entirely in character with the man who earlier embraced the opportunity to take on a new part as an "adventure." As Laurie Maguire observes, Antipholus of Syracuse "finds himself by losing himself to Luciana."[30] Meanwhile, the marriage of Antipholus of Ephesus and Adriana is left far more inconclusive. Antipholus of Ephesus, whose experience of the play has only been one of exclusion, is left in what appears, by comparison, to be a state of emotional paralysis, unable to renew his relationship with Adriana. As many critics have noted, his final lines are not to his wife but to the courtesan:

> COURTESAN. Sir, I must have that diamond from you.
> ANTIPHOLUS of Ephesus. There, take it, and much thanks for my good cheer.
> (5.1.393–94)

Even allowing for the inclusive benevolence of the comic ending, Antipholus's blatant and apparently unselfconscious reference to his "good cheer" are hardly the words of a repentant husband.[31] Such a conclusion would seem to chime closely with the spirit of participation fostered by the revels. For the students who were involved in the state of Purpoole, it was the opportunity to experiment with new parts, improvising unfamiliar roles, which not only offered them hope of future re-creation in terms of social and professional advancement but also bound them into the corporate body of Gray's Inn. Hence the revellers' jockeying for position on the dais where they could most fully participate as an acting audience. Thus in both performances it is a willingness to "entertain the offered fallacy" that is the precondition to social and institutional integration.

Indeed, social identity is an extremely prominent concern in *The Comedy of Errors*. The play is run through with an interrogation of the various relationships and communities in which individuals are invested and through which they seek to forge their identity, whether it be the blood ties of family, the union of marriage or the financial bonds that permeate the mercantile society of Ephesus. Antipholus of Syracuse's experience of stepping into his twin's part is one of being immediately integrated into a whole series of social relationships. As he tells Dromio,

> There's not a man I meet but doth salute me
> As if I were their well-acquainted friend,
> And everyone doth call me by my name.
> Some tender money to me, some invite me,
> Some other give me thanks for kindnesses.
> Some offer me commodities to buy. (4.3.1–6)

It is no wonder that Balthasar's warning against possible damage to Antipholus of Ephesus's social reputation struck such a chord. His identity is clearly constituted by his position within a series of overlapping mercantile and friendship networks. Thus the props of chain and rope that haunt the twins not only hold together the play's increasingly tortuous plot but also come to symbolize the bonds that bind Ephesian society. To begin, the chain represents the union of marriage between Antiopholus of Ephesus and Luciana; Luciana tells

Adriana "you know he promised me a chain" (2.1.107). However, on being shut out of his own house, Antipholus announces that he will instead give the chain to the hostess of the Porcupine:

> That chain will I bestow—
> Be it nothing but to spite my wife—
> Upon mine hostess there. (3.1.118–20)

Luciana is now to be presented with a "rope's end" (4.1.16), suggestive of her future punishment, but also an image of their broken relationship. In its movements throughout the play the chain also becomes implicated in Antipholus's business relationships. Thus Angelo explains to the merchant,

> Even so the sum that I do owe to you
> Is growing to me by Antipholus,
> And in the instant that I met with you
> He had of me a chain. (4.1.7–10)

The chain is bound up in the systems of credit that underpin the economic life of Ephesus. It is, moreover, not only an object in these negotiations but, as in its role in the exchanges between Antipholus, Adriana, and the hostess of the Porcupine, itself also a potent symbol of the bonds of trust that sustain the mercantile networks of the city. This point is made explicitly by Antipholus of Ephesus when he complains to Angelo,

> You promisèd your presence and the chain,
> But neither chain nor goldsmith came to me.
> Belike you thought our love would last too long
> If it were chained together, and therefore came not. (4.1.23–26)

As it literally travels from individual to individual, the chain embodies the profoundly social and, indeed, incorporated nature of the self in Ephesian life.

The comedy thus privileges a particularly social subjectivity, concluding appropriately enough, with a baptismal feast that celebrates the individual's place in the Christian community of the Church. Such an emphasis on community, of course, not only would have been entirely appropriate to the Inns but must also have been especially resonant in the institutional context of the revels. Moreover, of all the relationships explored in the play, it is fraternity, the bond of brotherhood, which seems to be the most potent. The primary force of the comic plot in *The Comedy of Errors* is not toward the conventional resolution of marriage, but toward the reunion of the two pairs of twins. It is, Egeon tells the Duke, primarily curiosity about his brother that inspires Antipholus of Syracuse to leave his home country:

> My youngest boy, and yet my eldest care,
> At eighteen years became inquisitive
> After his brother, and importuned me
> That his attendant—for his case was like,
> Reft of his brother, but retained his name—
> Might bear him company in the quest of him. (1.1.123–28)

It should then, perhaps, not come as a surprise that the main focus of the final scene of the play is the reestablishment of fraternal relationships. Indeed, the plot lines concerning the Antipholus twins' relationships with Luciana and Adriana are left inconclusive. No words at all are passed between Antipholus of Ephesus and Adriana after the confusion is resolved and while Antipholus of Syracuse's relationship with Luciana might seem more hopeful, his marriage proposal, "What I told you then / I hope I shall have leisure to make good" (5.1.376–77), is left unanswered. Shakespeare leaves these marriages hanging in the balance and turns the audience's attention decisively to the brothers as Antipholus of Syracuse tells his Dromio, "Embrace thy brother there. Rejoice with him" (5.1.415). It is then with an affirmation of fraternity that the errors of the play are resolved and the twins' identities finally restored:

> We came into the world like brother and brother,
> And now let's go hand in hand, not one before another. (5.1.427–28)

Such a celebration of fraternity would have been nowhere more appropriate than the Inns of Court. The vocabulary of brotherhood lay at the heart of the corporate language used by companies such as the city guilds, the merchant companies, and of course, the inns. Thus in guild and mayoral entertainments the trope of fraternity was always extremely prominent. Middleton's 1623 mayoral entertainment "The Triumphs of Integrity," for example, concludes with Integrity telling the assembled Drapers,

> May all succeeding honoured brothers be
> With as much love brought home as thine brings thee.[32]

Given that the revels were predicated on giving expression to the inns corporate existence, *The Comedy of Errors*'s final image of fraternity would have celebrated the very ethos of the *Gesta Grayorum*: an extended performance of institutional identity.

* * *

Situating Shakespeare's comedy in the broader performance culture of the revels, then, brings into focus the play's dramatization of the revels' concern with "taking part." Intriguingly, there is evidence that this is not just the case for later critics, whose temporal distance can make identifying thematic coherence a much easier, indeed one might say, temptingly inevitable, process, but that the inns audience too were sensitive to the affinities between the performance of the play and their revels. Thus in looking back over the chaos with which the Innocents' Night festivities opened and the performance of the play with which it closed, the description of the revels concludes: "So that Night was begun, and continued to the end, in nothing but Confusion and Errors; whereupon, it was ever afterwards called, *The Night of Errors*" (32).³³ The play *The Comedy of Errors* and the performance context of the revels are effectively merged into one extended performance. In other words, the audience of revellers themselves, in what seems to be a self-conscious recognition of both the resonances emerging between Shakespeare's comedy and the *Gesta Grayorum* and the complex relationship between observing and performing generated by the occasion, became engaged in the witty activity of eliding the gap between actor and audience, play and revels.³⁴

It seems, moreover, especially fitting that it is the concept of "error" that the revellers pick up on. In its alternative sense of "to wander," this term is, indeed, entirely fitting for a play in which at least half of the central characters have left their homes only to, quite literally, "wander in illusions" (4.3.43). And erroneous wandering also has resonance for the *Gesta Grayorum* in which the revellers have not only quite literally wandered from their seats but are, throughout the performance of the revels, pushing against the boundaries of artistic, social, and legal decorum. In both play and revels, however, it is precisely through this "wandering" that identity is reaffirmed. It is only in leaving their home country of Syracuse that the twins can discover new familial, social, and crucially, fraternal identities. Meanwhile, it is taking part in the Night of Errors in the Kingdom of Purpoole, both as actors and audience, which opens up new social and professional roles for the revellers.

Notes

I would like to thank Jennifer Low, Nova Myhill, and the participants in the seminar on Audiences at the SAA meeting in 2009 where this work was first presented. Their comments and discussion were crucial in developing my ideas. Peter McCullough, Michelle O'Callaghan, and Gillian Woods read drafts and provided extremely helpful thoughts and guidance. I am very grateful to Bradin Cormack and Lorna Hutson for sharing their work with me before publication.

1. Desmond Bland, ed., *Gesta Grayorum: or The History of The High and Mighty Prince Henry Prince of Purpoole*, English Reprints 22 (Liverpool, UK: Liverpool University Press, 1968), 31. All subsequent quotations from the revels are from this edition, incorporated into the text.
2. As Philip Finkelpearl points out, *revelling* was a term used in the period to refer to a whole range of activities, such as singing, dancing, making music, and performing various rituals associated with communal life in the inns, which would take place at a number of points throughout the year such as, for example, the Reader's feast. Philip J. Finkelpearl, *John Marston of the Middle Temple: An Elizabethan Dramatist in His Social Setting* (Cambridge, MA: Harvard University Press, 1969), 32–34. For discussion of the revels, see also Desmond Bland, ed., introduction to *Gesta Grayorum*; A. Wigfall Green, *The Inns of Court and Early English Drama* (London: Oxford University Press, 1931); Michelle O'Callaghan, *The English Wits: Literature and Sociability in Early Modern England* (Cambridge: Cambridge University Press, 2007); and Paul Raffield, *Images and Culture of Law in Early Modern England: Justice and Political Power, 1558–1660* (Cambridge: Cambridge University Press, 2004).
3. For a discussion of this text, see Bland, *Gesta Grayroum*, ix–xii.
4. David Bergeron's description of the multiple stages and audiences, which constituted Elizabeth I's royal entry and the dynamic, charismatic relationship that emerged between the queen (in her role as actor and audience) and the crowd (a participating audience), is entirely comparable with the many participating audiences in the *Gesta Grayorum*. See Chapter 7, "Charismatic Audiences: A 1559 Pageant."
5. Margaret Knapp and Michal Kobialka, "Shakespeare and the Prince of Purpoole: The 1594 Production of *The Comedy of Errors* at Gray's Inn Hall," *Theatre History Studies* 4 (1984): 70–81. On Shakespeare's stagecraft in *The Comedy of Errors* and in particular his use of space as it influenced the role of the audience, see Jennifer Low, "Door Number Three? Time, Space, and Audience Experience in *The Menaechmi* and *The Comedy of Errors*" in Chapter 4.
6. Reginald J. Fletcher, ed., *The Pension Book of Gray's Inn* (London: Printed at the Chiswick Press and published by order of the Masters of the Bench, 1901), 1:87.
7. On Crew, see Maija Jansson, "Sir Thomas Crewe (1566–1634)," in *Oxford Dictionary of National Biography*, ed. H. C. G. Matthew and Brian Harrison (Oxford: Oxford University Press, 2004).
8. Tiffany Stern, "Taking Part: Actors and Audience on the Stage at Blackfriars," in *Inside Shakespeare: Essays on the Blackfriars Stage*, ed. Paul Menzer (Selinsgrove, PA: Susquehanna University Press, 2006), 35–53, esp. 48.
9. On the pervasive, and sometimes indiscriminate, use of the term "theatricality" in studies of Renaissance England, see Thomas Postlewait, "Theatricality and Antitheatricality in Renaissance London," in *Theatricality*, ed. Tracy C. Davis and Thomas Postlewait (Cambridge: Cambridge University Press, 2003), 90–126.
10. William Shakespeare, *The Comedy of Errors*, ed. Charles Whitworth, *The Oxford Shakespeare* (Oxford: Oxford University Press, 2002), 5.1.237–40. All subsequent references to the play will be to this edition. Parenthetical references are to act, scene, and lines and are incorporated into the text.
11. Simon Palfrey and Tiffany Stern, *Shakespeare in Parts* (Oxford: Oxford University Press, 2007), 40–45. Palfrey and Stern are using the term *part* in the sense

of the written piece of paper that an actor would be given including his (and only his) speeches and cues. Andrew Gurr, *The Shakespearean Stage, 1574–1642*, 3rd ed. (Cambridge: Cambridge University Press, 1992), 99–100. See also Erika T. Lin, "'Lord of thy Presence': Bodies, Performance, and Audience Interpretation in Shakespeare's *King John*" in Chapter 6. As Lin explains, the process of "personation" involved actors becoming "physical incarnations" of the characters they were playing.

12. This seems, most likely, to have been Thomas Lambert, who was called to the bar in 1599 and called to the Grand Company in 1613. Fletcher, *Pension Book*, 1:142, 202.
13. Bland, *Gesta Grayorum*, 57, 101. The image of Helmes's signature in the Admissions Register is reproduced in Bland, *Gesta Grayorum*, x.
14. Charles Henry Hopwood, ed., *Middle Temple Records* (London: Published by the Order to the Masters of the Bench, 1904), 1:303–4. The episode is discussed in Finkelpearl, *John Marston*, 40. Again, there is a clear analogy with the "fiction-reality axis" that Bergeron identifies in Elizabeth I's royal entry in Chapter 7.
15. Bland estimates there would have been at least 140 participants in the revels. *Gesta Grayorum*, xiv.
16. For biographical information on William Holt, see Wilfrid R. Prest, *The Rise of the Barrister: A Social History of the English Bar, 1590–1640* (Oxford: Clarendon Press, 1991), 370.
17. On the relationship between leisure and pedagogy at the inns, see O'Callaghan, *The English Wits*, 23–27. On the revels as an opportunity to master the arts of courtly display, see also Douglas Lanier, "'Stigmatical in Making': The Material Character of *The Comedy of Errors*," in *The Comedy of Errors: Critical Essays*, ed. Robert S. Miola (New York: Routledge, 2001), 299–334, esp. 319–21.
18. Edward Waterhouse, *Fortescutus Illustratus* (London: 1663), 546.
19. Finkelpearl discusses the importance of "intramural jokes and local personalities" in the Middle Temple "Prince D'Amour Revels" of 1597–98 in *John Marston*, 52–55.
20. William Shakespeare, *Hamlet*, ed. Ann Thompson and Neil Taylor, The Arden Shakespeare, 3rd ser. (London: Arden Shakespeare, 2006), 3.2.99–100.
21. Tiffany Stern, *Making Shakespeare: From Stage to Page* (Abingdon: Routledge, 2004), 75–76. See also Peter Hyland's discussion of the relationships between actors and their roles in "Face/Off: Some Speculations on Elizabethan Acting," *Shakespeare Bulletin* 24, no. 2 (2006): 21–29.
22. Bland, *Gesta Grayorum*, xviii–xix.
23. O'Callaghan, *The English Wits*, 10.
24. Ibid., 24. As Bradin Cormack's work demonstrates, moreover, this assertion of communal identity was also bound up with issues of authority and governance. Thus Cormack convincingly argues that the revels need to be conceived of as a "jurisdictional exercise" that functioned to assert the inns' authority as self-regulating associations, and demonstrates how the revels performed both office and territory to stage the inn's self-governing status. Bradin Cormack, "Locating *The Comedy of Errors*: Revels Jurisdiction at the Inns of Court," in *The Intellectual and Cultural World of the Early Modern Inns of Court*, ed. Jayne Archer, Elizabeth Goldring, and Sarah Knight (Manchester: Manchester University Press, forthcoming). On the importance of the inns' corporate identity, see also Raffield, *Images and Cultures*.

25. For important recent work on legal modes of thought in *The Comedy of Errors*, see Cormack, "*Comedy of Errors*" and Lorna Hutson, "The Evidential Plot: Shakespeare and Gascoigne at Gray's Inn," in *The Intellectual and Cultural World of the Early Modern Inns of Court*, ed. Jayne Archer, Elizabeth Goldring, and Sarah Knight (Manchester: Manchester University Press, forthcoming), and Lorna Hutson, *The Invention of Suspicion: Law and Mimesis in Shakespeare and Renaissance Drama* (Oxford: Oxford University Press, 2007), esp. 147–57. For readings of *The Comedy of Errors* in the specific context of the *Gesta Grayorum*, see also Maureen Godman, "'Plucking a Crow' in *The Comedy of Errors*," *Early Theatre* 8, no. 1 (2005): 53–68; Lanier, "'Stigmatical in Making,'" 322–23; and Robert S. Miola, "The Play and the Critics," in *The Comedy of Errors: Critical Essays*, ed. Robert S. Miola (New York: Routledge, 2001), 1–51, esp. 28–29.
26. Eamon Grennan, "Arm and Sleeve: Nature and Custom in *The Comedy of Errors*," *Philological Quarterly* 59, no. 2 (1980): 150–64.
27. The case for the play being written specifically for performance at Gray's Inn is made by Charles Whitworth in his introduction to *The Comedy of Errors*, 1–10. An alternative perspective is offered by David Bevington, who argues that Shakespeare's stagecraft may well have been influenced by the requirement for the play to be performed in a variety of different locations. See "*The Comedy of Errors* in the Context of the Late 1580s and Early 1590s," in *The Comedy of Errors: Critical Essays*, ed. Robert S. Miola (New York: Routledge, 2001), 335–53, esp. 348–49.
28. Mark Bayer's essay in Chapter 3, "The Curious Case of the Two Audiences: Thomas Dekker's *Match Me in London*" offers a comparable reading of how different aspects of a play might emerge in performance before particular audiences.
29. Arthur Marotti, *John Donne, Coterie Poet* (London: University of Wisconsin Press, 1986), 26.
30. Laurie Maguire, "The Girls from Ephesus," in *The Comedy of Errors: Critical Essays*, ed. Robert S. Miola (New York: Routledge, 2001), 355–91, esp. 382.
31. As Laurie Maguire explains, these words are ambiguous and may be taken as "a termination of a relationship, a salacious reminiscence, or a genuine expression of gratitude." Ibid., 371.
32. Thomas Middleton, "The Triumphs of Integrity," ed. David M. Bergeron in *Thomas Middleton: The Collected Works*, ed. Gary Taylor and John Lavagnino (Oxford: Oxford University Press, 2007), ll. 309–10. See also Peter McCullough's discussion of Donne's play on brotherhood in his sermon at the funeral of Sir William Cokayne. "Preaching and Context: John Donne's Sermon at the Funerals of Sir William Cokayne" in *The Oxford Handbook of the Early Modern Sermon*, ed. Peter McCullough, Hugh Adlington, and Emma Rhatigan (Oxford: Oxford University Press, forthcoming).
33. As Robert S. Miola notes, the phrase "comedy of errors" soon became a common expression. "The Play and the Critics," 4. See also John Munro, ed., *The Shakespeare Allusion Book*, 2 vols (London: Humphrey Milford, 1932).
34. Cormack draws attention to the way in which the fit between Shakespeare's play and the "Night of Revels" is so neat that there is a strong suggestion that the disruption on Innocent's Night was itself a staged event. "*Comedy of Errors*." See also Ann Hurley, "Interruption: The Transformation of a Critical Feature of Ritual from Revel

to Lyric in John Donne's Inns of Court Poetry of the 1590s," in *Ceremony and Text in the Renaissance*, ed. Douglas F. Rutledge (London: Associated University Presses, 1996), 103–22. As Hurley points out, the 1597–98 Middle Temple revels feature a comparable interruption when the embassy from Lincoln's Inn have to leave abruptly because there is not enough room. See Benjamin Rudyerd, *Le Prince D'Amour or The Prince of Love* (London, 1660), 88.

CHAPTER 9

Bleared Vision in
The Taming of the Shrew

James Wells

A fixture of recent work on Shakespeare's audience is the insistence that non-naturalist techniques of early modern acting coupled with the technological limitations of the stage hindered the theater's power to create realistic illusions. In his recent work on audience response, Jeremy Lopez implies that our awareness of a non-naturalistic theater would have surprised neither playwrights nor the audience in Shakespeare's day, claiming that "the drama and its audience were very much aware of the limitations of the early modern stage, and that the potential for dramatic representations to be ridiculous or inefficient or incompetent was a constant and vital part of the audiences' experience of the plays."[1] If we can judge by the responses of our own time, critics and audiences on the whole have little problem with Shakespeare's visual and technological limits, finding as they do ample compensation in the language and action of his plays. *Henry V* might be considered an instance of this compensatory technique: the Chorus may complain about the wooden O's inability to hold "the casques / That did affright the fields at Agincourt," but the same poetry that complains of the theater's limitations and the unrivaled drama of political intrigue that follows the Chorus' apology beggar realistic spectacle.

However, to say that Shakespeare abandons illusion's verisimilitude in favor of linguistic accomplishment grossly oversimplifies the matter. As far back as 1984, David Bevington and others were analyzing Shakespeare's ability to create and complicate visual meaning.[2] Still, there are important differences between visual complexity and verisimilitude, which visually seems simple but experientially is complex. For an audience, a convincing and realistic illusion operates on an experiential division in which sense perception contradicts knowledge. Such complexity is central to *The Taming of the Shrew*, but it does not result from realistic illusion. In this play, Shakespeare recreates the experiential trickery of illusion through other means and in spite of forces that are explicitly working against illusion. He does so by creating onstage scenes that intensify the paradoxical experiences the audience undergoes by virtue of being in the theater. Central to *Shrew* is the paradox of character that results from the audience's being required perforce to carry out two opposing mental operations at the same time: (1) recognizing the actor as distinct from the character and (2) recognizing the actor as the character. In *Shrew*, Shakespeare intensifies this paradox by presenting a number of different scenarios that rehearse (and therefore exercise) the same faculty that allows audiences simultaneously to sustain the contrary possibilities of character and illusion. These scenarios generate false impressions of complementary kinds. In many cases, characters' real transformations turn out merely to be versions of the selves they already are. In a similar way, characters assume disguises that are less than fully distinguishable from the selves they supposedly conceal. At the same time, the real selves that are subject to disguise and transformation are themselves less stable and real than at first they would appear to be. These scenarios (and others similar to them in the play) create experiences like illusion, whereby audiences lose the spectacles they behold in the act of grasping them; yet paradoxically these scenarios provide a way of understanding the chronic difficulties inhabiting Kate's final speech.

In recent Shakespearean criticism, illusion has been noted for its power not just to fool audiences visually but also to beguile them politically. In her work on the connections between audience and actor, Bridget Escolme recounts how cultural materialist critics follow Bertolt Brecht in the assumption that realistic illusion charms audiences out of their natural defenses. Escolme quotes Brecht on this point: "Too much heightening of the illusion in the setting, together with a 'magnetic' way of acting that gives the spectator the illusion of being present at a fleeting, accidental, 'real' event, create such an impression of naturalism that one can no longer interpose one's judgement [*sic*], imagination, or reactions, and must simply conform by being one of 'nature's' objects."[3] The materialist critics quoted by Escolme judge Shakespeare's political merit in proportion to the extent to which he avoids the seductively disarming trappings of realism. Graham Holderness commends early modern theater because the audience was never "seduced by the oblivion of empathic illusion."[4] Like Holderness, Frances Barker admires the stage of Shakespeare's day inasmuch as the audience was "never captivated by the illusion because the spectacle never produced itself as other than it was."[5] Barker claims that those who malign the antirealist sensationalism of the Jacobean stage are "carrying out the belated cultural work of the bourgeois revolution."[6] By contrast, Catherine Belsey argues that the early modern theater presented a collision between an "emblematic mode [of presentation] and an emergent illusionism."[7] Together, these opposite forces were "capable of generating a radical uncertainty precisely by withholding from the spectator the single position from which a single and unified meaning is produced."[8] Thus, for materialists, early modern theater is an intermediate stage in the creation of the capitalist bourgeois myth of a unified self. In summary, Escolme holds that cultural materialists decry illusion as "productive of a unitary, self-contained and inward-looking subject."[9]

Although materialists may be correct about the political effects of illusion, their theory differs from what E. M Gombrich says about its psychological effect. Gombrich is well known among Shakespeareans primarily for his influence on Norman Rabkin's reading of *Henry V.* Unlike cultural materialists, Gombrich sees the mind under the influence of illusion to be at least as active as it is passive, as guarded as it is exposed. In the first place, Gombrich understands that the conspicuity cultural materialists praise as being particular to illusion in early modern theater to be a property of illusion in general, even the most realistic illusion. According to Gombrich, whatever effect of trompe l'oeil illusion achieves, "we are never tricked into mistaking the painting [of a seascape hanging on a museum wall] for an opening out into the real sea."[10] At a fundamental level, illusion may fool the eye, but it does not fool the mind. Although the idea is more speculative, Gombrich postulates that the faculty of the mind that allows us to mistake a collection of markings for a recognizable object is actually a defense mechanism—a "trigger" reaction that allows human animals to react to danger without having to make a full intellectual assessment.[11] If Gombrich is correct, then illusion does not lull its beholders so much as stimulate them.

However, the main "activity" of the mind experiencing illusion is one of simultaneity, where the mind entertains mutually exclusive propositions at the same time. Gombrich builds on Socrates's assertion about illusion in Plato's *Republic,* where he attempts to discredit poetic imitation for appealing to the irrational part of the mind by analogizing it in terms of the optical illusion created when one places a stick in a limpid pool:

> And the same things appear bent or straight to those who view them in water and out, or concave and convex owing to similar errors of vision about colour, and there is obviously every confusion of this sort in our souls. And so scene painting in its exploitation of this weakness of our nature falls nothing short of witchcraft, and so do jugglery and many other such contrivances . . . And did we not say that it is impossible to "hold contrary opinions about the same thing"?[12]

By contrast, Gombrich suggests that the problem of illusion is precisely what Socrates says is impossible: it requires us to hold "contrary opinions about the same thing."[13] Such a problem appears most clearly in his discussion of the "notoriously ambiguous inkblot" that can be read as either rabbit or duck but not both at once, which figures prominently in Rabkin's reading of *Henry V.*[14]

Although Gombrich and Rabkin both claim that it is impossible to experience both "alternative readings" of this illusion at once, the entirety of Rabkin's discussions of illusion suggest otherwise.[15] The illusion may be constructed so that it is impossible to see both rabbit and duck at the same time, but the point of the illusion as a whole is that we never leave off experiencing mutually exclusive possibilities at once. We may not be able to see both, but we continue experiencing one even when we no longer see it. The experience of this inkblot illustrates in a more involved way the contrary opinions that viewers have when they encounter any illusion, even a realistic one. Although Gombrich uses the word "opinion" to describe the mental state when encountering an illusion, "operation" or "faculty" seem better fits. "Opinion" suggests attitudes that are voluntary and subject to change, whereas the mind encountering an illusion is locked into carrying out two opposing operations for the entirety of the time it beholds the illusion. And these operations are best described in terms of recognition. The experience of an illusion requires that we simultaneously recognize what an illusion purports to be and that it is merely illusion. For all practical purposes, this experience of illusion as a paradox of recognition is identical to the experience of fictional mimesis in general—in which the mind must recognize the object being imitated and that the same object is merely an imitation. But more to the point, the experience parallels the paradox of dramatic character, which requires recognition of the actor as both identical with and distinct from the character he or she plays. Therefore, it is little wonder that, much to his frustration, Gombrich often has trouble separating art and illusion, even though he knows that they are not the same.

The Taming of the Shrew is especially conducive to discussions of the effect of illusion. At several points in the Induction, characters make reference to realist illusions or boast of mastery in creating them. The Lord compliments a visiting actor on a recently played role that "was aptly fitted and naturally performed" (Ind.1.86).[16] That same lord also speaks assuredly of his young page's ability to mimic feminine behavior: "I know the boy will well usurp the grace, / Voice, gait, and action of a gentlewoman" (Ind.1.130–31). Additionally, as evidence of Christopher Sly's new identity, the Lord and his servants describe pictures of Ovidian scenes so accomplished that one would swear they were real. As a matter of fact, the point of the Induction as a whole is to create a convincing illusion of nobility, or one at least convincing enough to fool Sly's less-than-formidable wit.

The play correlates illusion closely with deception, a theme that is perhaps best summarized by the idea of "supposes." In the play by that title, from which Shakespeare borrowed his comic subplot, George Gascoigne defines "supposes" as "nothing else but mistaking or imagination of one thing for another."[17] Although critics have since built on his reading, Cecil C. Seronsy's important essay shows how this theme of supposes unifies the Induction with the play's subplot and main plot.[18] Yet, while deception permeates the play, in large part, this deception is not practiced against the audience. Quite the contrary, the play takes great pains to make sure the audience is in on the joke.[19] In the Induction, we witness the Lord's meticulously crafted devices meant to fool Sly. We hear Tranio and Lucentio's plan to infiltrate Baptista's keep, and we even get to watch them assume their disguises. In two soliloquies, Petruchio expressly announces the artifices he will use to woo and is using to tame Kate. Arguably, we could have been taken in by Bianca's pretense of modesty, but if we have been paying careful attention to her interactions with her sister, Bianca's spirited resistance and bawdy retorts to her new husband should not come as a surprise. In these ways, the play is like many early modern plays that, as Andrew Gurr says, "begin with prologues and inductions [that] openly acknowledge that the play which follows is a fiction."[20]

Although the play may bring the audience into its confidence about the tactics its characters employ to deceive others, it affects the audience in a way that is very similar to deception, and, surprisingly, it does so in and by the very process of revealing these tactics to the audience. The case of Sly illustrates this ironic effect. The Induction is notable not just for the trick the Lord plays on the drunken tinker but for the lavish detail it includes as the Lord sets up his illusions. The Lord minutely specifies how to set up Sly's environment and how to dress his page as Sly's wife, going so far as to offer instructions on how to produce false tears. Once Sly's transformation is complete, the play does not try to deceive the audience. Sly and the page's former identities remain conspicuous even in their new roles: Sly maintains his habitual appetite for small beer even after the more refined delicacies of sack and conserves are offered. And the page, who may have perfected the manners of a gentlewoman, when asked, does not even put forth the energy to invent a name.

Yet, in the process of making the audience informed participants in Sly's deception, the play dupes them in a way that is almost identical to the one the Lord practices against Sly. This irony becomes clearer when we examine more closely what is funny about Sly. The humor in the Induction rests on two apparently absurd premises: first, that a person can instantly change internal identity simply because his external circumstances (what people call him, what he wears and consumes, and where he resides) have changed and, second, that a man can take seriously as the object of romantic pursuit an adolescent boy dressed in woman's finery. Yet these are two basic premises early modern theater audiences must have taken seriously if they were to participate in the theater at all. In other words, for an audience to fully apprehend Christopher Sly as deluded lord, it must reject the very assumptions that allow it to apprehend Christopher Sly as deluded lord or any other character in this or any other play. Thus the

Induction divides the experience of participating audience members precisely between accepting and rejecting what they behold on stage, creating a situation whereby acceptance is already a form of rejection and rejection the form of acceptance the play necessitates. However, this paradoxical experience of acceptance and rejection is identical to the one that the audience is already having by virtue of being in the theater at all. To experience theater requires audiences simultaneously to accept the figures on stage as real and to reject them as mere artifice. Through Sly, the Induction presents an intensification of an experience of acceptance and rejection that theater audiences are already undergoing when the play begins.

Maynard Mack's terms "engagement" and "detachment" might best apply to what audiences are doing in the theater in general and in an intensified form with Sly. For Mack, the first term applies to those moments in Shakespeare's plays that compel us to suspend disbelief and the second to those that repel us by reminding us that drama is mere artifice. To illustrate the dynamics between these necessary components of theater, Mack points to Sly. The tinker's state of having been literally "engulfed" by the Lord's theatrical event reflects audience engagement in its most pure form, and the drowsy boredom with which he regards the play proper embodies detachment.[21] Although Mack is the characteristically attentive critic here that he is in all his work, he seems to overlook two things: first, that an instance might simultaneous engage and repel the audience and, second, that in drama, participating audience members are already fixed in permanent states of engagement and detachment at the same time. A given moment in any play may arouse one of these opposing experiential states. However, the phenomenon of Sly involves both states at once. When the audience must reject what it normally accepts to experience the scene it beholds, it becomes more firmly fixed in the paradoxical state of engagement and detachment. Yet this state intensifies an experience the audience would already be having with Sly, whereby the detaching presence of the actor on whom the experience of the character depends limits the engagement that must take place.

Therefore, through the experience of Christopher Sly, the play complicates the question of what the audience is looking at. On one level, the audience is seeing what it always sees: a character in a play whose identity is formed by external circumstance and who might reasonably find a character played by an adolescent boy in woman's clothing fit for romantic pursuit. But by having the audience reject its familiar experience, the play is rendering the familiar obscure by making it essentially unrecognizable as such. The play has hidden the rules that govern the dramatic character by exposing them in the broad light of day (or "with the lights on," with a nod to the slogan of Ralph Cohen's new Blackfriars Theater in

Staunton, Virginia). In this way, Shakespeare has used the conditions of being a spectator to destabilize further an already unstable position.

A third comic element in the phenomenon of Sly reproduces onstage another quality of the audience's experience of characters: the states of partial obscurity into which character and actor reciprocally cast each other. Although Sly may eagerly embrace his new role as a character in the Lord's drama in which he unwittingly participates, the presence of the actor behind the character continuously disrupts the performance and continues to provide humor throughout the second part of the Induction. But once again, the comic merely exaggerates what is normal for the audience. In order to experience dramatic fiction, the audience must look at actors presenting characters while simultaneously looking beyond them in order that characters might be seen. Focusing too narrowly on actor or character has serious consequences for the audience. The presentational acting style of early modern theater might have shifted the balance toward the actor more completely than it is in theater today, but the audience still had to see beyond the actor if it was to experience a play at all. In Sly's case, the inability to subsume his old self into his new, even in the most meager way, is another parodic recreation of the experience of dramatic character, whereby, even in the most ideal circumstances, audience members can never fully and permanently transform actors into the characters they present.

The insistent presence of Sly's old self in his new role rehearses the problem of transformation from actor to character in an obvious way. However, even without the change, Sly's supposedly real identity plays on this problem in almost exactly the same way and brings into relief how a full coalescence of actor into character is impossible in the perception of the audience. When Sly's real identity is examined more closely, it does not look any more stable and secure than his new one as a lord. Under pressure to adopt the new self that the Lord's crew is foisting on him, Sly feebly bases his old identity on a series of shifting and transforming jobs that, by the more rigorous standards of the guild mentality of Shakespeare's day, rise only marginally to the level of "profession": "Am I not Christopher Sly, old Sly's son of Burton-heath, by birth a peddler, by education a cardmaker, by transmutation a bearherd, and now by present profession a tinker?" (Ind.2.17–20). Of the four, only "cardmaker" carries the authority of "profession," but that occupation belongs to a former version of the self, not the one we are currently viewing. His professional clout notwithstanding, Sly is defined more by what he lacks than what he owns, more by what he does not do than by what he does. He has never taken conserves and owns no more shoes than feet. The only proof he can muster for his old self is "Marian Hacket, the fat alewife of Wincot," who will know him by his debts: "If she say I am not fourteen pence on the score for sheer ale, score me up for the lyingest knave in Christendom" (Ind.2.21–23). Taken in light of an identity based on dearth, his blunder of being descended from "Richard Conqueror" might be called an unhappy coincidence that points to his and to the audience's persistent inability to find the identity that Sly supposedly embodies. The process by which Sly's attempts to establish identity only result in its loss serves, therefore, to intensify the common experience with dramatic character, wherein real identities evanesce even as they are brought into existence. Sly may be the one who is drunk, but our vision of him never achieves greater clarity than his alcoholic haze affords him of his own world.

The play places the audience in a similar state of not knowing exactly what it is looking at when the action shifts from the Induction to the play proper. Here, however, the predicament arises from taking a character seriously rather than from rejecting one as silly. The play presents Lucentio as the sympathetic protagonist in a romantic comedy, not, as it does with Sly, as the ludicrous object of farce. However, Lucentio continuously flouts the goodwill the audience extends him in treating him as a figure worthy of sympathy. At issue is the nature of Lucentio's disguise, particularly the question of whether his disguise really ever amounts to one. Lucentio's transformation into Bianca's tutor Cambio is more complicated than it first appears by virtue of being less complicated than a disguise should be. Disguise requires a certain distance between actor and assumed role, a marked distinction between the identity of the person assuming the disguise and the identity that that person assumes. By lowering his status and changing his clothes with his servant, Lucentio's plan to present himself as a scholar certainly meets the rule of discrepancy. Still, Lucentio's disguise recreates the self that he had just announced himself as being a mere two hundred lines earlier when he told Tranio that his reason for coming to Padua was "to institute a course of learning and ingenious study" and to learn virtue (1.1.8–9). Lucentio goes from being a scholar to disguising himself as one. In other words, Lucentio becomes what he supposedly already is and so creates the question of what the audience is actually looking at when it beholds Lucentio as "the young scholar" he will appear to be in most of the play (2.1.79). For the audience, if not for himself, Lucentio is and is not in disguise, or he is and is not what he has disguised himself as being, depending on how one looks at it. Although one might object to equating tutor and scholar, Gremio uses the latter term when introducing the person he believes is "Cambio" to Baptista. Plus, the decision to keep Lucentio's disguise and identity close to each other seems deliberate on Shakespeare's part. In Gascoigne's *Supposes*, the figure of Erostrato, on whom Lucentio is based, is disguised more generally as a servant.

The ease with which Lucentio gives up his identity only to reestablish it in another form casts new light on the process by which he establishes his identity in the first place and reveals that, as with Sly in the Induction, what we are looking at has been less than clear all along. The audience comes to know his identity as a scholar by way of the clumsy and wooden exposition that Lucentio delivers when he arrives on stage:

> Tranio, since for the great desire I had
> To see fair Padua, nursery of arts,
> I am arrived for fruitful Lombardy,
> The pleasant garden of great Italy;
> And by my father's love and leave am arm'd
> With his good will and thy good company,
> My trusty servant, well approved in all,
> Here let us breathe and haply institute
> A course of learning and ingenious studies.
> Pisa renownèd for grave citizens
> Gave me my being and my father first,
> A merchant of great traffic through the world,
> Vincentio come of Bentivolii.
> Vincentio's son brought up in Florence. (1.1.1–14)

It is first worth noting that the terms by which Lucentio announces his identity (his birth, lineage, provenance, and education) are identical to the ones on which Sly tries to establish his. And no sooner than Lucentio has finished, Tranio begins putting pressure on this identity in a way resembling the one the Lord and company use to coerce Sly out of his inveterately accepted self. Tranio entreats his master, "Let's be no stoics nor no stocks, I pray" (1.1.31). Significantly, Tranio does not suggest simply that Lucentio give up being a scholar but advises him to carry out his scholarly pursuits in ways that undermine that identity at its very core—in ways that, if put into practice, would make him decidedly not the self he presents himself as being. He instructs him to "balk logic with acquaintance that [he has], / And practice rhetoric in [his] common talk" (1.1.34–35). In effect, Tranio revises the definition of scholar to the point that it is no longer recognizable as such. Tranio's suggestion, like Lucentio's self-duplicating disguise, already threatens to divide Lucentio into being and not being the self that he is long before he changes identity. Furthermore, the speed with which Lucentio accedes to Tranio's advice ("Gramercies, Tranio, well dost thou advise") suggests that his purported identity as a scholar had been more hopeful (or even misleading) than real even before he abandons it (in part) to pursue Bianca (1.1.41). The verbs Lucentio uses to depict his anguish ("I burn, I pine, I perish") fit his general state as well as the consuming quality of his love for Bianca. His identity is undergoing a constant process of consumption—of burning, pining, perishing. Lucentio's decision to give up his identity completely to pursue Bianca merely fulfills a process that has been happening throughout the scene whereby his identity is constantly unraveling even it is stitched together. Yet at the moment Lucentio's identity is about to be discarded entirely, Shakespeare restores it through the back door, so to speak, and in a way that complicates rather than repairs it.

Lucentio's redoubled paradoxical state of having assumed a disguise that duplicates a real identity that was already shaky from the start offers an instance of *Shrew*'s principle of intensification such as we have seen before with Sly. When Lucentio assumes a disguise that is the same as his real identity, he dramatizes how in staged plays the methods for creating disguise and establishing real identity are virtually indistinguishable. Although this feature does not seem marked with meaning in *Shrew*, the play provides instances of the general function of drama whereby establishing identity is no more difficult than donning a disguise. Kate's shrewishness, for example, does not require a setup nearly as extensive as the one it offers for Lucentio's identity as a scholar. One word in the title combined with one line from Hortensio ("To cart her rather. She's too rough for me.") and a couple of stinging barbs from Kate are all it takes to establish Kate's identity as a shrew so fixedly that the audience finds the prospect of her reformation unlikely (1.1.55). Likewise, Bianca's character (at least in Lucentio's mistaken estimation) emerges essentially from her having done nothing—an absence that accrues meaning in the context of the row that revolves around her desirable "silence . . . and . . . sobriety" (1.1.71). In the experience of a play, self and disguise present themselves in the form of an irresolvable paradox. Something very much like disguise provides the occasion for identity, yet identity cannot be reduced merely to disguise. Dramatic character may be best defined as an experience in which the real self is a disguise. The instability created by Lucentio's doubling of disguise and self intensifies the general fragility that already exists in the way audience members experience the identity of the figures they behold in drama. Both the source and the effect of this intensification are the inability to discern in drama exactly what we are looking at. In other words, by making disguise and self virtually indistinguishable, the play takes a general condition of dramatic character, in which the audience cannot know exactly what it is looking at, and makes the experience more intense. In Chapter 6 in this collection, Erika Lin points out a similar conflict between the content of a play and the conditions of being a theater of in her discussion of the problem of resemblance in *King John*: "Bodily resemblance is thus *always* complicated by corporeal presence in the theatre: just as, within the dramatic representation, the appearance of Arthur's body deceives onstage spectators, in the actual playhouse, appearance necessarily belies lineage because onstage bodies are never actually who they purport to be" (122). In *King John*, characters are deeply concerned with and the action hinges on resemblances that are impossible to establish in a practical sense for the audience watching the play.

In a much more obvious way, the overt theatricality of Petruchio's wooing scheme raises irresolvable questions of what the audience is beholding, namely, by making it impossible to tell precisely how the two characters feel about each other. Before the wooing scene begins, Petruchio lays out his contrarian plan to treat Kate's resistance as the opposite of what it appears to be:

> Say that she rail, why then I'll tell her plain
> She sings as sweetly as a nightingale.
> Say that she frown, I'll say she looks as clear
> As morning roses newly washed with dew. (2.170–73)

Long before this speech, Petruchio has identified himself as a mercenary lover, one who will do anything to obtain a rich wife. Both these facts threaten to compromise the sincerity of anything Petruchio says in his attempts to woo her. In "Could Kate Mean What She Says?" Terrell Tebbetts claims that Petruchio's extravagant and evasive rhetoric in his stichomythic encounter with Kate qualifies as "non-referential language." Tebbetts uses the term to designate language that in no certain way reflects what the speaker feels.[22] Tebbetts does, however, point out a couple of key places in the wooing scene in which Petruchio moves out of the nonreferential register and back into direct speech: namely, his threat ("I swear I'll cuff you if you strike again") and his digression on her beauty ("For by this light, whereby I see thy beauty—Thy beauty that doth make me like thee well") (2.1.220, 270–71). Tebbetts's observations are certainly appealing. It is true that the rules of romantic comedy strongly drive the audience toward believing that the two main characters in the plot will fall for each other despite the impediments posed by others or themselves. Nonetheless, the play raises real questions because those exceptional moments when Petruchio supposedly breaks out of acting still conform precisely to the plan that he has laid out. Petruchio's announcement of his own theatricality has made it difficult to know when he is being sincere and impossible for the audience to say exactly what it is looking at.

Petruchio's device for convincing Baptista of his successful wooing presents an on-stage instance of the larger way the play as a whole has been creating illusion's irresolvable complexity at the moment it exposes the mechanisms of illusion. When Petruchio tells her father that the two of them "have 'greed so well together / That upon Sunday is the wedding day," Kate threatens to topple his whole enterprise by vowing, "I'll see thee hanged on Sunday first" (2.1.294–96). Petruchio is able to score a coup by claiming, "'Tis bargain twixt us twain, being alone, / That she shall still be curst in company" (2.1.302–3). What Petruchio does to Kate is the same as what Lucentio has earlier done to himself; he has remade Kate's formerly real identity into mere disguise. And his scheme's effect on their in-play audience is the same bafflement the play has elsewhere extended to the theater audience. Kate's silence indicates that she is dumbfounded—for what could she say in objection that would not merely reinforce Petruchio's claim about their private agreement? In order to sell the scheme to what must be an incredulous Baptista, Petruchio must resort to paradoxical logic: "I tell you, 'tis incredible to believe / How much she loves me" (2.1.204–305). Although Baptista assents, his response, "I know not what to say," should be taken as more than mere convention (2.1.316). It fittingly articulates the inability to know how to respond when one beholds a spectacle that is incredible to believe.

It should be of little surprise that when he moves from wooing Kate to taming her, Petruchio employs a similar strategy for obscuring what otherwise seems clear. This kind of blearing, or blurring, is the result of Petruchio's treating a perfectly acceptable household (i.e., food, bed, and clothing) as if it is unsatisfactory in a way that converts "kindness" into pain (4.1.196). When Kate complains to Grumio about her lack of food and rest, she claims that what "spites" her more than all "these wants" is how Petruchio deprives her "under name of perfect love, / As who should say, if I should sleep or eat / 'Twere deadly sickness or else present death" (4.3.11–14). What Petruchio has been able to do is set up an environment that is (to use a word he uses to describe himself) "peremptory" because Kate is unable to confirm what should be obvious: that her new husband is mistreating her. It is not so much that she believes Petruchio's protection is sincere as that she cannot think of how to argue against it.

The method Petruchio chooses to test his taming provides an explicit instance of the question "What are you looking at?" As proof of her subservience, Petruchio prompts Kate to ask this very question when he contradicts reality by calling the sun the moon. However, Kate's responses in this scene transfer the question of what one is looking at from Kate to Petruchio and ultimately to the audience. This transmission takes place because Kate gives Petruchio what might be considered a surplus of obedience. The surplus is subtle at first, but it becomes more obvious as the scene progress. When he insists, "I say it is the sun," Kate responds, "I know it is the sun" (4.5.16). Although she appears to agree, the form of her agreement preserves the authority of her disagreement that she initially reinforced by distinguishing between assertion and knowledge:

PETRUCHIO. I say it is the moon that shines so bright
KATE. I know it is the sun that shines so bright. (4.5.4–5)

The same surplus defines her response to his sudden reversal to calling the sun what it is: "Then God be blessed, it is the blessèd sun, / But sun it is not when you say it is not / And the moon changes even as your mind" (4.5.18–20). In her response, Kate not only agrees but goes a step further in granting Petruchio the absolute power to change the environment at a whim. But at the same time, she obliquely implies that Petruchio is both capricious and perhaps delusional in the way he whimsically ignores reality. Thus, she grants him authority in a way that, if viewed too closely, negates the authority it provides. Therefore, Petruchio resolves his question of his wife's obedience not so much on his ability to confirm that Kate is agreeing with him as he does on his inability to confirm that she is disagreeing with him. In this way, Kate is able to place Petruchio in the same position he had placed her when she was unable to mount an argument against a treatment she knew to be wrong. It is little wonder that Petruchio orders another test when Vincentio appears. In this test, in which Petruchio moves his wife to call Vincentio a woman and then retract her claim, Kate offers the same surplus of obedience and oblique compliance that defies her husband's efforts to confirm that she is not doing what she asked: "Pardon, old father, my mistaking eyes, / That have been so bedazzled by the sun / That everything I look on seemeth green" (4.5.44–46). She certainly retracts her claim and blames herself, but does naming the bedazzling sun as the fault for her mistake yield to Petruchio's earlier authority (Was it the sun or the moon at last count?) or assert her own?

Of course, the audience begins experiencing the question of what it is looking at the same instant that Kate does. For sun it is not, or moon it is not, until someone—a character, an author, a stage direction—calls it one way or the other or until the presence or absence of sun or moon becomes significant in the play.[23] Once Petruchio asserts and denies the moon's presence, he doubles the process by which the illusion of sunlight is created, even on a sunlit stage, and complicates the provenance of all fictional light. For the original audience, there would have been an additional layer to the joke, assuming that the Theater, like the Globe, was equipped with a "heavens" on which both sun and moon would have been painted. In this case, the audience would have been unable to deny the accuracy of Petruchio's claims about the moon shining above. Even so, it is safe to say that when Petruchio begins his test, audiences then and now are for this moment, as they are at so many other times in the play, left staring into space, unable to discern exactly what they might be looking at, even as it is being pointed out to them.

The hope here is that moments of confusion such as the one produced in Petruchio's test shed their own bedazzling light on the resolutions to the main plot and subplot. The lead-up to the climax has not gotten as much attention as the debate between Kate and Petruchio. The climax of the comic subplot pursues the idea of self as disguise in the most conspicuous way so far. Upon arriving in Padua, and inadvertently threatening to thwart his son's scheme to marry Bianca, the real Vincentio is unable to establish his real identity as Lucentio's father. Like so many other characters, Vincentio has been cast into an environment that is hostile to his real identity and effectively converts the real self into a disguise. Petruchio calls Vincentio's claim to his real identity "flat knavery," and the always-loquacious Tranio accuses Lucentio's father of being mad (5.1.35). With the exception of Grumio, the entire company believes Vincentio is falsifying his true identity. Although Grumio, who is much foxier than a pantaloon should be, correctly discerns the "right Vincentio" when pressed by Lucentio, he too must confess that he does not "dare" to "swear" Vincentio is the real one. As is customary for comedy, the issues of plot and identity are resolved by Lucentio's apparently divine deliverance:

> Here's Lucentio,
> Right son to the right Vincentio,
> That have by marriage made thy daughter mine,
> While counterfeit supposes bleared thine eyne. (5.1.107–110)

Yet this resolution is less than complete. Vincentio is wholly unsatisfied by Lucentio's explanation, as he is by his subsequent appeal that "love wrought these miracles": "I'll slit the villain's nose, that would have sent me to jail" (5.1.116, 123–24). Baptista and the rest of the Minola party leave the stage in a clamor, and resolution, to the extent that it occurs, happens in the significantly less tricky world offstage.

Vincentio's dissatisfaction anticipates the inadequacy of "supposes" as an explanation for the play's psychological trickery, for there are more than supposes that are blearing the audience's eyes. "Supposes," as mistaken identity, depend on a stable point of reference. For a "suppose" to work, there must be a fixed identity from which deception originates. To borrow Gasgoigne's language, the "one thing" that the imagination must mistake "for another" must have a certain degree of fixity before mistaking can take place. Yet *Shrew* repeatedly undermines the stability of references through duplication (in which the disguise and self are the same) and erasure (in which the self who animates the object of a "suppose" never materializes). Yes, characters get mistaken, but what they were before and what they become after complicate the very idea of supposes on which the play's action and resolution depend.

The problems of duplication and erasure that are inherent in the paradox of the self as disguise form a powerful context for understanding the chronic and most contentious problem of the play: the sincerity of Kate's final speech. The play has presented a series of characters for whom the real self is rendered a disguise. Although Kate is not in disguise, the perennial and seemingly irresolvable debate over her sincerity at the end of the play is in many ways an effect of witnessing a phenomenon in which the self and disguise cannot be distinguished. In the same way that Petruchio earlier presented Kate's "real" shrewish self as a disguise, his presentation of Kate as an obedient wife duplicates the ambiguity of the self as disguise. Those who assert that Kate is sincere at the end are correct when they point out that nothing Kate says in her speech or that she does after presenting it confirms irony. In other words, the speech contains sincerity. By the same token, those who distrust her can cite a clear separation of her self from the role that she plays in the scenes leading up to the finale, in which Kate makes assertions she does not appear to believe. Yet the play undermines the doubt it provokes by the very method it uses to provoke it. In the sun/moon test, Kate's surplus of obedience creates doubt about whether her compliance reflects her real self. However, in the next scene, where Kate hesitates to kiss Petruchio in public and he threatens to take her home once again, her surplus of obedience suggests that her compliance comes from the real self: "Nay, I will give thee a kiss. Now prithee, love, stay" (5.1.140–41). By calling Petruchio "love," Kate once again gives him more than he asks for and suggests that she has real affection for the man she kisses. In other words, the evidence for the true self and the evidence against it arise from the same place. The effect of this paradox is identical to that of the self as disguise, in which the same actions point in opposite directions. The upshot of Kate as a realization of the self as disguise is that her words, even if spoken sincerely, can never be tied to her with surety. As a matter of fact, this paradox has a self-negating effect: the more sincerely Kate performs her role at the end of the play, the more she generates the suspicion that she might be other than sincere.

For Kate, as for other characters in the play, the paradox of the self as disguise is an intensification of the larger paradox of theatrical illusion. In "Induction and Inference," Barry Weller notes how the theatrical medium itself as presented in *Shrew* prevents us from achieving fixity in Kate's final speech. Weller argues that "[i]naccessibility to psychological investigation becomes the essence of the theatrical situation and, strangely enough, uncertainty about motive and character does not impoverish the play but protects it from reductiveness."[24] A corollary to Weller's argument is that Kate remains inscrutable at the end because she has reproduced the conditions of being a character in a play for whom self and disguise are one and the same. Like all characters in the experience of the audience, to borrow from Weller, Kate "opens up the possibility that she is just acting and teases us with the metaphysical impossibility in theatre that appearance and reality can ever coincide."[25] Yet, in an altogether different sense, appearance (as in mere appearance) coincides perfectly with Kate's reality at the end because as a dramatic character she must embody both or her reality can never be more than appearance.

Other critics have noted the instability of Kate's identity at the end of the play and have related it to theater in similar ways. Michael Shapiro has argued that the audience's metatheatrical awareness of the cross-dressed page in the Induction undermines the certainty of Kate's "demonstration of obedience" in the final act.[26] Although Shapiro's central point is accurate, the popular term "metatheatrical" does not account for the phenomenon I'm describing here inasmuch as the concept usually requires and posits an awareness or reminder that we are watching a play. On a fundamental level, the audience is always aware that it is watching a play. This general fact is even more pronounced in the unavoidably exposed theater for which *The Taming of the Shrew* was created. More important, the intensification of the experiential paradoxes of dramatic character does not require such reminders. In fact, depending on the level of interruption, were the action of a play continually reminding us that it was merely a play, it could negate these intensified effects. A fitting analogy for the experiential intensification of the play is sensual or erotic stimulation. Not only are reminders unnecessary for those experiences, they can also be real turn-offs. Shakespeare is able to stoke experiences central to the audience by recreating them in other forms often more suggestive than overt. What is more, Shakespeare generates these experiences in a theater in which the atmosphere seems hostile to them.

The inability of Kate to prove herself sincere points up another self-negating quality of realistic illusion that Shakespeare is invoking at the end of play. The closer illusion comes to duplicating reality, the more it reinforces its status as artifice. The play actually provides instances of this effect in the absent paintings the Lord proffers as evidence of Sly's noble status. In these paintings, brooks run, sedges wave in the wind, blood drips, and tears fall. The general point of the paintings is to convince Sly of the reality of his incredible environment by appealing to a verisimilitude that could only exist in art of the finest quality. However, the combination of crisp detail and energetic movement in the pictures suggests another pertinent meaning. This combination implies counterintuitively that attaining a certain degree of illusory realism actually leads away from clarity and toward opacity because it prevents the viewer from fixing on what should become clearer as an illusion becomes more realistic. Shakespeare has achieved this ironic effect in Kate's final speech. Like a running brook in a painting, Kate constantly moves even as we fix upon her. In this way, the experience of Kate for the audience resembles the one produced in Lucentio upon first seeing Bianca, when Tranio politely reminds his master of the condition that Baptista had placed upon Bianca's eligibility: "You looked so longly on the maid / Perhaps you marked not what's the pith of all" (1.1.166–67). In the case of Kate's final speech, the longer we look, the less pith we mark. This is the paradoxical nature of realistic illusion, and Shakespeare creates this experience even though the limitations and conventions of his theater mean that such realistic illusions are no more available for the audience than they are for Sly.

For an image of how the theater audience experiences Kate's final speech, we can turn to her audience on stage. On one hand, Kate's audience is thoroughly convinced of her transformation from a shrew to a compliant wife. Even before her speech, Baptista offers Petruchio "[a]nother dowry to another daughter," claiming that Kate "is changed, as she had never been" (5.2.118–119). On the other hand, the word that is used to describe Kate's transformation is less certain than the sentiment it seems designed to convey. Lucentio twice calls Kate a "wonder": once when Kate first comes in obedience to her husband's call (5.2.110) and once after her speech, in the final line of the play. The term contains a certain internal tension insomuch as it suggests a kind of incredulity that comes from having to accept (or being unable to deny) something truly incredible. Lucentio, however, may not be the most trustworthy authority on the language of the supernatural, having earlier referred to his and Bianca's love using the related term "miracle" (5.1.116). Still, despite the poverty of Lucentio's judgment, the play provides no better word for capturing the paradoxical state the audience experiences when seeing a character who is disguised as herself and who, therefore, truly is incredible to believe.

Notes

1. Jeremy Lopez, *Theatrical Convention and Audience Response in Early Modern Drama* (Cambridge: Cambridge University Press, 2003), 2.
2. David Bevington, *Action is Eloquence: Shakespeare's Language of Gesture* (Cambridge, MA: Harvard University Press, 1984).
3. Bertold Brecht, "From the *Mother Courage* Model," in *Brecht on Theatre: The Development of an Aesthetic*, ed. and trans. John Willett (New York: Hill and Wang, 1964), 219, quoted in Bridget Escolme, *Talking to the Audience: Shakespeare, Performance, Self* (New York: Routledge, 2005), 11.
4. Graham Holderness, *Shakespeare's History* (Dublin: Gill and Macmillan, 1985), 212, quoted in Escolme, *Talking to the Audience*, 18.
5. Frances Barker, *The Tremulous Private Body* (1984; repr., Ann Arbor: University of Michigan Press, 1995), 17–18, quoted in Escolme, *Talking to the Audience*, 11.
6. Barker, *Tremulous Private Body*, 14.
7. Catherine Belsey, *The Subject of Tragedy: Identity and Difference in Renaissance Drama* (London: Methuen, 1985), 26.
8. Ibid., 28.
9. Escolme, *Talking to the Audience*, 11
10. E. H. Gombrich, "Illusion and Art," in *Illusion in Nature and Art*, ed. R. L. Gregory and E. H. Gombrich (New York: Charles Scribner's Sons, 1973), 194.
11. Ibid., 202–10.
12. Ibid., 193.
13. Ibid., 219.
14. Ibid., 221.
15. E. H.Gombrich, *Art and Illusion: A Study in the Psychology of Pictorial Representation* (1960; repr., Princeton, NJ: Princeton University Press, 2000), 205.
16. All citations of *The Taming of the Shrew* refer to Shakespeare, *The Taming of the Shrew*, in *The Complete Works of Shakespeare*, 6th ed., ed. David Bevington (New York: Pearson, 2008).
17. George Gascoigne, *Supposes*, in *The Tudor Period*, vol. 1 of *Drama of the English Renaissance*, ed. Russell A. Fraser and Norman Rabkin (New York: Macmillan, 1976), 102.

18. Cecil C. Seronsy, "Supposes as the Unifying Theme in *The Taming of the Shrew*," *Shakespeare Quarterly* 14, no. 1 (1963):15–30.
19. My use of this phrase is not meant to invoke Shirley Nelson Garner's "*The Taming of the Shrew*: Inside or Outside of the Joke," in which the author argues that whether one thinks the play is good or bad depends on the extent to which that person sees himself as inside or outside the joke that is being played on Kate. My use of the phrase refers only to the cognizance of the stage illusions; Garner refers to empathy with the characters. In Maurice Charney, ed., *'Bad' Shakespeare: Revaluations of the Shakespeare Canon* (Rutherford, NJ: Fairleigh Dickinson University Press, 1988), 105–19.
20. Andrew Gurr, *The Shakespearean Stage: 1574–1642*, 3rd ed. (Cambridge: Cambridge University Press, 1992), 180.
21. Maynard Mack, "Engagement and Detachment in Shakespeare's Plays," in *Essays on Shakespeare and Elizabethan Drama in Honor of Hardin Craig*, ed. Richard Hosley (Columbia: University of Missouri Press, 1962), 276.
22. Terrell Tebbetts, "Could Kate Mean What She Says?" *Publications of the Mississippi Philological Association* (1987): 14.
23. To a different end, Marianne Novy makes a similar point: "Since, as the mechanicals in *A Midsummer Night's Dream* know, it was impossible literally to bring in moonshine, the Elizabethan audience depended on the dialogue for indications of whether a scene was set in day or not. They must have frequently watched a nighttime scene set in literal sunlight and used their imagination," "Patriarchy and Play in *The Taming of the Shrew*," *English Literary Renaissance* 9 (1979): 272. In "The Naming of the Shrew," Laurie Maguire takes the point about the imagination a step further. She discusses at length an Oxford Shakespeare Company production in which the actor who portrays Sly plays double roles to the point of absurdity. In the climax of the subplot, the actor is playing a number of characters (Vincentio, Pedant as Vincentio, Baptista, and the jailor) so that "every time a character addressed Sly . . . or emphasized a gesture toward one of these characters, he gestured toward a blank space." To the point, Maguire says that "in theater, 'this' is what you say it is, even when 'this' is nothing." Laurie Maguire, "The Naming of the Shrew," in *The Taming of the Shrew*, ed. Dympna Callaghan (New York: Norton, 2009), 131.
24. Barry Weller, "Induction and Inference: Theater, Transformation, and the Construction of Identity in *The Taming of the Shrew*," in *Creative Imitation: New Essays on Renaissance Literature in Honor of Thomas M. Greene*, ed. David Quint et al. (Binghamton, NY: Medieval and Renaissance Texts and Studies, 1992), 323.
25. Ibid., 328.
26. Michael Shapiro, "Framing the Taming: Metatheatrical Awareness of Female Impersonation in *The Taming of the Shrew*," in *The Taming of the Shrew: Critical Essays*, ed. Dana E. Aspinall (New York: Routledge, 2002), 228.

CHAPTER 10

Fitzgrave's Jewel

Audience and Anticlimax in Middleton and Shakespeare

Jeremy Lopez

One of the most vexing problems for modern teachers and students of early modern drama is the too-tidy ending, where an ostensibly moral order is suddenly and arbitrarily restored—where compellingly antisocial characters are rounded up and expelled while bland figures of authority reassert themselves and stamp out the last embers of theatrical energy. Such moments in their sheer prevalence seem to call attention to the different expectations and desires of audiences "then" and audiences "now." Are we supposed to be glad that Vindice is punished at the end of *The Revenger's Tragedy*? Were audiences in 1607 glad, and if so, should we feel bad that we are not? Does Malcolm, or Richmond, really deserve our enthusiasm as the successor to Macbeth, or Richard III? Approaching the problem through irony—interpreting sudden and tidy endings as satirical or self-undermining—can be so easy as to seem disingenuous or expedient; but taking these endings at face value and reading them as transparent expressions of the playwright's, and his culture's, view of the relationship between morality and dramatic form is both aesthetically and ideologically unsatisfying.

My concern in this essay, then, is not only with historical or contemporary audience response to moments of moral ambiguity or chaos but also with the way scholarly language attempts to come to terms with that ambiguity or chaos and either define it as such or give it a new, more coherent form. My central text will be Thomas Middleton's *Your Five Gallants*, a play whose frustratingly anticlimactic ending takes shape around the triumph of a scholar and scholarly language. *Your Five Gallants* is also a play with a complex textual and editorial history. An epitome of the ironic conundrums that scholars of early modern drama face regularly, the 1608 Quarto of this intricately plotted play is in various places quite possibly corrupt: apparent transpositions or lacunae make it difficult to ascertain the authority or completeness of various sequences of action. But at the same time there is no actual evidence for textual corruption; the 1608 Quarto is the only early text, so there is no control against which to assess its integrity and authority; moreover, as I shall attempt to demonstrate, it is possible to read the Quarto as theatrically and thematically coherent. Textual corruption might, like moral ambiguity, be merely a figment of the scholarly imagination—a productive fiction that allows the strange historical artifact to be domesticated within the paradigms of academic discourse.

In the first part of this essay I discuss the dramatic structure of *Your Five Gallants*, and the relationship between its anticlimactic ending and some problems of sequence that have been perceived and corrected by editors and textual scholars. My primary interest here is in demonstrating how the totalizing language of scholarship can engender its own resistance. In the second part of the essay, I attempt to read against the grain of both Middleton's anticlimactic ending and conventional editorial theories of textual corruption. I do so by tracing the uncertain career of a crucial object—a jewel the protagonist Fitzgrave receives from his beloved Katherine—and creating for it both an imaginary future and a history of composition. The essay's conclusion frames the methodological problems raised by the first two parts within a comparison between Shakespeare and Middleton; here, I consider the surprising historical career of an early modern play text called *The Puritan Widow* in order to illuminate some of the critical and spectatorial fantasies of identity that inform our contemporary conception of and responses to early modern anticlimax.

* * *

In the second scene of *Your Five Gallants*, we learn that Fitzgrave, a gentleman, is the favorite suitor of Katherine, daughter of a recently deceased knight. Fitzgrave gives Katherine a chain of pearl as a pledge of his love, and she gives him a jewel. Katherine is also being sued to by the titular gallants—Primero, Frippery, Tailby, Pursenet, and Goldstone—who all appear in this scene after the exchange of love tokens. Rather than simply telling the gallants that she has chosen Fitzgrave, Katherine says that she needs time to make up her mind: at a month's end she will invite them all "to that election, / Which, on my unstained faith and virgin promise, / Shall light amongst no strangers, but yourselves" (1.2.59–62).[1] The gallants are satisfied with this plan and disperse. Fitzgrave is left alone on the stage and announces, to the audience, that he will disguise himself as a "credulous scholar, easily infected / With fashion, time, and humour" (93–94).

This will allow him—as well as Katherine and the audience—to see what he and Katherine (and we) surely already know: "Whether their lives from touch of blame sit free" (97). Of course the gallants' lives very much do not sit free from touch of blame, and in the ensuing action we are treated to them behaving badly in a variety of ways, each according to his character: bawd-gallant, broker-gallant, whore-gallant, pocket-gallant, cheating-gallant.

What we do *not* see, however, is the promised satire of the credulous scholar come to London. Although Fitzgrave, now under the pseudonym of Bowser, is introduced to the gallants by Goldstone as "Piping hot from the university; he smells of buttered loaves yet; an excellent scholar, but the arrantest ass" (2.1.57–59), he is never cheated or deceived by them or entangled in their plots. Fitzgrave is no Bartholomew Cokes. At one point Pursenet tries to rob him, and Fitzgrave overcomes Pursenet with force; at another point Goldstone steals his cloak while Fitzgrave is in bed, but Fitzgrave almost immediately gets it back. He is not, even in his affected scholarly persona, subjected to satirical ridicule. Quite the contrary, his affected scholarly persona is the mainspring of his triumph over the gallants. Because they think he is a scholar, the gallants ask Fitzgrave-Bowser to write a masque in which they might proclaim their worthy characters to Katherine. Fitzgrave agrees and writes a masque that reveals the true, blameful characters of the gallants who, unlike Katherine, cannot understand the Latin mottos that they bear upon their heraldic shields. Contrary to what the rest of the play would lead us to expect with its rollicking dramatization of improvisatory proteanism, Fitzgrave's assumed scholarly identity is not revealed *as* a disguise but rather proves to constitute his identity: he is able to write the Latin mottoes that humiliate the gallants and in doing so expresses, in both the most narrow and the most final terms, their identities. In act 5, scene 1, at the rehearsal for the masque, the gallants cannot translate the mottoes, and Fitzgrave gives them mistranslations, each of which is some form of ironic inversion of the actual translation: for example, Frippery's motto, *En avis ex avibus*, "one bird made of many" (5.1.109) is mistranslated, to the gallant's satisfaction, as "I keep one tune; I recant not" (5.1.178). Frippery's idea of himself, Fitzgrave's idea of Frippery, and Fitzgrave's idea of Frippery's idea of himself: nothing lies beyond the comprehension of the scholar's language. In the end, the gallants are forced to choose between marrying their courtesans or suffering "the indignation of the law" (5.2.70); the bawd Primero and his boy are ordered to be whipped, and Fitzgrave the gentleman-scholar gets the girl. As if intuiting that the spectators who have spent the last two hours enjoying the freewheeling antics of the gallants might be frustrated that Fitzgrave has come out so unequivocally on top, Katherine concludes the play with a confidently uncharming couplet: "And I presume there's none but those can frown / Whose envies, like the rushes, we tread down" (5.2.98–99). Anticlimax is discovering that the gentleman-scholar had matters in hand all along.

Fitzgrave's triumph is unsatisfying for a number of structural reasons as well. First, it is foreordained and perfunctory: Katherine makes a promise to Fitzgrave in act 1, scene 2, and she makes good on that promise in act 5, scene 2; Katherine and Fitzgrave do not interact in the interim (indeed, Katherine appears only in 1.2 and 5.2), and so the "plot" of their romance is merely a frame around the rest of the play's action. Second, although Fitzgrave and the gallants are presented as rivals in act 1, scene 2, the scenes that intervene between act 1, scene 2 and act 5, scene 2 do not in any way dramatize a contest between these rivals for Katherine's hand. Rather, those scenes dramatize the daily lives of the feckless, wanton gallants, whose utterly trivial interactions and transactions are given the liveliness and buoyancy the Fitzgrave-Katherine plot lacks by Middleton's comically suspenseful, intricately sequenced plotting. There is a remarkable moment in act 2, scene 1, for example, where, amid a great deal of complicated but diegetically clear action involving the theft and transfer of various jewels between gallants and courtesans, Goldstone's servingman Fulk enters to show his young master a pair of ornate drinking glasses:

> FULK. May it please your worship. They're done artificially, i'faith, boy.
> GOLDSTONE. Both the great beakers?
> FULK: Both, lad.
> GOLDSTONE. Just the same size?
> FULK. Ay, and the marks as just.
> GOLDSTONE. So, fall off respectively now. (2.1.211–15)

This exchange occurs out of earshot of the rest of the characters on the stage, so we know it must be significant, but we are given no way of understanding what the significance is until three scenes later, in act 2, scene 4, when the gallants meet at the Mitre tavern (at Goldstone's suggestion) for an evening of drinking and dicing. The Mitre, it turns out, has some very nice beakers that Goldstone has had his eye on for some time; he and Fulk steal these beakers and replace them with the counterfeit beakers from act 2, scene 1. Such patient plotting, where an object casually introduced becomes the nexus of a developing plot with which it is the audience's pleasure rapidly to catch up, is pervasive in *Gallants*. Other particularly rewarding instances include the series of scenes where Goldstone goes to extraordinary lengths to steal a saltcellar (4.1–4.5) and the series of scenes where Goldstone steals a cloak from Fitzgrave and pawns it to Frippery, who is then attacked by Pursenet, who was earlier attacked by Fitzgrave (3.1, 4.1–4.2).

The kind of detail-oriented reading (theatrical or textual) encouraged by such plotting loses some of its savor if one cannot be certain that the text as printed represents events in the order the playwright intended: if the process of textual transmission and reproduction may have jumbled sequences of intricately plotted action, how can we begin to imagine what kinds of theatrical effects an early modern audience experienced when watching Middleton's play—or expected to experience when watching any Middleton play? Problems of sequence in *Gallants* have been a concern for readers of the play since the earliest editions. Both Dyce (1840) and Bullen (1885) believed that two adjacent passages in act 2, each about 25 lines long, had been wrongly transposed. In Q, toward the end of what the Oxford text calls act 2, scene 1, the whore-gallant Tailby is alone onstage with a Novice courtesan, who gives him a ring. A stage direction announces that the pair *Exeunt*, after which point Fitzgrave appears, complaining about a jewel that was stolen from him earlier in act 2, scene 1. Fitzgrave is onstage for about 25 lines, and when he exits, Tailby reenters, singing a song of comic sorrow about having to leave the Novice: "O the parting of us twain, / Hath caused me mickle pain" (2.3.1–2). Tailby is met by the bawd-gallant Primero, who leads him, after about 25 lines, offstage for an assignation with another woman, Mrs. Newcut. The next scene (2.4) begins with the stage direction *Enter all at once*—the gallants are arriving at the Mitre tavern—and Primero, who was the last to speak at the end of the previous scene is the first to speak here. Tailby is the next gallant to speak, in the scene's fourth line.

Working on the assumption that Renaissance dramatists did not violate the "law of reentry" (an anachronistic but reasonable, and demonstrably consistent, "rule" of staging whereby no character who exits at the end of one scene can enter at the beginning of the next) Dyce and Bullen assumed that there should be intervening action between Primero and Tailby's exit at Primero's house and their reentrance at the Mitre. Nothing in the plot requires that Tailby and the Novice leave together after she gives him the ring, and his song makes as much sense if she exits without him as it does if he enters without her. Since the Fitzgrave scene and the Primero-Tailby scene are of approximately equal length, and since the Fitzgrave scene would act as a kind of rhythmic alteration between the two gallants' scenes, it "seems quite possible," as Baldwin Maxwell wrote in 1951, "that the order of two sheets was accidentally reversed or, if the play was written on both sides of the sheets making up the copy, that the printer erroneously set the later side first."[2] Dyce and Bullen therefore reordered Q so that Fitzgrave's complaint about his lost jewel intervened between Primero and Tailby's exit to see Mrs. Newcut and their entrance to the Mitre; the first twentieth-century edition of the play, by C. Lee Colegrove, followed Dyce and Bullen.[3]

In 1999, however, John Jowett rejected as merely speculative Dyce, Bullen, and Colegrove's emendation and Baldwin Maxwell's supporting argument about reversed sheets.[4] Jowett's argument has since been applied to the editing (by Jowett and Ralph Alan Cohen) of the new Oxford text of *Gallants*, which restores the two scenes to their original Quarto positions. The basis of Jowett's argument is not a "law"—an immutable principle of composition that circumscribes the playwright's creativity—but rather a sensitivity to theatrical effect, to what a playwright might have wanted an audience to think about his or her characters. Implicitly attaching the impetus toward editorial regularity to Victorian prudery, Jowett suggests that Dyce and Bullen's problem with Q's ordering of scenes stems from the resulting implausible—or perhaps simply distasteful—representation of Tailby's sexual prowess:

> The Novice and Tailby exeunt together, and the scene with Fitzgrave is a short interlude occupying the time that, we will guess, they spend in sexual activity. Tailby then enters as from this encounter . . . only to be joined together immediately with Mistress Newcut. Worse still from the viewpoint of sexual propriety, there is an immediate dramatic continuity from Tailby going in with Mistress Newcut to him coming out on stage at the Mitre with, amongst others, the two original courtesans. But Tailby's sexual excesses should be kept entirely distinct from textual corruption.[5]

Instead of corruption, Jowett sees dramatic innovation and experimentation—the sustained development of theatrical effects by surprising or counterintuitive scene ordering. He argues that Tailby's rapid exits and entrances in act 2 are of a piece with a later sequence where Tailby mentions to Pursenet that he's taking a ride out to Kingston to meet a woman, then exits, at which point Pursenet decides to rob Tailby in Coombe Park (which is on the way to Kingston), and then—at least as it can be inferred from the Quarto—seems simply to cross the stage and put a scarf around his face in order to establish that the location now *is* Coombe Park and that he is lying in wait for Tailby.

> [T]he sequence plays against theatrical convention, to create a momentary jar in our sense of time and place, and so to make a comic point about the arbitrary representation of these things in the theatre. In Act 2, just when we think Tailby is occupied with Mistress Newcut, time is elided so that we see him protesting his loyalty once again to the courtesans. His sexual affairs are practically simultaneous with each other, and the moment of achievement almost literally becomes the moment for furthering other exploits. With Pursenet, the moment of planning almost literally becomes the moment of putting the plot into effect.[6]

Quite convincingly, the logistical entanglements that seem to originate in the intricacies of a 400-year-old printing process become, in Jowett's argument, the source of the play's newly discovered self-reflexive theatrical life—a means by which the play *plays*. The harmoniousness of Jowett's conception of Middleton's innovation with modern thinking about the theater and theatrical conventions can be seen clearly in the filmic analogy Cohen uses while discussing such sequences in his introduction to the Oxford text: "Middleton has treated his

Blackfriars audience to a theatrical 'jump cut' that derives its humour . . . from the elasticity of theatrical time."[7]

Jowett's argument about the scenes in act 2 proceeds from the polemical assumption that, in the absence of definitive textual evidence for transposition, the critic is obliged "to consider anew whether the text might . . . play successfully" as it is printed.[8] This argument, which is consistent with twenty-first-century interpretive conventions—and which has enabled fresh editorial and critical attention to a whole host of fascinating texts once considered "bad" (Q1 *Hamlet*, for example)—renders somewhat surprising Jowett's treatment of another scene-ordering problem in *Gallants*, one not noticed by Dyce or Bullen but given sustained attention by Maxwell. The problem is that the scenes Dyce and Bullen label act 4, scenes 1 and 2, signatures F2r–F3v in Q, seem actually to belong, if the plot is to make sense, right after the dicing scene, which ends in the middle of signature E1r in Q. In the editions of Dyce and Bullen, the dicing scene—one of whose comic set pieces is Tailby pawning his clothes in order to keep playing—is immediately followed by a scene (they label it 3.1) where Tailby reads a letter from a woman in Kingston who asks him to visit her because her husband is out of town. Over the course of act 3, Tailby heads to Kingston via Coombe Park, where he is robbed by Pursenet. Then, twenty pages later, in Dyce and Bullen's act 4, scenes 1 and 2, Tailby is awakened by his servant after a late night of dicing, where he's gambled away his clothes and pleasantly surprised to be sent by his various female admirers a new suit, a new hat, money, and a letter. Quite reasonably, Maxwell argued that the scenes where Tailby is awakened after a night of dicing ought to follow upon the dicing scene itself, so that his being robbed in Coombe Park was the climactic (rather than intermediate) action in a sequence of events originating at the Mitre. Colegrove followed Maxwell in setting up his edition, and Jowett agreed in 1999 that the position of the later Tailby scenes in Q "interrupts the time-line, and in doing so it makes the plot unintelligible."[9] The Oxford edition of *Gallants* emends Q accordingly.

Jowett's agreement with Maxwell on this point is surprising because it requires him to avoid completely the question whether the text as printed can play successfully. Indeed, Cohen's introduction to the Oxford text begins by announcing that the 1608 text printed by George Eld "breaks the promise of the title-page to give the reader the play 'As it hath been often in Action at the Black-friers' by transposing two of the play's scenes and thereby badly knotting up a story with an already tangled narrative line."[10] But it seems worth remembering that neither Dyce nor Bullen, such careful readers as to insist on reordering two short scenes whose transposition has a negligible effect upon the plot, caught the apparently much more consequential jumbling of the later Tailby scenes. Very possibly these Victorian editors, disgusted or impatient with

Middleton's episodic prurience, saw the epitasis, or busy part of the subject (as Jonson has it in *Every Man Out*), as simply one long series of self-contained, disconnected episodes, where the gallants act according to their predetermined characters; and while we might object to the prudishness or humorlessness behind their reading, we cannot say that it is a *misreading*. Indeed, with only a minimal shift of emphasis, it is possible to see the position of the later Tailby scenes as Dyce and Bullen might have seen them *and* with the same critical subtlety that Jowett brought to the sequence of earlier Tailby scenes.

While the scenes involving Tailby getting out of bed after a night of gambling during which he lost his clothes, and receiving both clothes and a letter from his mistresses, might certainly be said to *repeat* action that we might *infer* occurred between the end of the dicing scene and the beginning of act 3 (which begins with Tailby reading a letter from a mistress), it is an overstatement to say that the position of the scenes in Q renders the plot unintelligible. Perhaps a spectator's momentary sense that, in Jowett's words, the play has "looped back in time" is meant to be an alienating dramatization of the relentless (if comic) *sameness* of the gallants' lives: on any given day Tailby might be expected to wake up late, to recall that he pawned away his clothes while gambling, to depend on the tawdry generosity of mistresses, whom he must then repay with sexual favors.[11] Further, in the Quarto, these scenes—which begin with Tailby offstage and still in bed, while his servant receives a satin suit on his behalf—are followed by a closely parallel scene where Fitzgrave-as-Bowser, offstage and still in bed, is called to by Goldstone, who steals Fitzgrave's cloak before the latter gets out of bed. The Tailby scenes end with Tailby newly outfitted and meditating on what a good life it is to be a whore-gallant, while the Fitzgrave scene ends with Fitzgrave in his shirt, wondering how to get his cloak back from the gallant who cheated him. One might argue that this is the only time in the play where Fitzgrave's decision to participate in the world of the gallants actually entangles him within that world. The apparent temporal shift and the interscene parallels are, when looked at in this way, entirely playable: what seems like an obvious discontinuity in the exposition of the plot might in fact be understood as a deliberately disorienting form of structural integrity. Tailby's waking up to live virtually the same day all over again might be a climactic joke about the gallant's character even as it thwarts the narrative drive or build we might expect from a more linear plot sequence.

Jowett and Cohen's relocation of Q's F2r–F3v to a position that makes more sense in narrative terms is entirely reasonable and probably makes the play easier for an audience to follow, on the page or on the stage. But the same is probably true of the Dyce and Bullen emendation of the earlier sequence, and as I have tried to demonstrate with my reading of the later scenes, the decision to make either editorial move cannot be based on an idea about making the Quarto text more playable, interpretable, or even simply more legible: the imagination and flexibility of contemporary scholarly methods, as Jowett and Cohen demonstrate with the scenes on C3v–C4v, allow the Quarto text to *be* legible, interpretable, and playable as it is. (And to be perfectly honest, the first time I read this play was in Bullen's edition, and I do not recall noticing that the later Tailby scenes were out of order.) The problem of deciding which is the "best" or "most theatrical" text, and whether those are the same thing, is a familiar one in Renaissance studies—the case of *Hamlet* being perhaps the most obvious example. What is particularly interesting in the case of *Gallants* is that the apparent textual problems are problems of sequence and seem urgent to sort out if we are to take the full measure of Middleton as a comic playwright: as I noted at the outset, there is a frustrating tension between Middleton's characteristically meticulous plotting on the one hand and the confusing state of the Quarto text on the other. My goal in this section of the essay has been to demonstrate how the work of trying to resolve this tension can make evident some points of overlap between problems of critical interpretation and problems of audience response. Jowett and Cohen's revision of Maxwell, Dyce, and Bullen on the transposed scenes, and my revision of Jowett and Cohen on the relocated scenes, might be said to enrich the text interpretively, but they also might be said to domesticate it—to refuse to admit the possibility of disorder, of a meaning or nonmeaning that remains beyond the comprehension of critical language. One way or another the text ends up representing Middleton as a consummately self-conscious plotter—even or perhaps especially when he least seems to be—and the scholar triumphs over the chaotic, competing creative energies and processes of the early modern playwright and printing house.

In the essay's next section, I attempt to find some alternatives to, or at least some ways around, the process of critical domestication by proposing an ironic, contingent reading of the play's overly neat closure, which itself depends on a highly contingent imagining of plot construction and textual production. My project in the second section is to trace the uncertain fortunes of the jewel Katherine gives to Fitzgrave in act 1, scene 2, a somewhat unruly object whose flickering presence in the text may or may not be closely related to the problems of narrative sequence and dramatic closure that I introduced in this section. In following Fitzgrave's jewel, I work to construct a critical narrative about the author Middleton himself and the process of composition for *Gallants* that might allow us to see the problem of the play's closure not simply as a contest between authorial intention and audience response, or between historical reception and modern literary criticism, but as a kind of suspension or oscillation—a point of intersection for divergent ideas of dramatic form that shimmers, briefly, like the jewel itself, and eludes our grasp.

* * *

In act 2, scene 1, Fitzgrave's first scene as Bowser, Pursenet's boy (who in 1.2 stole the chain of pearl Fitzgrave gave Katherine) "nims away Fitzgrave's jewel" (2.1.120 s.d.) while the disguised scholar is distracted with a musical performance. There is some very funny business later in the scene when Fitzgrave discovers that the jewel is gone but cannot say anything to the gallants for fear of revealing his identity. "The jewel! Heart, the jewel!" he exclaims to himself, and when Goldstone asks him what the matter is, Fitzgrave replies "Nothing, sir. / A spice of poetry, a kind o' fury, / A disease runs among scholars" (2.1.231–34). Briefly the play veers into a satire of Fitzgrave's scholarly persona that it otherwise seems generally to avoid. Left to his own apparently scholarly reverie by the other gallants who, in the meantime, are haggling over a ring Goldstone took from one of the courtesans, Fitzgrave worries aloud, for the benefit of the audience, about having lost Katherine's love token: "how can I gain her love / When I have lost her favour?" (242–43).

Fitzgrave's jewel *might* make its way in this scene from the Boy to Pursenet and from Pursenet to one of the courtesans, and that courtesan *might* give it to Tailby after Fitzgrave leaves the stage in act 2, scene 1. Katherine's chain of pearl is *definitely* given to another of the courtesans (see 2.1.143–53), who then gives it to Tailby (2.1.313), and this transaction is clear in the text. But the fate of the stolen jewel is much less certain: the Boy who steals it is directed to "exit" immediately after he steals it, and he says nothing to Pursenet about having stolen it. Later in the scene, the Second Courtesan clearly gives Tailby a "jewel" (2.1.326), and Cohen and Jowett's stage direction hypothesizes that it is Fitzgrave's, but they do not elsewhere indicate, with further editorial stage directions, how she came into possession of it. Q provides no help.

Cohen and Jowett's hypothesized staging makes sense for a play so concerned, as Jowett says, to dramatize the "fortunes or 'careers' of stage properties."[12] The immediate expectation once the Boy steals Fitzgrave's jewel is probably that it will, as happens with the chain of pearl, pass through the hands of more gallants, ultimately perhaps serving to undo them: at the end of act 4 Frippery shows Fitzgrave-Bowser the chain of pearl and asks the scholar to give him, in the masque, "a little touch above the rest . . . for I mean to present this chain of pearl to [Katherine]" (271–73). Frippery does not know the chain's provenance, and so when, at act 5, scene 2, line 25 he presents it to Katherine, she exclaims, "The very chain of pearl was filched from me!" and this is Fitzgrave-Bowser's cue to unmask. From previous cues in the play's plotting (including the attention Middleton lavishes upon the fortunes of the diegetically irrelevant beakers and saltcellar), it would be perfectly reasonable to expect the career of the jewel Katherine gave to Fitzgrave to come to a revelatory end in this scene as well: that is, in act 2, scene 2 Fitzgrave, while worrying about the jewel, encounters one of Katherine's servants, who is frantically looking for the chain of pearl; and in act 3, scene 1 Pursenet robs Tailby—who, in order to keep himself safe from bodily harm, gives an inventory of the wealth on his person that may or may not deliberately leave out the jewel: "there's a purse in my left pocket, as I take it, with fifteen pound in gold in't, and there's a fair chain of pearl in the other" (3.1.69–71). Both of these moments suggest that a public revelation about the theft of Fitzgrave's jewel is imminent, but in each case the revelation is avoided—delayed, we might think, for the sake of a climactic revelation in the final scene.

But the jewel is never mentioned after act 2, nor does it ever reappear. If we read this fact as a deliberate omission on Middleton's part, which he conceived as part of the expository and moral structure of the play, then we must imagine that the jewel simply ends up either with Pursenet's Boy or, if Cohen and Jowett's hypothetical staging is correct, with Tailby, and this latter possibility in particular might have significant ramifications for how we interpret the play's resolution. As with the Quarto's positioning of the scenes with Tailby waking up and Fitzgrave waking up, the jewel might allow these two polar-opposite characters to become echoes or doubles of one another, and perhaps we might glimpse in this doubling an ironic foreshadowing that exerts pressure on Fitzgrave's triumph: the irresistible whore-gallant, regularly sent for by women whose husbands are away from home, has ended up with Katherine's favor. Shadowed by his more sexually experienced opposite who seems always to recover what he's lost (in any version of the text, Tailby's bad night of dicing is always followed by his receiving a new suit), Fitzgrave is perhaps in danger of confronting, after his marriage, the humiliating problem faced by Bassanio and Gratiano at the end of *The Merchant of Venice*. In constructing this rather seductive interpretation, however, we must keep in mind that Middleton was himself a gentleman scholar and, like most satirists, undeniably a moralist. We might reasonably imagine that he was self-conscious enough about adopting arbitrary moral perspectives to be circumspect about conceiving Fitzgrave as a kind of surrogate playwright (indeed, as I discuss further in the essay's final section, the gentleman-scholar figure in *The Puritan Widow* is punished along with everyone else), but we would also have to acknowledge the possibility that he took the conception rather seriously. However disappointing it might be to admit, Middleton probably did not *want* the gallants to triumph, even ironically.

Moreover, the lost jewel is as likely as anything else to be a result not of deliberate design but of Middleton's own altered or discarded intentions. Indeed, we might reasonably suppose it to be a combination of both of these things. Perhaps Middleton knew from the moment he conceived the play that it would include the dicing scene at the Mitre, but he was not sure exactly where he would put that scene. Perhaps he conceived the device of the beakers while writing act 2, scene 1 and, impatient to get it onto paper, wrote the tavern scene as act 2, scene 2, realizing only sometime later that he had the same characters entering in the tavern scene who had exited in the previous scene. Perhaps he then hit on the idea of Fitzgrave's jewel being stolen, and a scene where Fitzgrave complained about it, which he could use to add some time between Pursenet and Tailby's exit with Mrs. Newcut and their entrance at the Mitre. And perhaps the fact that the stolen jewel and Fitzgrave's complaint were afterthoughts explains why (a) the transfer of the jewel from Pursenet to the courtesan is not specifically indicated in the text while the transfer of Katherine's chain of pearl from Pursenet to the courtesan is; (b) Fitzgrave's first realization that the jewel is gone involves satirical comedy against scholars that for the most part does not occur elsewhere in the play; (c) the text does not indicate that the jewel reappears later even when its twin the chain does; and (d) the placement of the scene where Fitzgrave complains about the lost jewel, and the reentry of the just-exited gallants at the beginning of the tavern scene, seemed odd to Dyce, Bullen, Maxwell, and Colegrove—perhaps, indeed, the sheet on which that scene was written was inserted loosely into the manuscript and shifted about before printing.

All of this is hugely speculative, of course, but it seems to me to have the advantage of imagining in a plausible way the role played by the creative process itself, and not only the vagaries of audience response within theaters and across centuries, in producing density as well as superfluity of meaning. That is to say, the problem of determining or imagining the ethical perspective we or a historical audience are meant to adopt at the end of *Gallants* might very well have as much to do with Middleton's own uncertainty (or inattention) as with his desire to cultivate uncertainty in his audience. If we must imagine something to account for the way the play's plot is represented in the text (and imagine we must, for there is no external evidence), it is perhaps productive to go beyond imagining a narrative solely of textual production, where the vagaries of the printing process intervene between the author's finalized intentions and an ever more distant posterity. Too, we might imagine a narrative of textual composition, where the text is the result of what a critic in another field has called "an intense, hazardous process . . . in which a developing work 'seeks to maintain its own integrity,' even against whatever initial intentions the writer may have had for it"—and where the text might very well be "the result of more than one creative process, one or more of which may never have been completed."[13] In this way it might be possible to see Fitzgrave's jewel not only as a function of what Foucault called the "principle of thrift"[14]—a marker of irony that returns us to the author's intention—but also as a manifestation of the principle of excess that lies within any act of composition, where the centrifugal movement toward form is as likely to send ragged pieces of content flying in unexpected directions as it is to smooth their edges and keep them in orbit around an authorial center of gravity.

* * *

Symptoms of formal excess (and encouragements to interpretive excess) like Fitzgrave's jewel are numerous and familiar in the works of Shakespeare: Antonio's unresolved imprisonment in *Twelfth Night* for example, the fate of Aaron's baby in *Titus Andronicus*, or the silence of the female characters at the end of *A Midsummer Night's Dream*. Moments of odd or redundant sequencing, with more and less fathomable textual explanations, are fairly common as well: consider the twice-narrated news of Antonio's troubles in *The Merchant of Venice* act 3, scene 2 or the repetition of the lines about "gray-eyed morn" in act 2 of the Q2 version of *Romeo and Juliet*. The idea that any of these instances—even Q2 *Romeo*—can be explained and made to "work" with recourse to thematic or theatrical interpretation will not raise many eyebrows: critical discourse has created for the figure of Shakespeare a maximally capacious sense of irony. The deeply institutionalized notion of Shakespeare as the playwright of his audience means that narratives of textual production or composition created to explain apparent textual corruption in Shakespeare's plays matter chiefly insofar as they produce, rather than foreclose, further interpretive possibilities. This is a key difference between Shakespeare and Middleton: on some important level it still seems possible to know what Middleton meant his plays to mean.[15]

The idealization of Shakespearean indeterminacy is a relatively recent, peculiarly modern (postmodern, of course, but also to a large degree modernist) phenomenon and, as Paul Yachnin has argued in a superb recent essay, has developed partly out of an antibourgeois prejudice that defines great art as timeless and placeless.[16] Yachnin's touchstone for this argument is *The Puritan Widow* (1606), a play that today seems unquestionably Middletonian: its setting is urban, its mode is satiric, its satire is quite explicitly anti-Puritan, one of its central characters is a mischievous and protean gentleman-scholar who is based on a popular jest-book representation of George Peele,[17] and its ending has both the gentleman-scholar and the Puritans being punished for their hypocrisy in no uncertain terms by a heretofore unseen nobleman from the court, whose admonishments to morality are notably antitheatrical. In almost every conceivable way, *The Puritan Widow* seems *not* to achieve the transcendence of place and time—its seventeenth-century London theatrical milieu—or the indeterminacy of meaning and authorial perspective that we imagine characterizes and explains Shakespeare's more enduring dramatic art. And yet, this play was attributed to "W. S." in its first printing of 1607, was included in the Shakespeare Folios of 1664 and 1685, and was accepted as Shakespeare's well into the eighteenth century.

Working both to problematize the figure of the capaciously ironic Shakespeare and to catch a glimpse of what underlies the concerted cultural effort to construct such a singularly ironic authorial figure and vision, Yachnin on one hand demonstrates that Shakespeare and Middleton might be more similar than they first appear: both use Puritans as "scapegoats for the players and playwrights' own profitable but problematic situation between the entertainment market and the system of rank. These Puritans are like the players in that they seek recognition and advancement from their social superiors, and unlike them, because they do it so poorly."[18] And on the other hand, Yachnin suggests that there is an ironic, perhaps self-aggrandizing myopia behind our modern inability to imagine how *The Puritan Widow* could be attributed to Shakespeare rather than Middleton: Middleton's "upmarket, fashionable" play is now condescended to because of its un-Shakespearean emphasis on the representation of bourgeois city life, while Shakespeare, the "great bourgeois retailer of elite culture," is considered the serious artist.[19] The play Yachnin uses to connect these two points is *Twelfth Night*, which seems to epitomize Shakespeare's "attenuation of topical meaning"—his interest in "characters who seem to live inside themselves before they live in any kind of social setting," which "has seemed to purify his drama of mundane interests and ... helped to elevate it into the realm of 'serious art.'"[20] Shakespeare's treatment of Malvolio, Yachnin goes on to say, "seems to lead us away from familiar standards of judgment, into the undiscovered territory of individual history and uniquely situated, subjective views of the world"; but it would nevertheless have been more common in the early modern period "to gauge Malvolio by the measure of his rank and overweening ambition, and less usual to see him by his own lights."[21]

Yachnin's argument suggestively links a utopian conception of artistic value with a post-Renaissance (indeed, a postmodern) spectatorial fantasy of classlessness; I would like, by way of conclusion, to suggest some ways in which this link can help us to understand, in both historical and posthistorical terms, the origin of the problems of interpreting anticlimax with which this essay began. I would like to suggest that the anticlimactic endings of Shakespeare's plays have become a fruitful source of highly ironized, self-subverting readings in part because they ask to be experienced from the point of view of characters who have succeeded—and whose success is almost without exception figured as a form of social advancement that comes, implicitly, at some spiritual cost: Malcolm or Richmond; Viola and Olivia in *Twelfth Night*; the Duke and Isabella in *Measure for Measure*. These anticlimactic endings allow us not only to see dramatic narrative as a means to attaining and expressing a powerful new identity whose most apt metaphor is "nobility" but also to revel in a voluptuous ennui born of the suspicion that this identity, for all the power it confers upon the individual, might be hollow.

Middleton's anticlimactic endings, on the other hand, ask to be experienced from the point of view of the characters who lose. Dramatic narrative has very little to do with social advancement in a literal or metaphorical sense, and the spiritual cost of characters' actions is evident at every moment throughout the plays: as we see in the case of *Gallants*, Fitzgrave's elevation above the gallants is both a fact and a foregone conclusion even before the action of the play begins. Middleton does not allow his characters to bear the weight of the spectator's fantasies all the way to the end. (If there is any purely thematic or intertextual argument for Middleton's authorship of *The Revenger's Tragedy*, this might be it: Vindice does not even hope to become duke, merely to be applauded by one, and his quite deliberate revelation of his theatrical identity as a revenger seems infinitely more wasteful than Hamlet's stumbling into the opportunity for vengeance and self-apotheosis.) The inverse of Viola, whose riddle of the children of her father's house both reveals (on the one hand) the secret that she's of the appropriate status and gender to marry Orsino and also (on the other) allows for the possibility that the secret will remain forever concealed, Middleton's five gallants are constructed in the end by riddles they don't understand and that encode only the open secret of their baseness. Like the nonaristocratic spectators for whom Viola's aristocratic birth is a metaphor for personal, psychic fulfillment, the gallants play at fluency with a language of privilege that, when the fiction is concluded, only works to exclude them. The characters of Middleton's anticlimaxes embody the perspective and the predicament of the late-modern consumer of Shakespeare's bourgeois fantasies of elite culture: we cannot be a part of Viola's world any more than Malvolio can—or any more than the gallants are part of Fitzgrave's because he let them act in his play. But in Shakespeare's play Malvolio is exiled from the resolution, and if we do not experience this as the comic catharsis it seems intended to be, we might at least entertain the notion that the revenge Malvolio promises is that of living well. Middleton's characters, on the other hand, remain onstage to take their lumps. Like the spectators, they have not been changed by the action of the play; recognizing ourselves in these pretenders is a disappointment.

Notes

1. Unless otherwise noted, all references to *Your Five Gallants* are from Thomas Middleton, *Your Five Gallants*, ed. Ralph Alan Cohen and John Jowett, in *The Collected Works of Thomas Middleton*, ed. Gary Taylor and John Lavagnino (Oxford: Oxford University Press, 2007). Parenthetical citations refer to act, scene, and lines.
2. Baldwin Maxwell, "Thomas Middleton's *Your Five Gallants*," *Philological Quarterly* 30 (1951): 31.
3. See C. Lee Colegrove, *A Critical Edition of Thomas Middleton's* Your Five Gallants (New York: Garland, 1979). Colegrove's edited text was his 1961 doctoral dissertation at the University of Michigan and was reprinted as part of the Garland Renaissance Drama series.

4. John Jowett, "Pre-Editorial Criticism and the Space for Editing: Examples from *Richard III* and *Your Five Gallants*," in *Problems of Editing*, ed. Christa Jansohn (Tübingen, Germany: Niemeyer, 1999), 137–49.
5. Ibid., 141.
6. Ibid., 142.
7. Ralph Alan Cohen, introduction to *Your Five Gallants*, in *The Collected Works of Thomas Middleton*, ed. Gary Taylor and John Lavagnino (Oxford: Oxford University Press, 2007), 596.
8. Jowett, "Pre-Editorial Criticism," 141.
9. Ibid., 143.
10. Cohen, introduction, 594.
11. Jowett, "Pre-Editorial Criticism," 143.
12. Ibid., 138.
13. The two quotations in this sentence are from Hershel Parker, *Flawed Texts and Verbal Icons* (Evanston, IL: Northwestern University Press, 1984), 24, 50. The quotation within the first quotation is from Murray Krieger, *Theory of Criticism* (Baltimore, MD: Johns Hopkins University Press, 1976). Parker's book is about the relationship between textual variation and critical interpretation in American literature, but his method and his conclusions—particularly chapter 2, "The Determinacy of the Creative Process"—have been very influential for my thinking in this essay and are pertinent to the study of early modern drama in a way few critics have recognized.
14. The phrase is from "What Is an Author?" *Bulletin de la Société Française de Philosophie*, 44, no. 3 (1969): 73–104. The text in which I read this essay is *Language, Counter-Memory, Practice: Selected Essays and Interviews by Michel Foucault*, ed. Donald F. Bouchard (Ithaca, NY: Cornell University Press, 1980), 113–38.
15. James Wells's reading of *The Taming of the Shrew* in Chapter 9 complements and intersects with my arguments in this final section about spectators' identification with characters, and it also demonstrates quite clearly some dominant critical and methodological assumptions about the unfathomability of Shakespeare's intentions and/or the "real" meaning of his plays.
16. Paul Yachnin, "Reversal of Fortune: Shakespeare, Middleton, and the Puritans," *English Literary History* 70, no. 3 (2003): 758.
17. The jest-book is *The Merrie Conceited Jests of George Peele* (London, 1607). For a discussion of this text and Middleton's *The Puritan Widow*, see Mildred G. Christian, "Middleton's Acquaintance with the *Merrie Conceited Jests of George Peele*," *PMLA* 50 (1935): 753–60.
18. Yachnin, "Reversal of Fortune," 758.
19. Ibid., 759.
20. Ibid., 783.
21. Ibid., 783.

Contributors

Mark Bayer is an assistant professor of English at the University of Texas at San Antonio. He is the author of the forthcoming *Theatre, Community, and Civic Engagement in Jacobean London* and numerous articles discussing early modern drama and culture and the long-term worldwide authority of Shakespeare's plays.

David M. Bergeron, professor emeritus of English, University of Kansas, has published extensively on civic pageantry. His well-known book *English Civic Pageantry 1558–1642* has been republished in a revised edition (Arizona State Medieval and Renaissance Studies, 2003). His most recent book, *Textual Patronage in English Drama, 1570–1640* (Ashgate, 2006), focuses on epistles dedicatory and addresses to readers in dramatic texts. He has published widely on Shakespeare, Renaissance drama, and the Stuart royal family, including *Shakespeare's Romances and the Royal Family* (1985), *King James and Letters of Homoerotic Desire* (1999), and *Practicing Renaissance Scholarship* (2000).

Erika T. Lin is an assistant professor of English at George Mason University. Her articles have appeared in such venues as *Theatre Journal* and *New Theatre Quarterly*, and she is currently working on her first book, *Shakespeare and the Materiality of Performance*. A portion of this project, published as "Performance Practice and Theatrical Privilege: Rethinking Weimann's Concepts of *Locus* and *Platea*," received the Medieval and Renaissance Drama Society's 2008 Martin Stevens Award for Best New Essay in Early Drama Studies. In addition, she has also begun preliminary research for a new book on the performance dynamics of seasonal festivities and early modern theatre.

Jeremy Lopez is an associate professor of English literature at the University of Toronto and the theatre review editor for *Shakespeare Bulletin*. He is the author of *Theatrical Convention and Audience Response in Early Modern Drama* (Cambridge, 2003) and numerous essays on the works of Shakespeare and his contemporaries.

Jennifer A. Low, associate professor of English at Florida Atlantic University, is the author of *Manhood and the Duel: Masculinity in Early Modern Drama and Culture* (Palgrave, 2003). She has published several articles in such journals as *Comparative Drama* and *Philological Quarterly*, and her most recent essay, "Violence in the City," is forthcoming in *Thomas Middleton in Context* (Cambridge University Press). She is currently working on a transhistorical study of the shaping force of staging and stage design on audience experience.

Paul Menzer is an associate professor at Mary Baldwin College, where he is the director of the MLitt/MFA program in Shakespeare and Performance. He is the editor of *Inside Shakespeare: Essays on the Blackfriars Stage* (Susquehanna, 2006) and author of *The Hamlets: Cues, Qs, and Remembered Texts* (Delaware, 2008) and has contributed essays on text, performance, and theatre history to such journals as *Shakespeare Quarterly*, *Renaissance Drama*, and *Shakespeare Bulletin*.

Nova Myhill is an associate professor of English at New College of Florida, where she teaches British literature before 1700 and drama from all periods. She has published essays on audience and reception in Foxe's *Acts and Monuments*, Massinger and Dekker's *The Virgin Martyr*, and Shakespeare's works. She is currently working on projects on female spectatorship in city comedy and the relation between theatrical spectatorship and early modern public punishment.

Meg F. Pearson is an associate professor in the Department of English and Philosophy at the University of West Georgia. Her most recent publications have addressed the function of infamy in Marlowe's *Edward II* and have argued for a pedagogy of revenge in *Titus Andronicus*. Pearson is currently working on a book-length project comparing the relationships of early modern painters and playwrights to their spectators.

Emma K. Rhatigan, MA, DPhil, is a lecturer in early modern literature at the University of Sheffield. She is currently completing the monograph *Preaching at Lincoln's Inn* and is editing a volume of Donne's Lincoln's Inn sermons for *The Oxford Edition of the Sermons of John Donne*. She is coeditor, with Peter McCullough and Hugh Adlington, of a forthcoming volume, *The Oxford Handbook of the Early Modern Sermon*. She has written articles on Donne, early modern sermons, and the relationships between the pulpit and the stage in early modern London.

James Wells is an assistant professor of English at Muskingum University. He has published essays on *Macbeth* and *Coriolanus* and has others forthcoming on *A Midsummer Night's Dream*, *Henry V*, and Shakespeare's language. He has also edited *The Second Part of Henry the Fourth* (2009) and *The Merry Wives of Windsor* (forthcoming) for the New Kittredge Shakespeare.

Index

Plays and other works are listed as subentries under their authors.

ab Indagine, Joannes
  Briefe Introductions . . . vnto the Art of Chiromancy, or Manuel Diuination, and Physiognomy, 126, 133n30
acting, 1–2, 4–7, 12–13, 19–20, 25–27, 29, 35n21, 38–42, 44, 46–51, 53n17, 56, 58, 60, 69n6, 72–74, 76–78, 87, 101, 103, 110, 114–17, 119, 121–23, 129–30, 136–37, 139, 140–41, 147, 148n5, 148n19, 151–57, 159–61, 162, 165, 166n11, 166n20, 171–72, 174, 176–78, 181, 185, 188n23
  presentational acting, 177
acting companies
  Children of Paul's, 61, 70n24, 106
  King's Men, 43, 58
  Lady Elizabeth's Men, 58
  (Lord) Admiral's Men, 19, 60–61
  Pembroke's Men, 103, 111n47
  Prince Charles's Men, 58
  Prince Henry's Men (formerly Admiral's Men), 61
  Queen Anne's Men, 11, 57–59, 61, 69n6
actor's body, 12, 25–27, 29, 39, 108n15, 129, 154–55, 180
Alfield, Thomas, 94, 108n8
Alleyn, Edward, 19, 111n47
Althusser, Louis, 128
anticlimax, 14, 189–90, 192, 203
antirealist, 172
antitheatricality, 3–5, 20, 31–32, 43, 166n9, 202

apprentices, 11, 24, 56–57, 59, 61, 63–64, 66–67
Ariosto
  I Suppositi, 158
Armstrong, Alan, 132n18
Arnheim, Rudolf, 109n23
art history, 97, 109n22
Astington, John, 69n12
audience
  as characters in plays, 37–39, 41–52, 77–79, 128, 166n8, 186
  behavior of (*see* crowd; collective behavior; spectatorship; theatrical competence)
  Caroline, 11, 37–38, 43–44, 46, 52, 53n15, 53n20, 53n22, 53n25, 60, 69n6
  collectivity vs. individuation, 23–24
  diversity/heterogeneity of, 2, 7, 9, 11, 26–27, 39, 56, 67, 240
  dramatic characterization of, as imagined by playwrights, dramatists, theater industry, 1, 9, 25–28, 33, 38, 96
  Elizabethan, 21, 24–26, 28, 35n27, 38, 43, 46, 79, 188n21
  female, 44, 48, 51, 54n27, 54n31
  homogeneity of, 2, 11
  in private theaters, 11, 37–40, 42–44, 46, 52, 53n4, 53n8, 53n11, 53n24, 55, 57, 59–60, 63, 70n24
  interactions with actors, 5–6 (communicated agreement/theatrical frame), 25–26, 29 (spectacular separation), 116

audience (*continued*)
  numbers of members attending theatre performances, 25, 30, 41
  playgoers, 2, 4, 7–9, 11–13, 17n41, 26, 31, 34n3, 36n61, 37, 40–44, 55, 58, 60, 62, 67, 68, 80, 96, 114–17, 121–23, 128
  playhouse riots (*see* riots)
  response as shaped by physical parameters of theater and staging, 12, 24, 28, 47, 71–75, 77–80, 83–87, 88n18, 89n22, 89n23, 89n24, 89n32, 116
  routinized playgoing (*see* habituation)
  seated on stage, 25, 37, 40–41, 48–49, 52, 53n16, 153
  stratification of, 58–59
  visibility of, 39–40, 105

Babington, Anthony, 96
Bacon, Francis, 23
  Advancement of Learning, The, 34n18
Bailey, Amanda, 130n3
Baker, Richard
  Theatrum Redivium, 44
Barker, Frances, 172, 187n5, 187n6
Barroll, Leeds, 19, 34n2
Bayer, Mark, 11, 53n25, 69n10, 69n15, 71, 168n28
Beacham, Richard C., 73, 87n6, 88n8
Beaumont, Francis, 32, 35n36, 36n48
  Knight of the Burning Pestle, 49, 54n31, 55, 66, 69n2, 135–36, 147n3
Beeston, Christopher, 43, 57–60, 63, 69n11
Bellamy, John, 111n55
Belsey, Catherine, 91n43, 133n32, 172, 187n7
Belting, Hans
  Likeness and Presence, 114, 130, 130n4
Bentley, G. E., 69n8
Bergeron, David M., 13, 96, 120, 147n2, 147n3, 148n7, 148n16, 148n17, 149n20, 149n23, 149n24, 152, 154, 166n4, 167n14, 168n32

Bergson, Henri, 83, 90n30
Berry, Herbert, 53n16
Berry, Ralph, 35n35
Bevington, David, 34n4, 87n1, 107n3, 111n44, 168n27, 171, 187n2
Biernoff, Suzannah, 109n29
Bland, Desmond, 155, 166n1, 166n2, 166n3, 167n13, 167n15, 167n22
Bloom, Gina, 131n7
Blumenberg, Hans, 85, 91n42
body language/image, 74, 97, 98, 100, 103, 105, 108n16, 113–19, 187n5, 187n6
  see also actor's body
Bowers, Fredson, 33n1, 68n1, 69n1
Bradbrook, Muriel, 35n35
Brathwaite, Richard, 32
  English Gentleman and The English Gentlewoman, The, 36n58
Braunmuller, A. R., 53n22, 108n18, 110n33, 110n34, 118, 131n10, 131n15, 132n15, 149n22
Brecht, Bertolt, 172, 187n3
Bristol, Michael, 32
Brome, Richard, 7, 11, 38, 44, 46, 53n7
  Antipodes, The, 5, 16n19
Brooks, Douglas A., 131n12
Browne, Thomas
  Religio Medici, 22
Bruster, Douglas, 39
Bryson, Norman, 109n23
Buckhurst, Lord, 158
Bullen, A. H., 35n40, 193–97, 200
Burbage, Richard, 111n47, 136
Burleigh, Lord, 158
Burre, Walter, 136, 147n3
Butler, Martin, 9, 17n41

Campion, Edmund, 84, 108n8
Canetti, Elias, 28
Caroline drama, 39, 43, 46
Cartelli, Thomas, 17n43, 101
Cartwright, Kent, 101, 110n38
Casson, Lionel, 78, 88n11
Catesby, Robert, 111n56

Cawarden, Thomas, Master of Revels, 138
Cecil, Robert, 158
Chambers, E. K., 53n19
Champion, Larry S., 69n1
Chapman, George
  Blind Beggar of Alexandria, The, 19
characters, 9, 12–13, 16n14, 43, 194, 196–97, 199–203, 204n15
  actor as character, 172
  antisocial vs. authority, 14, 189
  audience's experience of, 176–77, 178, 180–81, 188n23
  audience response to, 4, 6
  matching on stage to public persons 45, 155, 161, 165, 167n11, 167n17
  casting actors by type/characterization, 154–55
charisma
  defined, 145
  lineage, 141
charismatic circularity, 140, 143–47
Chaucer, Geoffrey, 21
Chettle, Henry
  Kind-Hartes Dream, 25, 35n25
Cholmley, Ranulph, 142
Christian, Mildred G., 205n17
citizen comedy, 61
city comedy, 61, 87, 208
Clare, Janet, 101, 111
Clark, Stuart, 98, 109n29, 133n31
Clerkenwell, 55, 59, 68
Cocles, Bartolommeo della Rocca
  A Brief and Most Pleasau[n]t Epitomye of the Whole Art of Phisiognomie, 125–26, 132n25,133n29
Cohen, Ralph A., 110n36, 176, 194–95, 197–99, 204n1
Colegrove, C. Lee, 194–95, 200, 204n3
collective behavior, 22–23
Compton, Lord, 158
convention, 5, 13, 15n1, 15n3, 16n26, 16n33, 20, 40, 43, 49, 193
  Dutch genre paintings, 84
  Roman, 72–73,76, 80, 83, 89n22

Cook, Ann Jennalie, 9, 17n41, 17n42, 20, 29, 33, 34n3, 36n61, 136, 148n4
Cooke, John, 59, 69n6
  Greene's Tu Quoque, 59
Cooper, Thomas
  Cry and Reuenge of Blood, The, 132n20
corporate and institutional identity, 38, 157–58, 162–64, 168n24
Cousin, Geraldine, 133n33
Crane, Mary Thomas, 72, 87n3, 90n41
Cranley, Thomas, 36n55
Crombie, A. C., 109n29
crowd
  behavior of, in historical record, 9, 11
  civic control of crowd, 21–24, 32, 111n55
  definition, 23
  theater industry control of crowd, 1, 9, 10, 19, 21, 25–28, 33, 38, 96
cultural poetics, 10
Cumber, John, 58
Cumberland, Earl of, 158
Curren-Aquino, Deborah T., 131n7

Davies, John, 27, 31, 35n38, 36n56
Dawson, Anthony, 8, 16n28, 34n19
Day, John
  Travels of the Three English Brothers, 59
Deats, Sara Munson, 108n28, 110n39
de Beaumanoir, Philippe
  Coutumes de Beauvaisis, 107n7
Debord, Guy, 24, 28, 34n20
Dekker, Thomas, 60–61, 69n1, 70n20
  Gull's Hornbook, The, 27, 35n39, 40
  If This Be Not a Good Play the Devil Is in It, 26, 35n29, 35n39, 35n42, 68n1
  Match Me in London, 11, 53n25, 55–68, 71, 168n28
  Northward Ho! (with John Webster), 61
  The Roaring Girl (with Thomas Middleton), 33n1, 69n4, 70n26
  Satiromastix, 61, 70n24
  Seven Deadly Sins, The, 68n1

Dekker, Thomas (*continued*)
  Shoemaker's Holiday, The, 67, 70n26
  Strange Horse Race, 35n42
  Westward Ho! (with John Webster), 61
  Whore of Babylon, The, 89n24, 149n21
de Lairesse, Gerard, 84
Dessen, Alan C., 132n17
de Witt, Johannes, 20, 33
Diehl, Huston, 109
DiMatteo, Anthony, 111n50
disguise, 61, 172, 175, 178–81, 183–85, 187, 190–91
domesticated experience, 10, 21, 28–29, 32, 114, 132n28, 155–56, 197
Dorsch, T. S., 80, 84, 88n21, 90n41, 91n41
Drayton, Michael, 29, 36n47
Drury Lane, 11, 55, 57, 59, 68n1, 69n10
Duckworth, George E., 73–74, 87n5, 88n7, 88n14
Dundas, Judith, 109n29
Dusinberre, Juliet, 131n7
Dutton, Richard, 69n15, 70n25
Dyce, Alexander, 193–97, 200

Earle, John, 25, 30
  Micro-cosmography, 35n24, 36n52
editorial practice, 189–90, 194–98, 204n4, 204n8, 204n11
Elam, Keir, 5–7, 11, 16n15, 16n16, 16n17, 16n22, 16n27, 53n23, 87n2, 115, 130n6
Eld, George, 195–96
Eliot, T. S., 3
Elizabeth I, 10, 13, 25, 120, 136–47, 148n15, 148n16, 149n19, 154, 158, 166n2, 166n4, 167n14
emblematic mode, 66, 80, 106, 142, 172
engagement and detachment, 8, 12, 32, 68n1, 72, 94, 99, 152, 158, 176, 188n21
epilogue, 5–7, 16n20, 16n25, 27, 29, 38–39, 42, 44, 52, 145
Erasmus, 84
Escolme, Bridget, 172–73, 187n3, 187n4, 187n9

Essex, Earl of, 158
execution, 15, 94–96, 102–3, 105, 111n55

Falco, Raphael, 137–38, 147, 148n12, 148n13
fantasies of identity, 44, 154, 190, 202–3
fantasy, metatheatrical, 77–78, 135
Field, Nathan, 26, 35n36
Fiennes, Joseph, 33
Findlay, Alison, 131n8
Finkelpearl, Philip, 166n2
Finlay, Roger, 34n7
Fletcher, John, 32, 35n36, 36n48, 66
Foakes, R. A., 89n22
Foucault, Michel, 3, 201, 204n14
Fraser, Antonia, 111n56
fraternity, 157, 163–64
French Revolution, 22
Frisch, Andrea, 107n7, 108n7
Froissart, Jean
  Chronicles of Froissart, The, 21–22, 34n9
Frye, Northrop, 25, 35n23

Gardner, Martin, 88n17
Garner, Shirley Nelson, 188n19
Gascoigne, George, 168n25
  Jocasta, 158
  Supposes, translated from Ariosto's *I Suppositi,* 158, 174, 178, 188
Gaskill, Malcolm, 132n24
Gasper, Julia, 66, 68n1, 70n21
Geertz, Clifford, 136–37, 148n8, 148n11
Gent, Lucy, 109n29
Gesta Grayorum, 13, 152, 157–59, 165, 166n1, 166n2, 166n3, 166n4, 167n13, 167n15, 167n22, 168n25
Glapthorne, Henry, 36n55
Goffe, Thomas
  Careless Shepherdess, The, 38, 44, 53n10
Gombrich, Ernst M., 97, 173–74, 187n10, 187n15
Gosson, Stephen, 4–6, 19, 31

Plays Confuted in Five Actions, 4, 15n11, 26–27, 33n1, 35n30
Schoole of Abuse, 6, 16n21, 48, 54n29
Greenblatt, Stephen 3, 14–15, 15n7, 15n9, 15n10, 15n12, 17n45
Greene, Thomas, 57, 59, 188n24
Greenfield, Thelma, 39, 52n2, 53n14
Greenwich, 156, 158
Gregory, Brad, 95,108n10
Grennan, Eamon, 158, 168n26
guilds, 138, 154, 164
Guilpin, Edward, 30, 36n51
Gunpowder Plot, 111n56
Gurr, Andrew, 2, 9, 15n3, 15n4, 15n5, 19, 25, 34n3, 35n22, 53n16, 53n25, 69n3, 69n4, 69n11, 70n19, 79–80, 88n18, 130n5, 136, 148n5, 155, 167n11, 175, 188n20

habituation, 10, 21, 28, 52n3
as routine, 30–33
Halpern, Richard, 12n12
Hanson, Elizabeth, 108n9
Happé, Peter, 53n15, 54n27
Harbage, Alfred, 9, 15n4, 15n6, 16n39, 17n44, 21, 34n8, 35n29, 39, 68n1, 69n1, 136, 148n4
Harvey, Elizabeth, 15n8
Haynes, Jonathan, 35n27
Henslowe, Philip, 19–20, 24, 60–61, 68n1
Herbert, Henry, Master of Revels, 60, 63, 68n1
Heywood, Thomas 57, 59–61, 63, 114–15
Hill, Christopher, 22, 34n11
Histriomastix, 36n57, 44
Hodgdon, Barbara, 131n7
Holderness, Graham, 172, 187n4
Holinshed, Raphael
Chronicles of England, Scotland and Ireland, 96, 108n16, 111n45, 111n46, 115, 129, 133n34
Hollander, Martha, 84, 90nn34–39
Holton, Robert, 23, 34n14, 34n15

Honigmann, E. A. J., 131n13, 132, 132n15
Horrible Murther of a Young Boy of Three Yeres of Age, The, 123, 132n19
Horsman, E. A., 16n24, 53n21
Howard, Jean E., 15n2, 36n49, 131n7
Howard, Lord Thomas, 158
Hunter, G. K., 130n3
Hutson, Lorna, 107n5, 132n24, 166, 168n25

Ichikawa, Mariko, 79–80, 88n18
identity
corporate, institutional, social, 38, 157–58, 162–64, 168n24
as disguise, 178–79
as dramatic character, 180–82, 184, 186
internal, personal, old, 175–76, 187n7, 188n24
as likeness, resemblance, body presence, 114, 116, 119, 129, 130
new or formed on external circumstance, 176–77
as persona, 191, 198
spectorial, critical, 190
subjective, 23, 93: Althusserian, 128; of individuals, 117; social, 163
illusion, 101–2, 111n51, 165, 171–74, 181
as a paradox of recognition, 174
as realistic, 171–74: verisimilitude, 186
induction, 11, 14, 16n24, 37–41, 46–49, 52n2, 53n7, 53n18, 53n21, 54n28, 135–36, 147, 174–78, 185, 188n24
Inns of Court, 10, 31, 44–45, 47, 59–60, 107n5, 154, 158, 161, 164, 166n2, 168n24, 168n25, 169n34
Christmas revels at, 148n19, 149n19, 151–53, 154–55, 166n5, 166n6
Inns of Court
Gray's Inn, 13, 80, 148n19, 149n19, 151–53, 154–55, 156–58, 162, 166n5, 166n6, 168n25, 168n27

Inns of Court (*continued*)
  Inner Temple, 151
  Lincoln's Inn, 59, 169n34
  Middle Temple, 155, 166n2, 167n14, 167n19, 169n34
intensification, 176, 180, 185–86

Jackson, Ken, 131n7
James VI and I, 11, 62–63, 65, 68n1, 70n22, 70n23, 70n27
  Basilicon Doron, 62, 138
  True Law of Free Monarchies, 62–63
Jones, Ann Rosalind, 130n3
Jones, Inigo, 72
Jonson, Ben, 6–7, 11, 16n24, 16n25, 31, 38, 40, 43, 53, 61, 146
  Bartholomew Fair, 7, 16n24, 43, 53n21, 54n33, 135–36, 147
  Devil Is an Ass, The, 36 36n50, 40, 53n18
  Eastward Ho! (with Marston and Dekker), 29
  Every Man Out of his Humour, 196
  Magnetic Lady, The, 37–38, 41–47, 52n1
  Poetaster, 31, 34n5
  Sejanus, 20, 135
  Staple of News, The, 38, 44, 48–52, 54n27, 54n28, 54n32, 54n34
Jowett, John, 194–99, 204n1, 204n4, 204n8, 204n11

Kelly, William, 103, 111n48
Kernan, Alvin, 53n22
Kernodle, George R., 89n23
Kiefer, Frederick, 89n24
Kinney, Arthur F., 90n32
Kirby, Luke, 95
Knapp, Margaret, 153, 166n5
Knutson, Roslyn L., 111n47
Kobialka, Michal, 153, 166n5
Kolve, V. A., 132n17
Krieger, Murray, 204n13

Lake, Peter, 70n27, 95, 108n11
Land, Norman E., 109n23

Lara, Manuel Gomez, 112n58
Le Bon, Gustave, 22–23
Lefebvre, George, 22–23
legitimacy and illegitimacy, 105–6, 115–17, 121, 126, 128–29, 130n7, 131n8, 137, 158
Lenton, Francis, 36n55, 69n4
Levine, Laura, 15n13
Lewis, Joyce, 95, 133n33
Lin, Erika T., 108n21, 110n37, 167n11, 180
London, 3, 8, 10, 15, 19, 25, 29, 33, 153, 158, 191
  citizens of, 15, 21–22, 147
  guilds, 138
  immigration, 30
  life in, 21, 30 (*see also* crowd)
  livery companies, 139
  playhouses, 9, 20, 28 (*see also* theater)
  spectators, 148
  streets and city of, 10, 136–42, 146–47
  theater audiences and theatrical milieu, 9, 23–24, 29, 202
Lopez, Jeremy, 8–9, 13–14, 15n1, 15n3, 16n26, 16n33, 104, 171, 187n1
Loseley Manuscripts, 138
Low, Jennifer, 12, 110n37, 130, 165, 166n5
Lunney, Ruth, 96, 104, 108n20, 111n42, 111n52

MacIntyre, Jean, 130n3
Mack, Maynard, 176, 188n21
Maguire, Laurie, 161, 168n30, 168n31, 188n23
Marlowe, Christopher
  Doctor Faustus, 11, 33, 107n2, 111n44
  Edward II, 12, 93, 94, 101–7, 108n20, 110n39, 111n42, 111n44, 111n47, 111n48, 111n51, 111n52, 112n56
  Jew of Malta, The, 19
  Tamburlaine the Great, Part I, 93
Marotti, Arthur, 161, 168n29
Marston, John, 166n2, 167n14, 167n19

Eastward Ho! (with Dekker and Jonson), 29
Jack Drum's Entertainment, 35n28, 35n46
materialist critics, 115, 172–73
Matthew, St. (gospel of) Beatitudes, 143
Maus, Katharine, ix, 15n8, 36n49
Maxwell, Baldwin, 193–95, 197, 200, 204n2
McAdam, Ian, 104, 111n51
McCarthy, Kathleen, 87n4
McClelland, J. S., 21–22, 34n6, 34n10, 34n17
McLeod, Randall, 117, 131n9
McLuskie, Kathleen, 63, 70n28
Menzer, Paul, 10–11, 52n3, 53n20, 69n7, 128
Merleau-Ponty, Maurice, 82, 89n28
Middleton, Thomas, 14, 61, 109n27, 205n16
　Changeling, The (with William Rowley), 66
　No Wit, No Help Like a Woman's, 58–59, 69n13
　Puritan Widow, The, 190, 199, 201–2
　Roaring Girl, The (with Thomas Dekker), 33n1, 69n4, 70n26
　Triumphs of Integrity, The, 164, 168n32
　Women Beware Women, 66
　Your Five Gallants, 189–201, 203, 204n1
Milton, John
　Paradise Regained, 22
mottoes, 144, 191
Mounteagle, Lord, 158
Mountjoy, Lord, 158
Muir, Kenneth, 34n12
Mukherji, Subha, 107n5
Mulcaster, Richard
　Quenes Maiesties Passage through the Citie of London, The, 138–41, 143–47, 148n15
Myhill, Nova, 11, 130, 165

Nashe, Thomas, 26, 33n1
Neill, Michael, 37–39, 43–44, 52n3, 53n4, 53n8, 53n11, 53n24
Nelson, John, 95
Nicoll, Allardyce, 89n22
Nixon, Paul, 78, 88n16
Norbrook, David, 70n27
Nordlund, Marcus, 109n27
Northbrooke, John, 4–5
Northumberland, Earl of, 158
Norton, Thomas. *See* Sackville, Thomas and Thomas Norton
Novy, Marianne, 188n23

O'Callaghan, Michelle, 157, 166n2, 167n17, 167n23
Olivier, Lawrence, 33
Orgel, Stephen, 108n18, 110n33, 136, 148n6, 149n22
Osborne, Laurie E., 54n31
Overbury, Sir Thomas, 4, 16n14
Owens, Margaret E., 108n16, 108n17

pageants, 1559 royal entry, 13, 29, 32, 61, 90n37, 129, 136–47, 148n7, 148n17, 149n19, 149n20, 149n23, 152, 166n4
Palfrey, Simon, 154–55, 167n11
Panofsky, Erwin, 89n24
Parker, Hershel, 204n13
Parrat, John, 144
part and participation, 136, 158–65, 166n4, 166n5, 166n8, 167n11, 167n15, 175–77, 196
　See also role
Patrides, C. A., 34n12
patrilineage, 115–22, 125, 127, 129
Peacham, Henry, 33n1
Pearson, Meg, 12
Peele, George, 202, 205n17
Percy, Thomas, 111n56
Perkins, Richard, 58
personation, 155, 157, 167n11
physiognomy, 125–26, 132n25, 132n57, 133n30
Piesse, Amanda, 72, 87n3

Plato's *Republic*, 173
Plautus
    Menaechmi, The, 12, 22, 71–79, 87,
        88n11, 88n16, 89n22, 91n41,
        158, 166n5
Porter, Martin, 133n28
Portpool, 152, 157
presence, 12, 40, 72, 83, 85, 93–94,
    113–23, 129–30, 131n14, 131n15,
    132n15, 138–39, 141, 144, 154,
    157, 159, 167n11, 176–77, 180,
    183, 197
presentational acting, 115
Preston, Thomas
    Cambyses, 106
Price, George, 61, 69n1, 70n20
Prichard, Carla Coleman, 112n57
Prince of Purpoole, 151–52, 155, 157–
    58, 166n1, 166n5
    See also Purpoole
prologue, 6, 30, 37–40, 42, 46–52,
    53n12, 56, 58–59, 93, 175
Proudfoot, Richard, 91n41
Prown, Jules David, 109n23
Prynne, William, 4
    Histrio-Mastix (*Histriomastix*), 31, 44
puritanism, 8, 202, 205n17
Purpoole, 162, 165
Puttenham, George
    Arte of English Poesie, The, 26, 35n31
Pye, Christopher, 101, 107n4, 111n41

queen as audience and actor, 136, 144–
    47, 166n4, 167n14
Queen Elizabeth I. *See* Elizabeth I,
    Queen
Questier, Michael, 96, 108n11, 108n12,
    108n14, 111n55

Rabkin, Norman, 173–74, 188n17
Rackin, Phyllis, 130n7, 131n7
realism, 172, 186
representation, 12, 25, 26, 29, 38–39, 41,
    43–44, 50, 52, 63, 65, 67, 80, 84,
    89n24, 95, 107n5, 114–17, 122,
    129, 140–43, 146–47, 148n17,
    149n20, 171, 180, 194, 202
resemblance, 115–19, 121–22, 126,
    129–30, 141, 180
revelers, revelling, 13, 151–58, 161–62,
    165, 166n2
revels, 11, 13, 53n17, 58, 60, 68n1,
    69n6, 70n25, 148n19, 151
Rhatigan, Emma K., 13, 53n17, 148n19
Rich, Lord, 158
Riots, playhouse, 24–25, 57–59
roles, 73, 107n5, 111n47, 124, 165,
    166n4, 166n5, 167n21
    charismatic sovereign (*see* queen as
        audience and actor)
    creative process, 200
    doubling of, 114–15, 180, 183,
        188n23, 199
    dramatic, 65, 104, 159–63, 174–75,
        177–78, 185
    in revels, by office holders, 155–58
    of audience, 1, 3, 5, 7, 12, 75–76, 78–
        79, 87, 93–94, 101, 154–56,
Rowe, Katherine, 132n16
Rowley, William
    Changeling, The (with Thomas
        Middleton), 66
    Shoemaker, A Gentleman, A, 59, 67
    Travels of the Three English Brothers
        (with John Day and George
        Wilkins), 59
Rudé, George, 23

Sackville, Thomas, and Thomas Norton
    Gorboduc, 106
Salgado, Gamini, 81, 89n27, 89n29,
    90n31
Salingar, Leo, 87n1
Sanders, Julie, 54n27
Schiesari, Juliana, 125, 132n28
Schwarz, Kathryn, 131n7
semiotics, 5, 13, 16n15, 16n16, 16n17,
    16n22, 16n27, 53n23, 79, 83,
    87n2, 113–15, 119, 123, 126–28,
    130n3

signifier, 65, 104, 110n37, 113–17, 121, 123, 127
sign, 106, 113, 115, 122, 124, 126, 133n30, 136, 139–41, 143, 147
Serlio, Sebastiano, 72, 84, 90n37
Seronsy, Cecil C., 174, 188n18
Shakespeare, William, 7, 9, 12, 14, 56, 61, 66, 79–80, 83–84, 98, 114, 145, 159, 190
  As You Like It, 145
  Comedy of Errors, The, 12–13, 71–72, 79–87, 88n21, 88n22, 89n22, 89n23, 89n27, 90n30, 90n32, 90n33, 91n41, 148n19, 149n19, 152–55, 157–65, 166n5, 166n10, 167n17, 167n24, 168n24, 168n25, 168n26, 168n27, 168n30, 168n33, 169n34
  Coriolanus, 22–23, 34n12
  Cymbeline, 113–14
  First Folio, 130n1
  Hamlet, 96, 108n18, 156–57, 167n20, 195, 197
  1 Henry IV, 36n49, 99–101
  2 Henry IV, 145
  Henry V, 29, 33, 129, 131n7, 145, 171, 173
  Julius Caesar, 155–56
  King John, 12, 113, 115–16, 120, 124, 127–29, 130n7, 131n7, 131n10, 131n13, 132n15, 133n33, 167n11, 180
  King Lear, 68n1
  Love's Labor's Lost, 139
  Measure for Measure, 201, 203
  Merchant of Venice, The, 199, 201
  A Midsummer Night's Dream, 145, 188n23, 201
  Othello, 139
  Richard II, 70n22, 137
  Richard III, 98–99, 110n34, 133n28
  Romeo and Juliet, 33, 201
  Taming of the Shrew, The, 13–14, 171–87, 188n18, 188n19, 188n23, 188n24, 188n26, 204n15

Tempest, The, 6, 16n20, 145
Titus Andronicus, 201
Twelfth Night, 35n36, 155, 201–3
Shapiro, Michael, 185–86, 188n26
Shearman, John, 97, 109n23, 109n24, 109n28
Sheffield, Lord, 158
Sherwood, William, 29, 95
Shirley, James, 29, 32, 36n48, 60
  Ball, The, 63
Shrewsbury, Earl of, 158
Sidney, Philip
  Arcadia, 22, 62
Simons, Eric N., 112
Slater, Niall W., 73, 88n12
Southampton, Earl of, 158
spectacle, 3–5, 7, 11–15, 79, 93
spectacularization of space, 8, 10, 21, 24–25, 29, 94
spectatorship, 5, 37–38, 42, 93, 96–97, 101, 102, 108
Spenser, Edmund
  Faerie Queene, The, 22
  Shepheardes Calender, 62
stage, 37–41, 43–51, 53n16, 53n20, 56, 60, 71–75, 77, 79, 138
Stallybrass, Peter, 130n3, 131n9
Steggle, Matthew, 53n7
Stern, Tiffany, 40, 53n20, 154, 155, 166n8, 167n11, 167n21
St. Giles in the Fields, 59
Stirlin, Brent, 34n12
St. James, 59, 68n1
St. Paul, 85, 137, 139
St. Paul's Cathedral, 21, 144–45
Sturgess, Keith, 60, 69n17
Stymeist, David, 102, 11n43
subjectivity. *See* identity: subjective
Sweeney, John Gordon III, 16n25

Taine, Hippolyte, 23
Tassi, Marguerite, 98, 109n32
Tebbetts, Terrell, 181, 188n22
technology of separation, 28
textual corruption, 190, 194, 201
theater, nonnaturalistic, 181

theaters
    Blackfriars, 14, 32, 37, 39–41, 43, 48–49, 51, 53n16, 53n20, 55–56, 60, 154, 166n8, 195–96
    Cockpit, 11, 43, 55–68, 68n1, 69n10
    Curtain, 20, 33
    Fortune, 11, 46, 69n12, 70n26
    Globe, 39, 43, 58, 79, 138, 183
    Phoenix, 60 (*see also* theaters: Cockpit)
theaters (*continued*)
    private, 11, 37–40, 42, 44, 46, 52, 52n3, 53n4, 53n8, 53n24, 55, 57, 59–60, 63, 70n24
    public, 12–13, 16n25, 24, 39, 56, 60, 79–80, 136–37Red Bull, 11, 20, 43, 46, 55–61, 63–68, 69n6, 69n12
    Rose, 19–20, 33, 79, 80
    Salisbury Court, 44
    Swan, 20, 33
    Theatre, 33, 183
theatrical competence, 5–7, 11
Theophrastus, 30
Thomas, Sidney, 88n21
Thompson, James, 95
Tomkis, Thomas
    Albumazar, 56, 69n5
Torrey, Michael, 133n57
Tower of London, 136, 140, 146
Trinity College, 56
trompe l'oeil, 173
Tuan, Yi-fu, 81
Tupper, Frederick, 34n12
Two Merry Milkmaids, 56, 69n6

van Eck, Caroline, 97, 109n22, 109n27
van Eyck, Jan, 95, 97–98, 109n25
van Mander, Karel
    Het schilder-boeck, 84
verisimilitude, 132n18, 171, 186
vision, 3–7, 13, 42, 44, 45–46, 49–50, 51, 80, 94, 98, 102, 109n22, 109n23, 109n27, 129, 133n31, 171, 173, 178, 202

W., C.
    Crying Murther, The, 124, 132n23
Ward, John, 97, 109n24
Waterhouse, Edward, 31, 32, 36n53, 167n18
Webster, John, 26
    Devil's Law Case, The, 56
    Northward Ho! (with Thomas Dekker)
    Westward Ho! (with Thomas Dekker), 61
    White Devil, The, 20, 34n4, 56, 69n7
Weimann, Robert, 39, 53n12, 53n13, 108n21, 110n37, 131n7, 136, 148n9
Weller, Barry, 185, 188n24
Wells, James, 13, 84
Westminster, 57, 60, 136, 145–47
Whitehall, 59
Whitney, Charles, 9, 15n3, 16n37, 148n5
Whitworth, Charles, 88n21, 166n10, 168n27
Whorf, Benjamin, 80, 89n25
Wilson, J. D., 132n15
Wilson, Robert
    Three Ladies of London, The, 25, 35n26
Windsor, Lord, 158
Winters, Edward, 97, 109n22
witness, witnessing, 29, 94–98, 146
    theatrical 12, 29, 59, 93–94, 96, 138, 175, 184
Womack, Peter, 131n7
Woodhouse, Thomas, 95
Worth, Ellis, 58
Wright, James, 69n14

Yachnin, Paul, ix, 8, 16n28, 24, 34n19, 108n19, 201, 205n16

GPSR Compliance

The European Union's (EU) General Product Safety Regulation (GPSR) is a set of rules that requires consumer products to be safe and our obligations to ensure this.

If you have any concerns about our products, you can contact us on

ProductSafety@springernature.com

In case Publisher is established outside the EU, the EU authorized representative is:

Springer Nature Customer Service Center GmbH
Europaplatz 3
69115 Heidelberg, Germany

www.ingramcontent.com/pod-product-compliance
Lightning Source LLC
LaVergne TN
LVHW091538060526
838200LV00036B/659